Francis Amasa Walker

First Lessons in political Economy

Francis Amasa Walker

First Lessons in political Economy

ISBN/EAN: 9783337080419

Printed in Europe, USA, Canada, Australia, Japan

Cover: Foto ©Suzi / pixelio.de

More available books at **www.hansebooks.com**

AMERICAN SCIENCE SERIES—ELEMENTARY COURSE

FIRST LESSONS

IN

POLITICAL ECONOMY

BY

FRANCIS A. WALKER, Ph.D., LL.D.

PRESIDENT MASSACHUSETTS INSTITUTE OF TECHNOLOGY
AUTHOR OF "THE WAGES QUESTION," "MONEY,"
"LAND AND ITS RENT," ETC.

NEW YORK
HENRY HOLT AND COMPANY
1893

Copyright, 1889,
BY
HENRY HOLT & CO.

PREFACE.

This book has been prepared for use in High Schools and Academies. In writing its pages, I have been well aware that the object sought is the most difficult at which an economist can aim. Whether this effort to reach the minds of pupils of fifteen, sixteen or seventeen years has been successful, will only be learned on actual trial.

In preparing a text-book for students in the period of life indicated, I have not thought it necessary to make the work childish. It is no "Primer of Political Economy" which is here offered; but a substantial course of study in this vitally important subject. I can only hope that it will be found that those for whom it has been designed will be able to follow that course to their own satisfaction and with good results.

In adapting the tone of discussion to younger readers than those for whom I have heretofore written, it has not seemed to me desirable to avoid words as long as are necessary fully to carry the meaning intended. In a treatise on political economy written in "words of two syllables," the author must avoid questions of prime importance, or else he will be driven to roundabout forms of expression and to highly artificial phrases. It is not the length of words, but obscurity or confusion in the mind of the writer, which will make a treatise on political economy difficult to youthful readers.

What has been attempted in the preparation of this little work is a clear arrangement of topics; a simple, direct and forcible presentation of the questions successively raised; the avoidance, as far as possible, of certain metaphysical distinctions which the author has found very perplexing to students of even a greater age; a frequent repetition of cardinal doctrines; and, especially, a liberal use of concrete illustrations, drawn from facts of common experience or observation. How far this attempt has been successful is now to be submitted to the judgment of others, and to the tests of the school-room.

For one, I am fully persuaded that it is as easy to teach political economy to students of fifteen, sixteen or seventeen years of age, as it is to teach geometry or quadratic equations, which are actually taught, and with complete success, within that period of life. But this can only be done by the master taking as much pains with his classes as he would take in teaching the latter subjects. There is not one scholar in five, perhaps in ten, who would go satisfactorily through geometry or quadratic equations by himself, using simply the text-book. The great majority of pupils require the active assistance of the teacher, at every stage of their progress. The master must continually search the minds of his pupils to see what they have apprehended, and what they have failed to apprehend. He must go back to fundamental principles just as often as he finds it necessary in order to fix these firmly in the mind. He must do more, much more, than hear recitations: he must positively and actively teach, if his scholars are to learn. He must illustrate, emphasize and enforce every successive lesson.

If political economy is to be taken up in such a spirit, in schools of the grade to which reference has been made, it can be successfully taught out of such a book as this was intended to be. Take, for example, the principle set forth in Chapter X, and made of such extensive use in later chapters: the principle that normal value is determined by the cost of production "at the greatest disadvantage." One who has mastered this has already learned the harder half of political economy. Yet there is nothing in it which cannot be made perfectly clear, by proper explanation, due iteration, free illustration, to the mind of a boy of sixteen, or, for that matter, of fourteen. A class might, however, get through that chapter, for the purposes of a routine recitation, under a master who was not himself interested in the subject, without thoroughly grasping the principle and giving it such a place in their minds as would enable them to use it in subsequent discussions regarding the distribution of wealth.

Another thing requires to be noted regarding the plan of the present work. Inasmuch as it is intended for youthful students, and is designed quite as much to interest them in the study of political economy as to make them proficient in it, the author has not held himself, as strictly as he has sought in previous works to do, to the treatment of political economy as a science, to be distinguished from the art of political economy. He has allowed himself great freedom in assuming that certain results are desirable in themselves, and certain other results undesirable: and he has sought to show how these may be avoided and those attained. Much, which, in his other works, has been treated as belonging to the Applications of political economy, is wrought into the substance of the present treatise.

It scarcely requires to be said that any one who should undertake to teach political economy, with the aid of this or any other work of an elementary character, should prepare himself for the task by studying more advanced textbooks. In this connection the present writer would recommend John Stuart Mill's Political Economy, and Marshall's brief but excellent Economics of Industry. He trusts he will not be deemed egotistical if he mentions his own fuller treatise on political economy, and, also, his Wages Question.

The teacher would be greatly assisted in preparing himself, both generally and for individual recitations, by using Problems in Political Economy, by Prof. W. G. Sumner of Yale University; Institutes of Economics, by President E. B. Andrews of Brown University; and Outline of Lectures upon Political Economy, by Prof. Henry C. Adams of the University of Michigan.

The habitual reading of the Quarterly Journal of Economics (Harvard University) is strongly recommended. The publications of the American Economic Association will be found highly useful.

While the chapters of this work are intended to be studied in the order in which they appear, some teachers may find it better to omit paragraphs 106 to 146, inclusive, on first passing through the book, reserving those sections for subsequent study.

MASSACHUSETTS INSTITUTE OF TECHNOLOGY,
    BOSTON, October 14, 1889.

TABLE OF CONTENTS.

PART I.
PRODUCTION AND EXCHANGE.

CHAPTER		PAGE
I.	Wealth and Value,	3
II.	The Cause of Value,	12
III.	The Production of Wealth,	17
IV.	Land,	22
V.	Diminishing Returns in Agriculture,	25
VI.	Labor,	34
VII.	Labor, Continued. The Organization of Industry,	50
VIII.	Capital,	60
IX.	The Relation of Cost of Production to Value,	72
X.	Production at the Greatest Disadvantage,	85
XI.	Money,	95
XII.	Primitive Forms of Money,	103
XIII.	Credit: The Standard of Deferred Payments: The Tabular Standard: Bimetallism,	109
XIV.	Banks and Bank-money,	122
XV.	Political Money: Inflation,	143
XVI.	Protection or Free Trade,	164

PART II.
DISTRIBUTION AND CONSUMPTION.

XVII.	The Problem of Distribution,	181
XVIII.	Rent,	189
XIX.	Rent, Continued. The Ownership of Land,	205

CHAPTER		PAGE
XX.	PROFITS,	215
XXI.	PROFITS, CONTINUED. CO-OPERATION,	225
XXII.	INTEREST,	237
XXIII.	WAGES,	251
XXIV.	THE ECONOMIC EFFECTS OF IMPERFECT COMPETITION,	261
XXV.	WHAT MAY BE DONE TO HELP THE WORKING CLASSES,	272
XXVI.	THE PAUPER LABOR ARGUMENT FOR PROTECTION,	283
XXVII.	THE CONSUMPTION OF WEALTH,	291
XXVIII.	FALSE NOTIONS ABOUT CONSUMPTION,	301

PART I.

PRODUCTION AND EXCHANGE.

POLITICAL ECONOMY.

CHAPTER I.

WEALTH AND VALUE.

1. Political Economy is the Science of Wealth.—Political economy, or economics, is the science of wealth.

Political economy has to do with nothing but wealth. This warning should be carefully heeded. A great part of the confusion which has existed on this subject has arisen from the fact that many writers on political economy have allowed their attention to be diverted, here or there, now or then, to some other social object besides wealth, and have perplexed themselves and misled their readers by discussing questions which do not belong to them, as political economists.

When we say that the political economist, as such, has to do with nothing else besides wealth, we are not saying that wealth is the most important matter in the world. We simply say that, if wealth is important enough to be investigated, it should be investigated by itself. The best and surest way by which to increase our knowledge of any subject, is to isolate it and study it long and carefully, by itself, from all sides. This is just as true of a social problem as of a chemical problem. The great difference between the two cases is that in the social problem it is not possible to keep out all foreign elements. Hence we can never expect to reach the same degree of assurance in political economy as in chemistry. But that constitutes no reason at all for not excluding foreign elements so far as we can, and keeping the thing we are studying, namely, wealth, as closely in view, all the time, as the nature of the case will permit.

2. Relation of Value to Wealth.—I have said that political economy is the science of wealth. But what is wealth ? I answer, Wealth comprises all articles of value and nothing else. Everything which has value is wealth. Nothing is wealth which has not value. In the language of the philosophers: Wealth is the *substance,* of which value is the *attribute:* that is, we always and everywhere attribute value to the substance, wealth.

If wealth and value are thus indissolubly joined together, the reader may ask, Why, when, should we not call political economy the science of values ? I answer, It would be perfectly proper to do so. Some writers have done so. One reason, however, for calling political economy the science of wealth, is that many persons who would not be in the least interested on being asked to listen to a lecture, or read a book, on the science of values, would be very much interested on being told that the subject was the science of wealth. Wealth is a word which appeals to all, poor or rich, low or high, ignorant or educated. No one is above, no one is below, an interest in this subject. It is, therefore, a good term to use in describing political economy.

3. Value Defined.—But what is value ? This is a question which needs to be carefully answered; and the reader should always keep the definition clearly in view. It will not do to think loosely about value.

In common speech we use the word in more than one sense. Thus, we might say that the value of a horse is one hundred dollars, or that a certain book contains some valuable truths. In political economy, however, the word should always mean precisely one thing, and nothing else.

The definition which I have to give is a long one, and I must ask the reader to commit it carefully to memory. There are few things which it is worth while to commit to memory, word for word; but this is one of them:

VALUE IS THE POWER WHICH AN ARTICLE CONFERS UPON ITS POSSESSOR, IRRESPECTIVE OF LEGAL AUTHORITY OR PERSONAL SENTIMENTS, OF COMMANDING, IN EXCHANGE FOR ITSELF, THE LABOR, OR THE PRODUCTS OF THE LABOR, OF OTHERS.

It is proper, speaking briefly, to say that value is Power in Exchange; but whenever we say this, we must have in mind all that is stated above.

4. Two Exceptions.—What do we mean by saying, "irrespective of legal authority or personal sentiments"? This will be best shown by illustrations, as follows:

The Emperor of Russia or of Germany can, by a few words, compel two millions of men to come from all parts of his empire, to serve in his army He can command them to make the greatest exertions, to submit to the most painful sacrifices, involving hunger and fatigue, and even wounds and death. At his will, they must march, watch, fight, or die. Political economy has nothing to do with this, because it is done by legal authority. This is not a case where value exists. These services are not economic.

On the other hand, the soldiers of England and the United States perform services which are economic. They are not compelled to enter the army. The government makes it worth their while to do so. It "goes into the market for labor," and hires men to leave their homes or their farms or their shops, and serve for one year, or three years, or five years, in the army. What they are to do there is not the question for us to consider here. So long as the government hires them, with clothes and food and money, and so long as they, on their part, freely accept these terms, we have a case of value, just as much as if they were hired to work upon harbor-improvements or in building roads. I do not say that it is just as well for the country to hire men to fight as it would be to hire them to build roads. I only say that, in each case, there is value. The clothing, food, and money of the government confer upon it the power to command, in a fair and free exchange, the labor of the workmen, or of the soldiers. The labor of the workmen, or of the soldiers, confers upon them the power of commanding, in a fair and free exchange, the clothing, food, and money of the government.

So much for "legal authority." How about "personal sentiments"? Again, let us proceed by illustrations. A mother gives her thoughts, her care, her labor, her time, her strength, day by day, without grudging and without reserve, to the rearing of her children; while, in their sickness, she drains her very life-blood to protect and save them. But this is not a case of value. Political economy has nothing to do with it. The mother renders these services to these children, because they are hers. She does it out of affection for them, and not for reward. On the other hand, the services of a hired nurse or of a paid physician are economic: they constitute a case of value.

5. **Value Not a Physical Property.**—The reader now sees why I said, "irrespective of legal authority and of personal sentiments." Leaving out these words, for the moment, let us see how our definition of value will read: Value is the power which an article confers upon its possessor of commanding, in exchange for itself, the labor, or the products of the labor, of others.

Value is not any material or physical property of an article. In any given place, at any given time, any given article may depend for its value upon certain physical or material properties in itself; but these properties are not the value. Softness is not value; hardness is not value. Some articles are more valuable, the softer they are; some are more valuable, the harder they are. Color is not value; absence of color is not value. Some articles are more valuable, the more highly they are colored; others become more valuable, the more perfectly free they are from every tinge of color. Tenacity is not value; ductility is not value. Some articles are more valuable, the greater their tenacity; others have value in proportion to the ease with which they can be drawn out. Sweetness is not value, acidity is not value. Honey is valuable in proportion to its sweetness, vinegar to its sourness. We see, then, that value is not any material or physical property of an article.

6. Transferability Essential to Value.—We have seen that value is power in exchange. Now, to an exchange, as to a quarrel, there must be two parties. An exchange requires at least two exchangers. Value, then, is a social phenomenon.

Again, in order that there shall be an exchange, there must not only be two exchangers, but the article to be exchanged must be such that it can be detached from one and made over to the other. That is, transferability is essential to value.

This point is of much importance, since it at once settles the relation to political economy of certain properties and qualities, which many persons have written about as if these were wealth, namely, health, intelligence, strength, skill, even personal honesty. If, however, we apply the test of our definition, we find that these properties or qualities are not wealth, since they have not value. They have not value, because they cannot be exchanged. A man cannot detach health, strength, skill, or intelligence from himself, and make them over to another person. They can, indeed, be taken away from the present owner, as by death or sickness; but they do not, in that case, become the property of another. The gouty millionaire cannot, with all that he has, purchase the robust health of the laborer by the wayside, or buy for his own empty-headed son the learning or the trained faculties of the humblest scholar.

7. The Use of Personal Qualities May be Sold.—But while these properties and qualities cannot be detached and transferred, and thus cannot be said to be wealth, the present use of them can be made over to another, and hence may become the subject of exchange. The rich invalid may command the services of the robust laborer in waiting on his person; he may hire the poor scholar to be tutor to his son. The use, therefore, of such personal qualities and endowments properly constitutes an item of wealth. By the force of contract, the possessor may even transfer the use of them for a definite period in the future, as when a man is hired by the week, the month or the year. Such a sale, however, of personal qualities or endowments is always a "contingent" one. It is always subject to the chance of death or sickness.

8. Better than Wealth, but Not Wealth.—If we ask why it is that so many excellent writers in political economy have insisted upon regarding health, strength, intelligence and skill as being wealth, we shall find that it is because these things seemed so good and desirable. But the fact, for example, that health is better than most forms of wealth, or that health may be the means of acquiring wealth, does not make it wealth. There are many things which are better than wealth, but are not wealth. "A good name," says Solomon, "is rather to be chosen than riches, and loving favor than silver or gold;" yet a good name is not riches, and loving favor is neither silver nor gold. And, at this point, we find that the popular use of the term coincides with the definition given it for scientific purposes. Plain men do not speak of such qualities or endowments as being wealth. No merchant or manufacturer or laboring man would include any one of these items in an account of his wealth, however precious he might esteem them.

9. The Desire of Wealth.—We have defined wealth. It will be seen that by this term is not meant great wealth; that the idea of luxury, or softness of living, is not necessarily implied in it. In common phrase, when we speak of a man as wealthy, we mean that he has great wealth; that he can, if he pleases, live richly. But the wealth of which the political economist speaks embraces the frugal fare and the small savings of the poor laborer, just as much as it does the sumptuous living and the vast accumulations of the millionaire.

It will be seen from the foregoing that the desire for wealth which leads men to labor and to exchange the products of their labor is not, in all cases, or in most cases, the same as that "love of wealth" which preachers or moral philosophers are wont to condemn. The desire of wealth, on the part of a poor laborer, means no more than his wish to provide decent and comfortable subsistence for those dependent upon him, and to save them from suffering, squalor and filth. On the part of one who is more fortunate, the desire of wealth may mean the wish to have his family respectably housed and decently clothed; the children well educated for the duties of life, and a fair provision made against sickness and old age. This is all which the desire of wealth means, in the case of nearly all human beings. On the part even of those more fortunate still, the desire of wealth may mean, not so much the taste for rich food, sumptuous apparel, gay equipage and social display, as an ambition to undertake great works, for which large resources are necessary; a wish to be esteemed strong, sagacious and masterful; or even the purpose, altogether benevolent, to use wealth in charity or for the promotion of learning, art and religion.

It will appear what a varied matter is the love of, or the desire for, wealth, alike in its origin and in its ulterior objects. It is probably because people have commonly thought of the desire for wealth as the greed of gain, as the passion for display, as the craving for luxury, as the miser's thirst for gold, or as the strong man's love of power and mastery, that political economy has so often borne a bad name. We have shown, above, how partial and how false such a conception is.

10. Political Economy does not Inculcate Love of Wealth.—Even where the desire of wealth becomes a strong appetite or a raging passion, political economy is not to be charged with any part of this. The political economist has not implanted a love of wealth in the human mind; nor, finding it there, does he seek to blow it into a flame. He simply takes it as he finds it; and, regarding it as a social force, he proceeds to inquire how this passion, or propensity, as it exists among men, influences their actions in respect to the production, the exchange, the distribution, the consumption, of that which we call wealth. His business is that of the professor of a science, viz., to trace effects back to their causes, to project causes forward to their effects, within the domain of wealth. Hence, we see how unjust is the sneer at political economy, when it is spoken of as the "gospel of mammon."

11. Political Economy Chastens Greed.—Not only has political economy not implanted a desire for wealth in the human mind; not only does it not inculcate greed of gain; but it would be easy to show that the study of political economy has done much, perhaps more than any or all other causes, to repress violence, fraud and rapine, as means towards the attainment of wealth. By showing how wealth is really best gained and kept, it has tended to banish a ravenous, ferocious greed, which seeks to snatch its objects by brutal force, with whatever injury to others; and has replaced this by an enlightened sense of self-interest, which seeks its ends through services and exchanges mutually beneficial, and which supports social order and national peace, as the conditions of general well-being.

Before Adam Smith published his great work, the "Wealth of Nations," in 1776, it was a maxim of public policy that only one party to a trade could profit by it: that all which one might gain the other must lose. Out of this root grew wars and commercial restrictions, which set man against man and nation against nation, making intercourse between even the most highly civilized states a game of deceit and violence. Adam Smith, by his masterly exposition of the mutual benefits to be derived from exchange, left the love of wealth in the human mind, not rebuked but enlightened. Men might still seek wealth as earnestly and ardently as ever, but no longer by the old, bad, brutal, heathen methods. Little more than a hundred years have elapsed since the appearance of the "Wealth of Nations": yet mankind have, within that time, made greater progress toward humane and mutually beneficial relations between states and nations, than during all other centuries of human history.

CHAPTER II.

THE CAUSE OF VALUE.

12. Utility Essential to Value.—We have defined value as, briefly speaking, power in exchange. We are now to inquire whence comes that power? Why is it that one article has value and another has not? Why is it that one article has great value, while another, perhaps more beautiful, perhaps more useful, has little value? These are questions we shall now try to answer.

We may certainly begin by assuming that no one will give for any article his labor or the product of his labor, unless he has a use for that article, or unless he is buying it for someone who has a use for it. Hence we say that usefulness, or utility, is an essential element of value. We need make no exception to the statement, that, wherever value is, there is utility.

But we must explain just what we mean by utility, or usefulness. That word, as we use it here, signifies no more than that an article meets a felt human want: that men have *a use* for it. But this is not the sense which the word always has. By it is sometimes meant that an article is beneficial: that it does good to the person who owns or consumes it, in making him stronger, wiser, happier or better; or, else, that it does good to the community. Now this would not answer, in the present case. An article may have utility, in the sense that men have a use for it, in the sense that it satisfies a want which men feel, and yet be harmful, perhaps in a high degree. Intoxicating drinks are, to most persons who buy them, very injurious: yet, so long as men will give for them their labor or the products of their labor, intoxicating drinks possess utility, in the economic sense. Many articles which are always used, or which are often used, in such a way as to injure the mind, or body, or both, are useful in this sense.

13. Value not Proportioned to Utility.—We have said that there is always utility where there is value. Is it, also, always true that there is value wherever there is utility? We answer, no. There cannot be value without utility, but there may be utility without value. Nothing is more useful than atmospheric air: there is nothing for which men have a more constant use, nothing of which they have a more intense need. Yet atmospheric air has, as a general thing, no value at all. Every man, even the poorest and meanest, takes of it what he will, without giving anything in exchange. Water, too, has a high degree of utility. Although men have a use for it in widely varying degrees, some water, more or less, every human being craves, with an eagerness which would soon result in delirium and death, were it denied. Yet water is generally to be had without giving anything in exchange for it. Men help themselves to what they want of it.

Not only is it true that there are some articles which have great utility and no value at all: but among articles which have both utility and value, the value is not always in proportion to the utility. Of two articles, both of which are very useful, both of which men desire and earnestly crave, either of which it would be pain to be deprived of, one may have a high value and the other a low value.

14. Difficulty of Attainment, the Second Element of Value.—We conclude, then, that there is another element of value. And, on reflection, we find that element to be difficulty of attainment, or, as it is sometimes called, scarcity. If we apply these two tests, utility and difficulty of attainment, we shall be able to explain every case of value which we meet, or of which we can conceive. We are sure, therefore, that our analysis is correct.

The reason why men do not, in general, give their labor, or the products of their labor, in exchange for atmospheric air or water, is not that these substances are not useful to them; but that there is, usually, no difficulty in obtaining as much of either as anyone can require. The moment there comes to be any difficulty in obtaining a sufficient amount of atmospheric air, that substance may fairly become the subject of exchange: that is, may acquire value. Air may be delivered to divers under the sea, through pipes or rubber tubes, at a fixed price per cubic foot. A great amount of labor and capital is often employed in supplying atmospheric air to miners under ground, where it is paid for at a high price. While one can always have in his house, for nothing, as much bad air as his family can breathe, pure air in a dwelling is often very costly. It is, indeed, one of the most expensive of all luxuries: so expensive that many persons who devote large sums to display and fashion do not feel themselves rich enough to have their own houses, and the churches, schools, concert halls and theatres which they or their children attend, decently well ventilated.

In general, as we said, water has no value. Indeed, a great deal is sometimes paid for merely getting rid of it: for pumping it out from cellars and mines and low lands, or for building dikes or levees against it, along the banks of rivers or upon the sea-shore. On the other hand, when, in desert countries or in great cities, water becomes difficult of attainment, in the quantities desired and in the right times and places, it comes to command a price, perhaps a high price.

Again, iron, although distinctly the most useful of all the

metals, in the extent and variety of its applications, has a much lower value than many others, simply because the difficulty of attainment is, in its case, less. The price which a man pays for a knife, for instance, does not measure the usefulness of the knife to him, but only the difficulty of attainment. He pays, in fact, fifty cents for the knife: but he would sooner pay $5, or $10, or even $50, than not have a knife.

15. Demand and Supply.—We have thus far spoken of the two elements of value, viz., utility and difficulty of attainment; but when we come to investigate the ratios of exchange, and to talk of buying and selling in the market, it will help us very much to substitute for these terms two others, viz., Demand and Supply.

The fact that an article is useful gives rise to the demand for it. The difficulty of attainment, in the case of any article, governs the supply of it. The value of an article depends upon the demand for it and the supply of it. A large demand does not necessarily mean a high price, since the supply may be practically unlimited. A small supply does not necessarily mean a high value, since the demand may, also, be small. But in the case of any article which is desired by men, and which can only be obtained through the exertions and sacrifices of economic agents, value is, at any time, fixed by the relation between supply and demand. *Other things equal, if demand increases, or supply decreases, value will rise. On the other hand, if demand decreases or supply increases, value will fall.* Inasmuch as the demand for any article and the supply of it are subject to frequent changes, sometimes great and sometimes small, sometimes one way, sometimes the other, it is not to be expected that its value will long remain the same. But this liability to change of value is very different in the case of different articles. Some move as rapidly and frequently as a weathervane; others have a certain degree of stability. But it is always to be borne in mind that, whenever any change of value takes place, it must be due to a change in demand, or in supply, or in the two unequally. We say unequally, since, if the change in demand were just equal to the change in supply, value would remain unaffected.

CHAPTER III.

THE PRODUCTION OF WEALTH.

16. Production Defined.—The term, production of wealth, embraces all those acts and courses by which it comes about (1) that an article which before had no value acquires value, or (2) that an article which before had a certain value now bears a higher value. The production of wealth is not the creation of matter, but the creation of value.

The word, production, is derived from two Latin words which mean drawing forth or bringing forward. The term is very significant as applied to wealth. Much of the production of wealth which takes place, as we shall see, consists merely in drawing things out from where they have no value and in bringing them forward for human use.

17. Three Kinds of Value.—A German economist (Prof. Knies) has said that the production of wealth embraces the creation of three kinds of value, time-value, place-value, and form-value. The distinction is not one which we shall need to carry through our study of political economy; but it is interesting at this point, as affording good illustrations of what is meant by the creation of values.

18. Time-value.—Time-value is created in the case of ice, when it is produced, kept along, carried over, from the winter, when nobody wants it, and when it is, perhaps, an obstruction and a nuisance, into the summer, when many people want it, and want it very much. Keeping the ice over from winter to summer, producing, extending it, with all which that requires of labor or of care, is the creation of value: is, therefore, the production of wealth. Wine and many other articles of human use may acquire greatly increased value with age.

19. Place-value.—This species of value is created whenever an article is safely transported from a point where it has no value to a point where it has value, or from a point where it has a certain value to a point where it has a greater value. Most of the values created by commerce are of this kind. Many commodities have two or three times the value in the markets of New York or London which they have in the regions from which they were brought. Timber which is worth eight or ten dollars a thousand feet in Georgia or Canada, will bring, without change of form, twenty-five dollars in Boston.

The addition to the value of articles due to transportation varies very widely. It is, of course, greatest in the case of bulky articles, like lumber and coal, and of perishable articles, like summer fruits. Some articles will, as the saying is, "bear transportation;" that is, their heightened value will repay the cost of transportation, for thousands of miles; other articles are not worth, in any market, as much as would be required to transport them a hundred miles, even by the easiest route. Of course, a great difference is made in the cost of transportation, according as the carriage is by water or by land;* according as it is done by carts and wagons, or by trains of cars; or, again, if it be by carts or wagons, according as it is over smooth and level roads, or over rough and steep mountain paths. It is an old saying that "resistance is distance;" and it is true that two places separated by a thousand miles of navigable water may be

---

* In his speech on the tariff, in 1824, Daniel Webster estimated the cost of bringing iron from Sweden, by water, to Philadelphia, to be no greater than the cost of carrying it from that port fifty miles into the interior.

nearer, economically speaking, than two places divided merely by the spur of a mountain chain.

20. Form-value.—The third kind of value which has been spoken of, namely, form-value, is that which is most important of all. By far the greater part of the operations which we call industry, are for the purpose of creating this species of value. Creating value, as we said before, not creating matter, since, generally speaking, the matter involved grows less as the value grows greater. A block of marble, which may be worth twenty dollars, comes under the hands of a sculptor. His whole work consists of chipping-off portions of the marble, which are thrown away. When the sculptor has finished his task, there is only one-half or one-third as much marble as at the beginning; but the statue is worth a hundred, a thousand, or ten thousand dollars, according to the skill and taste of the sculptor. Cotton has a certain value in the storehouse of the planter, along the Red River or the Yazoo. After the cotton has been ginned, i.e. cleaned by machinery, there is less of it: less, not only by the amount of seed and impurities removed, but less of actual cotton, since the ginning process involves some waste. Notwithstanding this, the cotton is worth more, although there is less of it. When the cotton is taken to the mill, and picked and carded and rolled and spun and woven, there is, at each stage of the manufacture, a loss of material, greater or smaller. Yet, in each case, what is left is worth more than the whole was, until we come to the point where the pound of cotton, which was worth eight cents in the planter's hands, is worth fifteen, or twenty-five, or fifty cents, in dress goods, in thread or in lace. When iron ore is made into pig-iron, there is a great loss of iron; when pig-iron is made into wrought-iron, there is a further loss; when wrought-iron is worked up into building or carriage hardware, the quantity is still more diminished; but at each stage there is an increase of value.

21. Wealth and Value, Again.—Always and everywhere, the production of wealth means the creation of value; and always and everywhere, value is power-in-exchange. It is not a question whether men ought to desire the articles produced; whether those articles make them better or wiser or healthier or happier. If, in fact, a man does desire any article sufficiently to give for it his labor or the product of his labor, there we have a case of value. Wherever and whenever, by whatever acts, in whatever ways, value is created, there and then wealth is produced.

22. The Three Primary Agents* of Production.—The three primary agents in the production of wealth are land, labor and capital. In every creation of values, all these agents are engaged, although the proportions in which they severally contribute to the production of wealth vary widely. In the production of a pound of cotton, worth ten cents, there is a large use of land. When that cotton is made into fabrics worth twenty-five cents, the additional use of land is comparatively slight, consisting mainly of the occupation, for a few seconds of time, of a very small part of the ground on which the factory is built, and of a few quarts of water falling through fifteen or twenty feet and helping to turn the great wheel of the mill. When the cloth, thus made, is cut and sewn and formed into a garment, the additional use of the land is probably smaller.

---

* When the reader shall reach the close of Chapter VII., it will be seen that we introduce a fourth grand agent in the production of wealth, under modern industrial conditions, viz. business ability; meaning, by that, business ability (both natural and acquired) in an exceptional and high degree, suited to the vast cares and responsibilities of production where the division of labor has been carried to a wide extent. This, however, cannot properly be termed a *primary* agent of production.

still, for each cent's worth of value added. Even in the creation of time-value and place-value, a certain use of land is required, whether for stores and warehouses, or for roads and the tracks of railroads, stations, wharves, etc.

In the same way, the proportions in which labor and capital contribute to the production of wealth vary widely. Two articles may be exchanged for each other, one of which has required the use of two times, five times, or ten times as much capital as the other. In that case, the other article has probably cost more, perhaps very much more, labor

CHAPTER IV.

LAND.

23. Land Defined.—The term, land, as used by the political economist, embraces all natural agents, of which use is made in the production of wealth. It has reference, not more to tilled fields than to pasture and meadow, to forest and mine. It embraces the water as well as the "dry land." Wherever a stream falling over a ledge gives the force which is used to drive the great wheel of the mill, there we have a case of the use of land, in the production of wealth. The fisheries of the deep sea and of the shallow bays and arms are closely related to such "extractive industries" as the cutting of timber and fuel from the forest, the raising of coal and metallic ores from the depths of the earth, or the gathering of ice from the frozen waters of fresh lakes and rivers. All these operations, even to the boring for petroleum or natural gas, relate to the land, as the economist uses that word.

24. The Quantity of this Agent of Production is Fixed.—The land—the aggregate of all the natural agents at the disposal of any community—is, unlike the capital that may be placed upon the land, unlike the laborers who may be called to work upon it—a fixed quantity. There is so much of it and there can be no more. It is not in the power of mankind to increase the breadth of the land, or to add anything to the sum of the natural agents which are subject to human uses. Men may, indeed, from time to time, discover resources in nature not previously suspected ; they may increase the dry surface at the expense of the water surface, as when a great part of Holland was redeemed from the ocean by dikes, built with prodigious labor ; as when lakes and swamps are tapped and drained, to become the fields of a flourishing agriculture. Again, whereas one generation only scratched the surface, to raise a scanty and precarious crop, succeeding generations may learn to plough and bring up the productive essences of the soil from great depths. Still again, by engineering skill and the invention of powerful machinery, shafts and galleries may be run through solid rock ; and substances, liquid and solid, of great usefulness to men, may be raised through the crust of the earth, to a distance of 1500 or 2000 feet. But in all this there is no addition to the sum of natural agents ; only a larger or a better use of those already existing. Sooner or later, later or sooner, human ingenuity and labor will reach the end ; and it will, thereafter, only be a question of the wise or the unwise use of the natural agents placed at the disposal of mankind.

25. All Use of Land involves a Certain Loss.—Not only do the productive properties and powers of the soil constitute a fund, which cannot be increased by human effort ; but there is involved, in all use of the land, a certain loss, which, so far as science enables us to foresee, is permanent and irretrievable.

That loss may, for any given production of wealth, be very small, under prudent management ; while recklessness, greed and ignorance may turn that necessary loss into monstrous and hideous waste. Many of the once fairest lands on earth, which supported large populations in comfort, are now little better than sterile deserts, owing to man's abuse of nature.

How, it will be asked, can this be so, if the modern scientific law known as "the conservation of energy" be true? How can any force be lost out of nature? I answer, No force can be lost; but force may, by purpose or accident, be transmuted from forms in which it has ministered to human wants, into forms in which it is useless to man, and even into forms which are injurious and destructive. A cottage, which has long sheltered a family, may, through the snapping of a coal, pass-off in heat and smoke; and in half an hour nothing will be left but a heap of ashes and blackened stones. There is just as much force in the world; but there is one cottage less. Almost any article that nourishes the human frame may be transmuted into more or less virulent poisons. The mere dissipation and scattering of valuable substances may deprive them of their usefulness. Such is the condition under which the human race occupies and enjoys the earth.

CHAPTER V.

DIMINISHING RETURNS IN AGRICULTURE.

26. The Great Law of Agricultural Production.—But, aside from the progressive diminution of the productive powers and properties of nature, through human use, we find that the land, at any given time, is cultivated or enjoyed subject to one universal condition, which we express by the term, the law of diminishing returns in agriculture. This law may be stated as follows:

AFTER A CERTAIN POINT HAS BEEN REACHED, IN THE CULTIVATION OF ANY TRACT OR FIELD, AN INCREASE OF PRODUCT CANNOT BE OBTAINED WITHOUT MORE THAN A PROPORTIONAL APPLICATION OF LABOR, OR CAPITAL, OR BOTH.

Thus, we may suppose that a field in Hampshire, England, is producing 24 bushels to the acre, under an outlay, by the farmer, in labor and capital, which we may represent by $24a$. Now, inasmuch as this field has long been under cultivation in a community where labor and capital are abundant, and inasmuch as the farmer knows all about the field, what is best to do with it, how it can be made to yield the largest crop for the least labor, we may fairly assume that the point of diminishing returns has been reached. If this be so, then it will be true that the farmer cannot raise the crop to 27 bushels, an acre, by simply expending $27a$ upon the land; still less can he raise the crop to 30 bushels, an acre, by expending $30a$; much less, still, can he raise the crop to 33 bushels by expending $33a$. Instead of this, he might find that 27 bushels would cost $28a$;

30 bushels, 32a; 33 bushels, 36a. The amounts of labor and capital required to raise the larger crops might even increase more rapidly, perhaps much more rapidly. To raise 33 bushels to the acre might cost, not 36a, but 40a; while to raise 36 bushels might cost 50a, and to raise 39 bushels might cost 60a. But, whether the increase in the amounts of labor and capital required be greater or be smaller, it is true that, whenever a certain point has been reached in the cultivation of any field, for the purposes of any crop, a more than proportional amount of labor, or of capital, or of both, will thereafter be necessary, in order to increase the produce, in any degree, however slight. This is what we mean by the law of diminishing returns in agriculture.

27. The Universality of this Condition.—The existence of this condition cannot be disputed. There is no acre of land on the face of the globe, on which 60 bushels of wheat can be raised with twice as much labor and capital; 90 bushels, with three times as much labor and capital; and 120 bushels, with four times as much labor and capital, as would be sufficient to raise 30 bushels. Every time a farmer breaks up a new field, in order to increase his crop, he bears testimony to the existence of this law, for, if that law did not exist, it would be easier for him to increase his crop by applying a larger amount of labor and capital to the old land. Generally speaking, the new land he breaks up is not quite so good as the old; yet it pays him better to raise the additional produce from poorer land than to "force" the cultivation of the older and the richer tracts. Every time a body of population leaves an old country to break up land in a new one, fresh testimony is paid to the existence of this law, which, indeed, has furnished the main motive force of the migrations which make up so large a part of human history.

And this law applies universally to all the produce of the land, whether in the form of "crops," or of ore from the mine, or of fish from the sea, or of timber from the forest, or of wool and flesh from the sheep that graze over the unbroken ground : only, in these latter cases, the operation of the law is more apt to be disguised, or hidden from view, by other causes.

Let us take, for illustration, the ore from the mine. The larger the quantity of ore which it is necessary to raise, the deeper must the miner go into the crust of the earth. The deeper the mine, the greater the labor of pumping out the water which continually tends to flood it ; the greater the labor required for ventilation, to force in fresh air and expel the poisonous gases which are every hour forming in the shafts and galleries ; the greater the labor required to hoist the ore, ton after ton, to the surface.

28. Importance of this Law.—The law of diminishing returns in agriculture must be mastered in all its bearings, if the student is to make progress safely in Political Economy. If this principle is not at the time understood, or is subsequently lost sight of, the most monstrously false opinions may be formed regarding the production of wealth and the conditions of human existence. But for the law of diminishing returns, thousands of millions of men might live in the United States as comfortably as tens of millions. As it is, all mankind dwell, and must forever dwell, under the shadow of this condition. After a certain point has been reached, land will only yield the material for food, clothing and shelter in continually, and after a while, rapidly, diminishing proportions, in return to man's effort.

And that "point" is not merely a theoretical one, or one which, while it might be, is not likely ever to be, attained. The point of diminishing returns has already been reached in most of the countries of the world. In many, it has long since been passed, with the result of misery, squalor and disease to helpless millions. Even the "new countries" of the globe are rapidly approaching that point.

Of course, when one is reasoning in regard to the operation of any force, he is always understood to mean "other things equal." Now, as other things seldom are equal at any given time, and as they tend to become more and more unequal from time to time, the conclusions one may reach, in writing of the operations of any simple force, will required to be understood, or to be qualified, or to be modified, or to be corrected, according as other things are unequal. The fact that other things, which affect the cultivation or enjoyment of the land, change greatly, from time to time, has obscured the law of diminishing returns, in the sight of the unthinking, and has even led some generally intelligent persons to deny its existence.

29. Causes which set back the Point of Diminishing Returns.—Thus, when we say that, after a certain point, the produce of the land can only be increased through a more than proportional application of labor and capital, we assume, among other things, that the art of agriculture remains the same. If improvements take place, these will not change the law, but they will change the point at which the law begins to apply. Let us illustrate. One hundred years, or fewer, ago, it was universally believed that, if a piece of land were to be cultivated every year, through a considerable period, it would become exhausted: that is, the land would lose its fertility and would thereafter be worthless. Consequently, it was held that, for one year out of three, or out of four, land should be allowed to lie "fallow," that is, uncultivated, and no demand be, for that year, made upon its productive essences. Now, under this condition, it might have happened that a community, with a certain number of people, cultivating, say, 6000 acres, had just reached and touched the point of diminishing returns; i.e., the number of laborers being what it was, the product, per laborer, was then greater than it would have been with a larger number of laborers. More laborers would, indeed, have produced more corn; but not enough more to make each laborer's share as large as before. Now, in the case of this community, it might have happened that, just at this point, the principle of the "rotation of crops" was discovered. What is that principle? This: that different crops do, to a considerable extent, draw different elements from the soil. Crop a takes element a; crop b, element b; crop c, element c. Consequently, a piece of land which had been cultivated, one year, in crop a, and the next year in crop b, might really be resting as to elements a and b, while producing crop c, the third year.

The discovery of this principle would clearly change the point of diminishing returns, in the case of the community we have supposed. Formerly, it may have been the custom to let the land lie idle one year out of three: in that case, only 4000 acres could be cultivated in any given year. Now, 6000 acres may be cultivated every year, *which gives the same result as if the land had been increased to* 9000 *acres*, without the rotation of crops. Consequently, the number of laborers may increase for a considerable time before they reach the new point of diminishing returns.

30. Effect of Agricultural Improvements.—One hundred years ago, land, in the most highly civilized countries, was cultivated by means of shabby little ploughs with, at best, an iron tip upon the share. Consequently, the soil was brought up by the plough from but a little depth; and it was almost, though not quite, the same as if the soil itself had been shallow. Our own President Jefferson is said to have been the inventor of the first iron plough. By little and little, the iron plough grew larger and stronger, bringing up the soil from greater and greater depths.

Now, an acre which is ploughed to the depth of sixteen inches may not, taking ten or fifty years together, produce twice as much as an acre which is ploughed to the depth only of eight inches, but it will certainly produce a great deal more in any year or during a term of years. If we suppose, then, that, in the community we have been talking about, the point of diminishing returns had again been reached, by the increase of laborers, in spite of the rotation of crops, it might happen that this point would be once more changed through the introduction of deep ploughing. The 6000 acres, cultivated to the depth of fourteen or sixteen inches, would be equal to 8, 9 or 10 thousand acres, perhaps, when cultivated to the depth only of six or eight inches.

Again, we might suppose that the vegetable species, up to this time cultivated, had been such as yielded a very large amount of root and stock, for a small amount of grain and fruit. If this were the case, the introduction of new vegetable species, yielding a large amount of edible matter, to a small amount of stalk and root, would be practically equivalent to increasing the amount of land: that is, a larger number of laborers could get from the soil as good a living as the smaller number had, before this change.

In the same way, in the case of a community raising sheep and cattle, the introduction of improved breeds instead of the little, rough, underbred animals which formerly yielded very little of flesh or of wool or of milk, for a large amount of grass consumed, might have the effect to move the point of diminishing returns much further off.

31. The Law Holds, None the Less.—As has been said, the introduction of new arts, and the improvement of familiar processes, from age to age, has obscured this great law of agricultural production. So much so that many writers, seeing a large population supported in comfort upon lands which once yielded a scanty subsistence to a small population, have been disposed to deny the existence of the law altogether. But this is an error. At any given time, the art of agriculture being as it is, the point of diminishing returns is liable to be reached by the increase of population. Nor can it be reasonably expected that improvements and inventions will indefinitely put-off that point, in the life of any community. Sooner or later, later or sooner, according to circumstances, that point must be reached; and if the number of laborers thereafter increases, each laborer must be content with a smaller product: that is, with meaner subsistence.

32. Effect of Diminishing Returns in Agriculture upon the Products of Manufacture.—The law that has been described governs all the productions of the land. How does it stand related to the products of manufacture? I answer: Only so far as the materials are concerned. All these are derived, more or less directly, from the land; and the cost of producing them, or their price in the market, inevitably feels the influence of the law of diminishing returns in agriculture. But all kinds of manufacture do not employ the same amount of materials derived from the soil, for a given amount of labor and capital: and, as the efficiency of labor and the efficiency of capital are not subject to the same law, it follows that different industries may be differently affected. The influence of this cause may be very great in one branch of industry, while in another it is so slight as to be scarcely worthy of notice. For example, iron ore and coal are products of the land, and consequently subject to this law. The greater the quantities required, the deeper into the earth's crust must mining operations be carried, the larger the amount of labor involved in getting out a ton of either. Now, pig-iron is a product of iron and coal, treated by labor, aided by capital, in a way which we shall hereafter be called to note. A large increase in the cost of coal and iron ore will cause a large increase in the cost of pig-iron. That increase, however, will not be so large, proportionally, in the latter as in the former case. The cost of the ore and coal required to make a ton of pig-iron may have been enhanced from $6 to $7; but, if the manufacturer of pig-iron can now sell his product for $13, instead of $12, as before, he will make himself good for the additional dollar which the coal and the iron ore have cost. In this case, the increase in the cost of the coal and the iron ore, due to the principle of diminishing returns, has been one-sixth; while, in the case of pig-iron, it has been only one-twelfth.

33. Apply More Labor Still.—Again, wrought-iron, in a great variety of forms and for many uses, is a product of pig-iron and coal, treated by human labor, aided by capital, as before. A ton of pig-iron, worth $13, might be worked up into hardware of many kinds, a part being worth 30 dollars a ton; other portions, 50, 75 and 100 dollars; other portions still, to which more labor and capital had been applied, 200 or 300 dollars; other portions still, i.e. fine cutlery, watch springs and surgical and philosophical instruments, being worth 500 or 1000 dollars a ton. Now, the reader will observe that, all through this process, it is only the increased cost of the original coal and iron ore, and of the small additional amount of coal or charcoal, for the shaping, welding or tempering heat required, which is due to the principle of diminishing returns. The same cause which would double the cost of pig-iron, might increase the cost of knives and watch-springs very slightly.

Again, if it became necessary to cultivate poorer fields, or to raise larger crops from the same fields, in order to supply the community with cotton, and the price of cotton were thereby increased from ten cents to twelve, a pound, this would have a great effect upon the cost of coarse cotton cloth, but a comparatively small effect upon the finer products, such as thread and lace. If the price of lumber were to be doubled by the necessity of going to distant forests, or by the necessity of resorting to smaller trees, the larger ones having been cut away, this would have an immense effect upon the cost of a rough shed; a smaller effect upon the cost of a neat cottage, where the boards should be planed and matched and fitted nicely; a much smaller effect upon the cost of an elegant mansion, where a great deal of labor is expended in carving and turning and polishing the material.

CHAPTER VI.

LABOR.

34. Labor, as an Agent of Production.—It was said that the three primary agents of production are land, labor and capital. We have now spoken, so far as is at present necessary, of land. Let us next speak of labor.

This term is applied to the efforts and sacrifices of human beings directed towards the production of wealth, i.e., the creation of values. Mere muscular exertion is not labor, in the sense of the political economist, since the muscular power of dumb animals belongs to capital. It is even a question whether the work of slaves should be treated as labor, in the economic sense. Some writers have insisted, not without reason, that, so long as human beings are bred and reared in servitude, made to work without their own consent, and not allowed to receive the reward of their own exertions, whatever they do in the production of wealth comes under the law of capital, as we shall hereafter see it. The question is one which is not important to discuss.

Not even all the muscular exertions of free human beings belong under the head of labor. As severe efforts are often put forth in sport or play or for the admiration of bystanders, as for the production of wealth. The sacrifices to which a boat's crew of young men submit, the exertions which they make during months of training, as well as the tremendous physical struggle to which these lead, are not labor, in the economic sense. On the other hand, the work of the professional ball-team, whether in practice or in their occasional contests, is labor, in the full economic sense, because it is directed towards the creation of values. Those sacrifices are submitted to, those exertions made, in order to draw to their games hundreds or thousands of spectators, each of whom pays his shilling, or his two shillings, for the pleasure of seeing an exhibition of high skill and great physical force.

35. What Does "a Day's Labor" Mean?—We have, in the last chapter, spoken of the application to land of certain "amounts of labor" for the production of wealth. It is, however, difficult to apply a universal measure to the quantity of labor made use of in any given case. When we speak of a "horse-power," we mean the force necessary to raise 33,000 pounds one foot upward into the air in one minute of time; and, inasmuch as the downward attraction of gravity is substantially the same on all parts of the surface of the earth inhabited by man, a "horse-power" means the same thing, the world over. But a day's labor * means a very different thing in one of the Pacific Islands from what it does in Bengal. It means a very different thing still, in Russia. It means a very different thing in Russia from what it does in England.

There is, then, no absolute, single measure by which we can determine and express "amounts of labor." But we can bring into comparison men of the same country, men even of different countries, under conditions, as to land and as to tools and machines, nearly enough alike to enable us to say that very wide differences, as to labor-power, exist between individuals of the same country, and between the men of one country, taken as a whole, and the men of

---

* In his history of England, Lord Mahon [Earl Stanhope] states that an English woodsawyer would do as much work in one day as thirty-two Bengalees, at the same business, under precisely the same circumstances.

other countries. These differences let us now try to explain.

Causes of Differences in Industrial Efficiency.

These causes are very numerous; but the chief may be mentioned as follows:

36. (I) Differences in Inherited Health and Strength.—No matter how it came about, whether as the result of the influences of climate, or as the result of other causes working in the past, it is true that the men living, at any given time, in one country were born with a greater capacity for exertion than those of another country. Even if supplied during infancy and childhood with the same food, and brought up in every respect under similar conditions, the men of the former country would, at 15 or 25 or 40 years of age, have a greater lifting or pulling strength, and would be capable of far more prolonged exertion, than the men of the other country. In every community there is a certain capability of labor inherited from the past; and that inheritance varies widely in different countries and in different races. In this respect compare the South Sea Islander or the Bengalee with the Englishman or the Irishman.

37. (II) Food.—Between individuals of the same nation and the men of different nations, who have inherited the same capability of labor, great differences as to labor-power would be caused by differences in the food-supply, both during the period of youth and growth, and during the period of active exertion. Take three men of the same natural powers, and feed one of them on the small amounts of rice which make up the diet of an East Indian; the second on the scanty supply of potatoes and buttermilk which is all the Irish peasant at home can hope to receive; the third on the great variety of vegetable and animal food which makes up the subsistence of a North American farmer, and you will have widely different results, in the three cases, as to the capability of severe and sustained exertions. To a very great extent, what a working man can do, in a given time, depends upon the quantity and the quality of food he has to eat. To neglect this consideration, in speaking of the labor of different countries, and often of different classes in the same country, is to make a great blunder.

38. Food is the Fuel of the Human Engine.—The food which is supplied to the laborer, to enable him to work, bears much the same relation to his efficiency, or work-power, as the fuel put into the furnace, beneath the boiler, bears to the efficiency of the engine. The stomach is, in a high sense, the furnace of the human machine. It is there all the power is generated which is to move the limbs in severe and protracted exertions for the production of wealth, just as the engine derives all the power it has to drive the wheels, which move the machinery of the mill, from the combustion of fuel in the furnace. Up to a certain point, the more fuel is fed to a furnace, the more steam power is created. Likewise, up to a certain point, the more food is given the laborer, the more labor power is developed.

Not only is it true that, up to a certain point, labor power increases with the increase of food; but labor power increases at a more rapid rate than does the food itself. It is the same with the fuel in the furnace. If we suppose that a furnace, of a certain size and pattern, required, for its best working, 100 pounds of coal, it would by no means follow that 50 pounds would do half as much work; it might do only one-third as much, or one-quarter as much. This, clearly, would be an uneconomical use of the machinery. If, again, the supply of coal were to be reduced to 25 pounds, the engine might not do enough work to make it worth while to use it at all. This would be a very uneconomical use of the machinery. If we suppose the amount of solid food, of a certain standard, which was required to keep an able-bodied man in condition to do his best work, was 250 oz. a week, it would not be true that with 200 oz. he would do four-fifths as much; with 150 oz., three-fifths as much; with 100 oz., two-fifths as much. On the contrary, the first hundred ounces might only suffice to keep him alive, doing no work at all. The next 25 oz. might enable him to crawl feebly about, working with little energy and through short periods of time. With 150 oz., he might easily do twice as much work as with 125 oz.; with 200 oz. twice as much as with 150.

Hence it will appear that it is a very uneconomical use of food to give it in such small amounts as 100 or 125 or 150 oz. per week. Every additional ounce of food, up to a certain point, creates more work power than any of the ounces which preceded.

39. Is there any Limit?—There is, of course, a limit to the increase of labor power through increase of food. After a certain point, the advantage resulting from a more liberal supply might be small; at a still further point, it might cease to be an advantage at all; a little later, the point might be reached where a still further increase of food might be positively deleterious, leading to physiological obstruction and disease. These successive points change according to the constitution and habits of individuals, according to climate, according to occupation, according to circumstances innumerable. But for each person, there is, at any time, an economic maximum of food, the consumption of which will, in his case, yield the largest amount of working power, for each unit of food. If more food be taken into the system, there may be a still further creation of laboring power; but the gain will be less than proportional. If less than this economic maximum of food be given, the amount of working power developed will not only be less, but less for each unit of food. As the supply is reduced, this loss of labor-force goes on at a ratio which is much more rapid than the ratio of the reduction of food. When a certain point has been reached, the amount of labor power generated by each unit of food is so small, that, speaking only with reference to the production of wealth, we may say that the food so given is wasted. Were it not human beings but dumb animals that were concerned, no one would hesitate to say that it would be more profitable to kill them than to feed them so low.

40. How Laborers are Underfed in the Old Countries.—It is very difficult for an American, brought up in the midst of plenty, in a land where the point of diminishing returns has not been reached, to realize how mean and poor is the subsistence of a great part of the inhabitants of the world. Except in a few favored countries, nearly all of them, like our own, " new countries," and except among the most favored classes in a few other countries, the laborers of the world receive far less than the economic maximum of food. In some countries, the amount of food going to the average laborer is so small as to fairly reach the point indicated by the last sentence of the preceding paragraph. As a matter of self-interest, it would not pay to keep horses and cattle at all, unless they were to be better fed than are hundreds of millions of our fellow-creatures.

The miserably inadequate diet of the people of China and India, keeping them all the time on the very verge of famine, is so familiar, from common report, as not to require to be dwelt upon here. I will quote a few facts from official reports or from the writings of well-known economists, regarding the food of the working classes in some of the more favored countries of Europe.

Of the industrial classes of France, Lord Brabazon wrote, in 1872: "Many a French factory hand has never anything better for his breakfast than a large slice of common sour bread, rubbed over with an onion so as to give it flavor." At about the same time, Mr. Locock wrote, from the Netherlands: "Meat is rarely tasted by the working classes in Holland. It forms no part of the bill of fare, either for the man or his family." From Belgium Mr. Pakenham wrote: "Very many have for their entire subsistence but potatoes with a little grease, brown or black bread, often bad, and for their drink a tincture of chiccory." Now, France, Holland and Belgium are not among the worst but among the best countries of Europe, industrially speaking. If we cross over the Channel to England, which is the richest country of Europe, we find, even there, that a large portion of the laboring class are kept below the economic limit of subsistence. "In the west of England," wrote Prof. Fawcett, about 1864, "it is impossible for an agricultural laborer to eat meat more than once a week."* Of the peasants of Devonshire, Canon Girdlestone wrote, a little later: "The laborer breakfasts on tea-kettle broth—hot water poured on bread and flavored with onion—dines on bread and hard cheese at twopence a pound, with cider very washy and sour; and sups on potatoes or cabbage greased with a tiny bit of fat bacon. He seldom more than sees or smells butcher's meat."

Bad as the state of things was when Prof. Fawcett and Canon Girdlestone wrote, it had been even worse in the

---

* And yet Prof. Fawcett could write that "it is physically impossible that any permanent rise in wages should take place without corresponding diminution of profits." If there were any physical impossibility in the case, it would seem to be the impossibility that such wretched peasants could be better fed without adding to the profits of their employers.

preceding generation. The poor law commissioners of 1833 reported, that at that time, while the British soldier was receiving 168 oz. of food, per week, according to a certain standard, and even the public pauper was receiving 151 oz., the agricultural laborer received but 122 oz. Now, it goes without saying that, when the laborer, toiling from morning to night in the field, receives a smaller amount of nourishment than the sense of public decency will allow to be given to paupers, the laborer is underfed, in the sense that he will and must underwork.

The reader will naturally ask why, if laborers receiving more food would do more and better work, employers do not furnish more ample subsistence. This important question can only be answered when we reach the chapters on distribution.

41. (III) Sanitary Conditions.—In order to secure the laborer's greatest efficiency, it is not only necessary that he should have an abundance of good food, but that there should be an ample supply of fresh air. After the food, which has been taken into the stomach, has been digested and turned into blood, that blood must pass into the lungs and be there purified. Carbonic acid is to be thrown off, and oxygen taken in from the air. But if the oxygen has been used up and the air is already loaded with carbonic acid, that purification cannot take place. The human being, so situated, becomes heavy and dull, his blood becomes foul, and the tissues tend to corruption. In such a case, a large amount of food taken into the system may even become a source of weakness and ill-health.

Moreover, in close and unventilated rooms are likely to be found the germs of active diseases which shorten life or permanently impair physical activity. So great is the effect of this cause that we have here the explanation of no small part of the differences of working force which are found among the laborers in different countries. The first great prison reformer, John Howard, shocked the world with the revelations which he made of the way in which the convict classes were housed; yet Mr. Edwin Chadwick could say, in 1842: "More filth, worse physical suffering and moral disorder than Howard describes as affecting the prisoners, are to be found among the cellar population of the working people of Liverpool, Manchester and Leeds, and in large portions of the metropolis."

Even the agricultural population was not much better provided for. The following is a description given by the poor law commissioners, of the cottages of the county of Durham: "The chimneys have lost half their original height, and lean on the roof with fearful gravitation. The rafters are evidently rotten and displaced, and the thatch, yawning to admit the wind and wet in some parts, and in all parts utterly unfit for its original purpose of giving protection from the weather, looks more like the top of a dunghill than a cottage. Such is the exterior; and when the hind comes to take possession, he finds it no better than a shed. The wet, if it happens to rain, is making a puddle on the earth floor. . . . They have no byre for their cows, nor sties for their pigs; no pumps or wells; nothing to promote cleanliness or comfort. The average size of these sheds is about 24 by 16. They are dark and unwholesome; the windows do not open, and many of them are not larger than 20 inches by 16; and into this place are crowded 8, 10, or even 12 persons."

In Scotland the case was scarcely better. Sir James Caird stated, that, in 1861, one-third of the people lived in houses of one room only; another third, in houses of two rooms only. Prof. Gardiner, writing of Glasgow, said: "Out of a population of 85,000 householders, 30,000 or 35,000 belonged to a class who are most dangerous in a sanitary point of view." The dwellings of Ireland were even worse. Mr. Inglis thus describes the city homes of 1834: "Hovels, cellars, mere dark dens: damp, filthy, unwholesome places, into which we should not, in England, put any domestic animal."

If it is in homes such as have been described, that children grow to maturity and get the size and strength which are to determine their quality as workers, what wonder that they become stunted, weazen and deformed! If it is in homes like these that laboring men have to seek repose and refreshment, after the day's work; that they breathe the air which is to oxidize their blood, and eat and digest the food on which to-morrow's work is to be done, what wonder that the blood of manhood becomes foul and lethargic, the nerves unstrung, the sight weakened or distorted, the whole tone of life and of labor depressed!

42. (IV) Intelligence.—The three causes we have thus far adduced, are physical, affecting the muscular power and endurance of the laborer. The cause now mentioned is mental. It is the laborer's intelligence which enables him to apply his bodily force to his work, not only with effect, but with the greatest effect. How great a factor in industrial efficiency the general intelligence of the laborer may be, is only seen when we consider the several elements which make up that efficiency.

(*a*) The intelligent laborer requires a much shorter apprenticeship; less of technical instruction. It is said that the recruits in the British army who can read and write learn their drill in one half the time taken by recruits who cannot read and write.

(*b*) The intelligent laborer requires far less superintendence. Superintendence is always costly. If an overseer is required for every ten men engaged on a piece of work, the product must pay for the time not of ten men, but of eleven. If the overseer, as is most likely, gets twice the wages of a common laborer, then the product must pay for the time and labor of twelve men. The employer could just as well afford to pay his men 20 per cent. more, could he dispense with the overseer.

(c) The intelligent laborer is far less wasteful of material. No product can be obtained by labor, even in agriculture, without the sacrifice of pre-existing wealth. Would you raise a crop of wheat? a bushel must be sown for every six or eight bushels to be reaped; and with it, perhaps, large quantities of costly manures. In mechanical industries, the value of materials used in manufacture is often as great as the amount of wages paid. Frequently the value of materials consumed is greater, sometimes much greater, than the amount paid in wages: in some cases, twice as much, in others, five times as much. If, then, an unintelligent laborer is going to waste, or spoil, or in any degree injure, the materials given him, he will soon do more harm than his labor is worth.

(d) The intelligent laborer can use delicate and intricate machinery to advantage, and he alone can. In most countries no machines are used in agriculture, but only the simplest and coarsest of hand tools. This is not, mainly, because the people are too poor to have machines, but because they are too ignorant to use them. Were the best peasant out of twenty to be given a mowing machine, or a reaper, he would bring it so quickly to wreck and ruin as to offset the value of his whole summer's work. The United States is, indeed, the only large country in which the ordinary agricultural laborer can be trusted with complicated machinery.

In manufactures, the difference wrought by intelligence or want of intelligence on the part of the working classes is even greater. In some parts of Eastern Europe, even the primary "mechanical powers" are not made use of. If the inhabitants wish to lift a weight, they do it by main force, instead of using the pulley, the windlass or the inclined plane. As to the complicated and expensive machines employed in factories, the ordinary European peasant has no fitness whatever for dealing with them.

43. (V) Cheerfulness and Hopefulness in Labor.—The cause now adduced is moral, affecting the will, which controls alike the physical and the mental powers of the laborer. Since severe and sustained exertions are naturally irksome,* cheerfulness and hopefulness in labor must grow out of the self-respect and social ambition of the laborer and his personal interest in the result of his work. It is here, that is, in the moral elements of industry, that we find the most potent cause of differences in efficiency. Cheerfulness and hopefulness in the laborer become the spring of exertions, in comparison with which the brute strength of the slave is but weakness. Chattel labor is always and everywhere ineffective and wasteful, because it has not its reward. As Adam Smith said, a person who can acquire no property, and does not even own himself, can have no other interest than to eat as much and work as little as possible. No matter how complete the power of the master over the person and over the life, he cannot command all the faculties of his slave. The slave may be made to work, but he cannot be made to think; he may be made to work, but he cannot be kept from waste; to work, indeed, but not with energy.

---

* Yet in this respect the races of men differ widely. It is one of the fruits of culture that the operation of the mental and physical powers becomes, every generation, less and less irksome, until, with the men of the best brain endowment, effort becomes actually pleasurable. But, for the vast majority of mankind, in their present stage of development, the statement in the text needs but slight qualifications.

Energy is not to be called forth by threats and blows, but by hope, ambition and aspiration. The whip cannot reach the parts of the man where lie the real springs of action. The slave cannot, if he would, work as if he were a freeman. The nervous force is only in a small degree under the control of the conscious will. It is only when some passion of the higher nature, love, gratitude or hope, is awakened, that a man can render his best service.

44. Unprofitableness of Slave Labor.—Had it not been for the impotence of the lash, the nations would have risen far more slowly from the almost universal condition of slavery. The slave has always been able to make it for his master's interest to sell him freedom. He could always afford to pay more than any one else could make out of him. Hence, the former slave-states of the American union, building their political and social institutions upon slavery, as the corner-stone, had to forbid or restrict the exercise of manumission. Even with the little the black could apprehend of the privileges of freedom, even with his feeble hopes and aspirations, condemned by his color to social exclusion, he could always buy himself, if allowed to do so. This unprofitableness of slave or bond labor, it was, which prepared the way for those great changes which transformed whole populations of slaves or serfs into nations of freemen.

Among free laborers, great differences in industrial efficiency are found to exist, according as the reward of labor is near and certain, or distant and doubtful. It is in the case of the proprietor of land, under just and equal laws, that the incentives to industry are found most acute. He knows that every stroke of his arm is creating value, which he, himself, and his children after him, will enjoy to the full. Neither bell nor whip is needed to drive him afield. He goes gladly to his work, at the first flush of morning; and the setting of the sun finds him still hoeing the corn, or tying up the vines, or tinkering the sheds, or caring for the cattle. Long as is his work-day, he is not worn out at the close. The waste of muscular force is, in such labor, at its minimum. Nervous exhaustion comes late and comes slowly to him who sees his reward manifestly growing under his hands.

It is not alone active exertion which is called out by the proprietorship of land. Of even more consequence is the care which is taken to prevent injury and waste; to keep tools and implements in order; to save the growing vines and plants from their thousand enemies; to keep the live stock at their best; to store and house the gathered crops.

45. Industry and Frugality Awakened by Ownership.—The familiar examples of industry and frugality, are those afforded by the peasants of France, Holland and Switzerland, in the cultivation and care of their little estates. A hundred years ago an eminent traveller, Arthur Young, wrote, of a certain district in France: "An activity has been here that has swept away all difficulties before it and has clothed the very rocks with verdure. It would be a disgrace to common sense to ask the cause: the enjoyment of property must have done it. Give a man the secure possession of a bleak rock and he will turn it into a garden: give him a nine years' lease of a garden, and he will turn it into a desert." Many of the vineyards which greet the eye of the traveller, along the Rhine, have for their entire soil earth which has been carried, in baskets, up the mountain side by the laborious peasantry. "When I used to open my casement," wrote Mr. Inglis of his stay in Zurich, "between four and five in the morning, to look out on the lake and the distant Alps, I saw the laborer in the fields; and when I returned from an evening walk, long after sunset, there was the laborer, mowing his grass or tying up his vines."

I said that it was the proprietor of land, under just and equal laws, who exhibited, in the highest degree, industry and care for the preservation of wealth. We have two very striking examples of the impairment of these qualities by unfair conditions or laws. It would certainly make any one laugh, to-day, to hear the Scotch people spoken of as indolent. Their energy and activity has been shown in all the corners of the earth; yet, a hundred and thirty or forty years ago, "the lazy Scotch" were a proverb throughout Europe for negligence and indolence. This was because of the system of short leases, then almost universal in Scotland, which robbed the laborer of a greater part of the proper fruit of his exertions. A single act of wise legislation, providing for long and secure leases, changed all this, and brought out the real energy and spirit which are innate in the Scottish character.

Only half as long ago, the Irish were known, in their own country, as hopelessly lazy. This was universally believed to be a part of their character. It was, in fact, the creation of unjust laws and a bad system of land tenure. When the Irish, emigrating under the pressure of famine, found themselves upon new lands, under strange suns, having an equal chance with others, they soon showed themselves the equals of any in hard and patient labor.

46. The Hireling.—We have thus far been speaking of men working for themselves, and entitled to receive all the fruits of their labor. Whenever men take the position of hired laborers, working for wages, some part of this hopefulness and cheerfulness in labor, which we have seen to be the fruitful source of strenuous exertions, is, by the very nature of the case, lost. If a man working at wages, for another, does not put into his work all the energy he would if working for himself, if he fails to exercise all the care of tools, implements, materials and product which he would were they his own, this is not wholly a matter of blame. We have already seen that not all the springs of activity are under the control of the conscious will; and it is scarcely possible for any man, no matter how sincere his intentions, to do all for another which he would for himself. At the same time, it must be said that there is a great difference among individuals of the same community, and also among the men of different nations and races, in regard to the capability of doing the work of others, as if it were one's own. There are men, there are even nations, that have this capability in a high degree.

It need not be said that these are the nobler nations; and that the spirit of fidelity and devotion to duty, thus carried into hired labor, has also its political reward, making these nations more strong and peaceful at home and more powerful abroad, than those which have a lower capability, in the direction of which we have been speaking.

CHAPTER VII.

LABOR CONTINUED—THE ORGANIZATION OF INDUSTRY.

47. The Division of Labor.—We have thus far spoken of the causes which produce differences in working force, or labor power, among individuals. We are now to consider certain causes which give to large bodies of laborers, whether individually weak or individually strong, a greatly increased power of production. These may be embraced under the title, organization of industry, though that term is not altogether satisfactory. Let us first speak of what is called the Division of Labor.

In a very primitive condition of industrial society, each man does, as a rule, what every other man does. The community is, indeed, divided on the line of sex, the women taking up certain duties which are considered more suitable to their strength and intelligence; but the men are all herdsmen, or all hunters, or all fishermen, or all tillers of the soil, according to the circumstances in which the tribe is placed. Each man's work is like every other man's, except so far as natural strength, skill, and courage enter to make distinction. After a while, however, in such a community appears the smith, under one name or another, cunning to make or repair the implements of the chase or of husbandry; to build boats, or to cover-over the humble dwellings of the tribe. The smith, by virtue of his skill, fares better than all the others, except the chiefs, yet the hunters or herdsmen or fishermen have more left to themselves, after paying for the smith's work, than they had when they tried to do smith's work for themselves and did it very poorly. As the tribe grows in numbers and in knowledge, more and more smiths appear; and these come, in time, to be divided into classes, such as the blacksmith, working upon metals; the carpenter, working upon wood, and the mason, working upon stone or brick. As wealth increases and the wants of the community become varied, a great number of occupations come to be recognized, until the members of a community are called by a hundred different names, to describe their ways of contributing, individually, to the production of wealth.

48. Advantages of the Division of Labor.—The advantages of the division of labor are many. The most important may be indicated as follows.

(*a*) The division of labor not only develops dexterity in general but it gives technical skill. In a primitive community, where each man, by turns, does a great variety of work, there is, commonly, little nicety of touch, agility of movement or accuracy of vision. To use a familiar phrase, it may be said of a member of such a community that his "fingers are all thumbs;" and that his senses are not subtle. It is, generally speaking, only when arts and trades become developed and are carried to a high point of perfection, that the qualities indicated become the common property of the community.

Not only do a people, among whom the division of labor has proceeded far, come to possess this general dexterity; but each person acquires a high degree of technical skill by applying himself, day by day and year by year, to his single avocation. Adam Smith stated, that, in his day, a good blacksmith, who had, however, practised but little in making wrought nails, could, by giving his whole day to the work, make, perhaps, two or three hundred nails, of a rather poor quality. A blacksmith who frequently made nails, but without having this for his sole or principal business, could perhaps make eight hundred fairly good nails in a day. But a man who gave himself wholly to making nails could turn off twenty-three hundred in a day, all of the best finish.

(*b*) The division of labor saves much time in apprenticeship. A man who had to perform a great variety of duties would never become a really skilled workman, but would die before he had learned any one of these well. Even after the division of labor had appeared and been carried far, it still required a great deal of time to thoroughly learn one trade. Seven years used to be the period of apprenticeship. When, however, owing to the still greater multiplication of arts and the still greater introduction of machinery, one of these former trades becomes broken up into half a dozen or more, the time required to fit a person to do his work in life is greatly reduced. It does not take nearly one-fourth as much time to learn to do one thing well as to do four things well. Indeed, many people could never learn to do four things well, who will yet learn to do one thing very well.

(*c*) The division of labor saves time that would otherwise be occupied in passing from one kind of work to another, and in laying down and in taking up the tools of different trades. This is a consideration, sometimes of great importance, sometimes of little importance.

(*d*) The division of labor promotes improvements and discoveries. Many a man, who, if he had been occupied in passing through a long succession of varied duties, would never have made any discovery or invention, has, by being shut up to one single kind of work, and having his attention concentrated upon that alone, come, in time, to devise the means of doing rapidly and easily that which before had been done slowly and painfully. It is true that many of the greatest inventions have been due to those who were not personally engaged in doing the work to which their new machines were intended to apply; but on the other hand, there has been an incalculable number of inventions which have been the result of confining one ingenious mind to a single difficult problem.

It is worth while to notice here, that, while the division of labor greatly promotes invention, it sometimes happens that, after this has been going on for a long while, invention comes in to change the course of things and actually to diminish the division of labor. Thus, when Adam Smith wrote, there were eighteen different operations involved in the making of a common pin ; and this extensive division of labor undoubtedly contributed to the steady improvement of tools and implements used by these different operatives. Sixty or seventy years later, some ingenious person invented a pin-making machine, by which the wire was drawn out, cut off, sharpened, headed, and all the successive processes of manufacture, down to sticking the pins into the paper, were performed upon the simple condition of moving a wheel.

(*e*) More important, perhaps, than any of the preceding, is the consideration that the division of labor permits the adaptation of physical powers and personal qualities throughout a great variety of work, and gives to almost every man, woman, or child a place in the industrial order. In a thousand industries of the present time, there is some part which a feeble or crippled person can perform : something which such a person can do just as well as the largest and strongest. In primitive states of society, the practice was often resorted to of exposing sickly or deformed children, while infants, to be devoured by wild beasts, or to die of hunger or cold. This seems horrible enough ; yet it is fairly a question whether there was not as much kindness as cruelty in it, when it is considered that to these unfortunates life only could have been protracted misery, since society had then no place in which they could work and earn their bread.

Secondary Advantages of the Division of Labor.

Such are some of the primary advantages of the division of labor. There are others which are, by one stage, more remote, but not less real or perhaps less important. Some of these may be indicated as follows:

49. (I) Competition.—Where each one of a number of persons is every day performing a variety of miscellaneous duties, now a little of this and then a little of that, it is difficult or impossible to measure the work done by the several persons so employed: to say that this one has done more, or less, than that one: to assign credit or blame according to real desert. It is, in such a case, moreover, difficult or impossible to say how much of the day's labor has gone to this piece of work or to that; and it is, by consequence, difficult or impossible to compare the labor-cost of things so produced. But when work is so divided and the parts so distributed that each man becomes charged with a certain definite task, it is not only possible to make comparisons between the amounts accomplished by different workmen within the same trade, and to make comparison between the labor-cost of different articles, but every one, at once, naturally, begins to do so. Such comparisons are made with ease and confidence; and with comparison enters competition. Every man compares himself with his fellow; every employer makes comparisons among his workmen, both as to the amount and as to the quality of the work; each producer looks carefully about, on every side, to see if there is not some article of equal value that can be made at a smaller cost of labor.

50 (II) A Standard of Performance.—With the laborers of a community distributed among different occupations, according to their powers and qualifications, and with such opportunities for comparison as we have just now shown to exist, there comes to be a standard for the performance of work, in each separate art or trade. Some mason, for instance, who is exceptionally true of eye and hand, one day lays a better wall than he, himself, had ever before done, more straight and even and firm. This immediately becomes a standard for the future, not only to him, but to every other mason in the neighborhood, and also to all persons who employ masons. It having been once seen that so good a wall can be made, all hereafter desire that their walls shall be made not less perfectly. After this standard has been reached by the craft, some mason, some day, goes ahead of this and builds an even better wall; which, in turn, becomes the standard of future work: and so the thing goes on. What men will do depends very much on what they try to do; what they will try to do depends very much on what they believe possible, or upon examples which they have themselves seen of the best work.

51. (III) Esprit de Corps.—With the formation of large bodies of laborers, devoting themselves to certain arts and trades, there soon arises a sort of public sentiment within the craft, which demands of every member that he shall at least approach the standard of performance which at the time exists, and that he shall not, by his actions, throw discredit on his fellow workmen. This public sentiment, within the trade, often exerts more influence on many workmen than competition alone would do. A great many, who would care little about pleasing their employers, will do, or will forbear, a great deal in order to keep the respect and goodwill of their fellows.

52. (IV) Industrial Environment.—By these somewhat hard words, I mean to express the influence, in addition to all that has been before spoken of, which is exerted upon the laborers of a community, in general, by their being placed in the midst of a great, powerful, and highly organized system of production. In such a community, the child is brought into the world half an artisan. From his parents he has derived handiness, aptness, quickness, and fertility of resource. Then, too, he becomes a better workman simply by being accustomed, through childhood, to see tools used with address, and through watching the alert movements, the prompt co-operation, the precise manipulation, of bodies of skilled workmen. The better part of industrial, as of every other kind of education, is unconsciously obtained. And when the boy goes himself to work, he finds examples, on every side, to imitate; if he encounters an obstacle, he has only to stop, or hardly even to stop, to see some older hand deal with the same; if he needs help, it is at his elbow; and, above all, he comes under impulses and incitements to exertion, and to the exercise of care and pains and ingenuity, which are as strong and constant as the impulses and incitements which a recruit experiences in a crack regiment, from the moment he dons the uniform.

53. Is there an Offset to this?—But, it may be asked, is not this increase of production at the expense of health and life? Does it not mean that the laborer will be the sooner and the more completely worn out? I answer, that, in part, this may be so; but that in part, probably the greater part, it is not true. It is not necessarily true in any degree. Two things are to be borne in mind.

(*a*) Mankind were made for labor, for patient, energetic

labor. Keen, persistent activity is, up to a certain point, not injurious. On the contrary, industry has its sanitary, not less than its economic reward. Neither idling nor dawdling over work is beneficial to health.

(*b*) A little of disorderly work is often more trying than a great deal of orderly work. Perhaps some one of my readers will remember a day of travel which was peculiarly tiresome. He may have been called up unnecessarily early, and have been not a little worn out by the suspense of waiting before it was time to start; then, at the last moment, it may have been discovered that something was lacking. This involved a deal of hurrying to and fro, and an anxious and excited search, followed by a sharp run to the railroad station. Here it was learned that the train was late, and the end of a half-hour of uneasy waiting and moving about saw the traveller on his way, already pretty well tired out. Further delay upon the track, by reason of a "hot-box," and a failure of connection at a railroad junction, completed the misfortunes of the morning; and the traveller arrived at his destination, after a really short journey, more used-up than would have been involved in making a well-ordered and fortunate trip of five times the distance. In the same way, the proper direction of industry will enable laborers to accomplish much more, with much less of nervous strain and muscular wear-and-tear. There are some countries where, if you were to enter a factory, you would think a small riot was in progress. Everybody seems excited and hurried, and there is a great deal of shouting and running to and fro; yet, as a matter of fact, the machinery is moving at a much slower rate than is customary in an English factory, and the "output," per hand, is scarcely one half as much. In an establishment where each person has his place and perfectly knows his duty; where work never chokes its channels and never runs low; where nothing comes out wrong end foremost; where there is no fretting or chafing; where there are no blunders or catastrophes ; where there is no clamor and no fuss, a pace may be maintained which would soon kill outright the operatives of a noisy, ill-disciplined, badly-organized shop.

54. (V) Mastership in Industry.—When the division of labor has been carried a great way, in any community, production receives a tremendous impulse from the fact that large bodies of labor and capital come under the control of individuals who have exceptional ability for the conduct of business. In a primitive state of society, the man of great brain-power and will-power moves but a single pair of hands. In an advanced industrial state, he may move a thousand. If his choices as to what shall be done, how it shall be done, when it shall be done, are judicious, there cannot fail to be a vast gain in the amount of work done and in the amount of waste saved.

The division of labor in its first stages does not require the introduction of the master class. When the forms of production are few, and the materials are simple; when only hand-tools are used, and the artisan, working at his bench, makes the whole of an article; when styles are standard and the consumers of a product live close at hand, the need of the employer is not greatly felt. Each artisan may carry on his work, in his own little shop, and keep up with the others.

But when the hand-loom gives place to the power-loom ; when great numbers of persons, of all degrees of skill and strength, are brought into the giant factory, each performing one simple operation, knowing perhaps nothing about any other; when powerful and delicate machinery is introduced; when costly materials have to be brought from the four quarters of the globe, and the product is to be distributed, by the agencies of commerce, throughout distant lands, then the employer becomes not only a necessity of the situation, but the master of the situation. If he have the genius to plan, he can find a thousand helpers, each of whom will do his own part perfectly, yet not one of whom but would have been utterly helpless and amazed in the face of the difficulties and dangers which only bring into keener exercise the powers of the real man of affairs.

55. Business Ability as the Fourth Grand Agent in Production.—At the close of Chapter III, we spoke of three great primary agents of production, viz., Land, Labor, and Capital; and that statement suffices for a primitive society. But when we undertake to account for either the production or the distribution of wealth, upon the vast scale of modern industry and trade, in all enlightened and progressive nations, it becomes necessary to introduce a fourth agent of production, viz., Business Ability; to admit a fourth claimant in distribution, viz., the Employer.

By Business Ability in this connection, we mean ability in more than the degree which is required to enable a single laborer or artisan to direct his own production and manage his own small affairs; in more, even, than the degree which is required by the employer of labor in that state of industry where the division of labor has proceeded but a little way.

By Business Ability, as a distinct economic agent, we mean the power, the capacity, the temper required to do business, with at least moderate success, in those later stages of industrial organization, when the division of labor has proceeded far, when production takes place upon the large scale, and with reference mainly to general, rather than to local, markets.

CHAPTER VIII.

CAPITAL.

56. The First Canoe.—We have thus far spoken of land and labor; we are now to speak of capital.

The capital of a community is that part of its wealth* which is devoted to the production of wealth.

A very simple illustration will suffice to show the origin and office of capital.

Let us take the case of a tribe dwelling along the shore and living upon fish caught from the rocks jutting into the sea. Summer and winter together, good seasons and bad, they derive from this source a scanty and precarious subsistence. When the fish are plentiful, the people live freely, even gluttonously. When their luck is bad, they submit to privations which involve suffering, sometimes famine. Poor as this condition of life is, it is not likely to grow any better. Unless some new force enters into the life of the tribe, their children and grandchildren will be found living just as meanly and precariously.

But let us suppose that one of these fishermen, moved by a strong desire to better his own condition, undertakes to lay-by a store of fish. Living as closely as will consist with health and strength, he denies himself every indulgence, even at the height of the season; and, so, by little and little, accumulates in his hut a considerable store of dried food. As the dull season approaches, he takes all he

---

* Excluding land and natural agents, considered as unimproved.

can carry and goes up among the hills, where he finds trees whose bark he detaches by sharp stones. Again and again he returns to his work in the hills, while his neighbors, who ate more freely than he during the fishing season, are painfully striving to keep themselves alive. At the end of the dull season, he brings down to the water a canoe, so light that it can be borne upon his shoulders, so buoyant that in it he can paddle out to the "banks," which lie two miles or ten miles from shore, where in a day he can get as many fish as he could catch from off the rocks in a week.

57. The Canoe-Builder.—The canoe is capital. Its owner is a capitalist. He can now take his choice of three things. (1) He may go out in his boat and bring home supplies of fish which will allow him to marry and rear a family in comfort and security, while, with the surplus, he hires some of his neighbors to build him a hut, their women to weave him blankets and nets, their children to bring water from the spring and to wait upon his family. (2) He may let out the boat to some one who will be glad to get the use of it by paying for it as much fish as one family could possibly consume; and he may himself stay at home in complete idleness, basking in the sun or on stormy days seeking refuge in his comfortable hut. In other words, he may thereafter "live upon his income." (3) He may let out the canoe, and himself turn to advantage the knowledge and the experience acquired by its construction, in making more canoes.

This last is what he is most likely to do. Again and again he comes down from the hills to the shore, bringing a new canoe, for which scores of fishermen clamorously compete. And it is to be noted that the later boats are made at a smaller cost of effort and sacrifice. He has found out the groves where the trees are largest and the trunks most clear of branches. He has acquired a knack which makes it almost a pleasure to strip-off vast rolls of tough, elastic bark. He no longer spoils the half-completed work by a clumsy movement or an ill-directed blow. Moreover, his personal toil and pains are reduced to a minimum, since, for a small part of the price of a canoe, he hires some of his neighbors to carry his burdens and do the heavy work.

58. The Increase of Canoes.—But soon the canoe-builder's gains are threatened. Thus far, in the possession of exceptional skill and knowledge, he has been a monopolist, and has reaped a monopolist's profits. Now, however, stimulated by the sight of such great wealth (that is, so great a command of other people's labor) acquired by one man, others begin to enter the field. As an essential condition, each must first save and accumulate enough food to support him while making his first boat: that is, must accumulate a certain amount of capital. This, however, is much less difficult than it was in the case of the original boat-builder (1) because fish have come, through the multiplication of boats, to be much more easily obtained; (2) because, with good models before him, the new builder has fewer experiments to make, and a far less ingenious man can now make a fair boat; (3) because certainty and nearness of success will inspire the labors of ten men, where one will be moved to exertion and sacrifice by a prospect that is distant and doubtful. Moreover, some of the shrewdest of the assistants of the old boat-builder, who have watched him at his work and whom he has trusted, more and more, to do even the nicer parts of the task, begin to desert him and to set up for themselves.

With this increase in the number of builders, the rent of boats falls rapidly and the profits of the business are greatly reduced. The first boat repaid its cost in a few weeks or even days. Indeed, the builder might, if he had chosen, have lived thereafter, so long as the boat lasted, in complete idleness, getting as much fish as he could eat simply by letting-out the boat to others. But now a boat only repays its cost in months, perhaps in years. Still the men who make boats get a better livelihood than those who use them; while those who use boats get a better livelihood, even after paying a high rent, than those who fish off the rocks.

59. The Parting of the Ways.—Now let us suppose that the manufacture of boats has proceeded so far that there is one serviceable boat for every four adult males of the tribe. At this point, one of two widely divergent courses may be adopted, with very important results to the future of the community.

1st. The multiplication of boats goes forward till each man is provided with a boat in which he can catch enough fish in an hour or two, a day, to keep himself and his family, summer and winter, good seasons and bad. The creation of capital has at least led to this result: it has put famine out of the question. There is always an abundance of cured fish, even in the meanest hut. All the time not occupied by fishing is spent in idleness or sport.

2d. The manufacture of boats stops at the point where fish for the whole tribe can be provided by one-fourth of its members. These toil early and late upon the banks; while the remaining members of the tribe work for them, in one capacity or another. Only so many boat-builders remain as are needed to repair and keep up the existing stock of boats. Many of the tribe become housebuilders, since no one is now willing to live in the paltry huts which formerly were thought good enough for anybody. Others become domestic servants in the families of the fishermen, of the boat-builders, and of the housebuilders. Others occupy themselves in making and fashioning trinkets and ornaments, which, in a semi-barbarous tribe, are always in great request.

Soon new wants emerge.

First, a taste for a diversified diet begins to appear. Whereas, formerly no man thought of anything better than to have enough of fresh or of dried fish to eat, the members of the tribe now crave other kinds of food; and many betake themselves to breaking-up the soil and cultivating vegetables, fruits and grains, which they exchange, on favorable terms, for fish, or for the work of the house-builder, or for menial services on the part of others. Some take to the mountains, and there snare or entrap the wild goats, which they bring down to the shore, feeding and tending and breeding them, and selling their milk, their flesh and their skins for the labor, or the products of the labor, of others.

Secondly, in addition to the taste for a diversified diet, there soon begins to be felt a desire for better dress. Whereas, formerly no one thought of more than to be covered against the cold, the men of the tribe now wish to have themselves and their wives and children clad in comely and even handsome garments; and many now betake themselves to preparing and fashioning skins and animal hair into dress, for their own use and for the use of other members of the tribe.

When we come to speak of the consumption of wealth, we shall see what are the effects of these new economic desires upon the welfare of the tribe which, so short a time ago, lived wholly upon fish caught upon the rocks along the shore.

60. The Law of Capital.—It is not necessary at present to trace further the increase of capital. At every step of its progress, capital follows one law. It arises solely out of saving. It stands always for self-denial and abstinence.

At the first beginning, savings are made slowly and painfully; and the first items of capital have a power in exchange (a power, that is, to command the labor of those who have not capital) corresponding to the difficulty with which they are secured. The first bow, the first spear, the first canoe, the first spade, much as they cost, pay for themselves in a few days, when once they have been made. Subsequent increments of capital are gained at a constantly diminishing sacrifice, and receive a constantly diminishing remuneration, until, in the most advanced countries, buildings are erected and machines constructed which only pay for themselves in ten, fifteen, or twenty years.

At every stage, capital releases labor-power which was formerly occupied in providing for the wants of the community, according to its then prevailing standard of living. At every stage, the members of the community make their choice, whether they will apply the labor-power, thus released, to the production of wealth in other branches, or will content themselves with living as well as before, with less labor, giving up the newly acquired leisure to idleness or sport.

61. The Three Forms of Capital.—In a rough way, capital may be said to exist in three forms: subsistence, tools, materials.

Subsistence.—In the earliest stages, capital consists mainly of the means of subsistence for the producer and his family. It was not easy, at the beginning, to lay-by enough of the game, or the fish, or the fruits, of one season to last until the next. For want of such a store of food many a tribe perished; many another was kept in a low, miserable condition, unable to shift its seat to more promising localities, and continually depleted by famine and disease.

But when once a tribe, by exceptional good fortune, or through prudence and self-control, acquired a reserve sufficient for a full year's subsistence, it became, in a degree, master of its conditions. It could shift its seat to better hunting or fishing grounds. It could pursue its avocations systematically and economically, not, as before, hurriedly and wastefully, under the stress of immediate want. Moreover, the physical strength of its members was kept at the highest point by regular and sufficient diet.

An ample year's subsistence forms the most important advance which a people ever make in their progress towards industrial prosperity. No subsequent step costs one-half, or a tithe, as much. Many peoples never find themselves able quite to accomplish this. The people of British India can hope for no more, in good years, than to be carried through into the next; while, once in every four or five years, a famine following upon a short crop sweeps away multitudes, through sheer starvation, or through the fevers which feed on half-famished populations. Even in Ireland, there was known, half a century ago, a period, two or three months long, preceding harvest, which was called by the peasantry "the starving season." The early Greek poet, Alkman, calls Spring "the season of short fare."

Tools.—The next purpose, in logical and generally, also, in historical order, for which capital is accumulated is the acquisition of tools. We use the word here in its largest sense, including all utensils, apparatus and machinery. The knife, the bow, the spear, the canoe, the net, are the tools of a certain stage of industrial society. The spade, the cart, the plough, the distaff, the forge, are the tools of a later stage. The loom, the lathe, the printing-press, the trip-hammer, the railroad and the ship, are the tools of to-day. The buildings which protect machinery from the weather, and the shops in which trade and manufactures are carried on, are, in this sense, tools.

The increase in productive power which takes place, as a

community acquires the capability of using complicated tools and apparatus, and of applying steam and water-power to move machinery, is immense, almost beyond our conception. One man with simple tools may do the work of ten men, equally strong and equally well fed, who have only their hands to work with. Ten men with the wood-working, cotton- and wool-working, or metal-working machinery of to-day, run by steam or water-power, may easily do the work of a thousand, with distaff, chisel, saw and axe. It s exceedingly important that the youthful student of economics should early be made familiar with some of the applications of tools, apparatus and machinery to manufactures, in order that he may come to appreciate how large a factor in the production of wealth this form of capital is. It would be fortunate if vists to large industrial establishments could be made a regular part of the system of instruction for children.

Materials.—The third form which capital takes is that of materials. The word, as here used, covers all kinds of wealth which are devoted to the production of wealth in any other way than as subsistence for the laborer, or as tools, to increase his power in production. In a primitive state, materials play a small part. The bait for the hook, among a tribe of fishermen; the corn saved for seed, in a planting community, are the most prominent materials in early industry. In a later age, a large part of the accumulated wealth of a community exists in this form.

62. Mutual Relations of the Three Forms of Capital.—We have said that the capital of a community may be classed under three heads: subsistence, tools, materials. In a certain sense, these three may be resolved into one, subsistence; as, indeed, all forms of subsistence itself may be resolved into one, food. Thus, the first simple tools of the barbarous community may be said to be exactly represented by the subsistence required by the laborers engaged in making the tools. The first materials produced by the aid of these tools may be said to be represented by the subsistence of the laborers using the tools, added to that of the laborers who made the tools. And so of the more elaborate tools and machines, and the more various and costly materials, of after ages : all may be said to represent the subsistence of the laborer while engaged in production.

Likewise, all the forms of subsistence, viz., food, clothing, shelter and fuel, may be reduced to one, food. The clothing of the laborer, for example, represents the food which he consumed while he was gathering the fibres of the wild grasses and weaving them into a blanket. The hut represents the food consumed during its erection. The fuel represents the food consumed while the laborer was gathering fagots in the forest.

But, while all the three forms of capital, viz., subsistence, tools and materials, may thus, in theory, be reduced to subsistence, and while the four forms of subsistence, itself, viz., food, clothing, shelter and fuel, may likewise be resolved into food, it yet makes a vast difference to the productive power of the community in what proportion its capital is actually divided among these different elements.

63. Fixed and Circulating Capital.—The economists have been wont to divide capital into two classes, fixed and circulating. The distinction has a certain value, although it is not always easy to say into which class a certain body of capital would fall.

Mr. Mill gives the following definitions of these classes :
" Capital which exists in any durable shape, and the return to which is spread over a period of corresponding duration, is called Fixed Capital."

" Capital which fulfils the whole of its office, in the pro

duction in which it is engaged, by a single use, is called Circulating Capital."

This distinction may be illustrated as follows. Here is a quantity of woollen yarn. Is it fixed or circulating capital? We answer, circulating capital, inasmuch as it does its whole work in production by a single use, that is, when it is woven, once for all, into cloth. On the other hand, the loom on which the yarn was woven, is fixed capital, because it exists to weave many and many a lot of yarn into cloth ; and the return to the capital invested in it is spread over a considerable period of time, several years at least.

Let us take another illustration. Here is a quantity of " stores" fitted to support a large body of laborers, viz., clothes, hats and shoes, meat, bread, groceries, and so forth. Do these constitute fixed or circulating capital? Circulating capital, because they can, as yet, be, so to speak, turned into any industrial direction : that is, they can be used in subsisting laborers who are engaged in making almost any conceivable thing, or class of things. Let us suppose that these goods are actually consumed in subsisting a gang of laborers engaged in building a bridge, or putting up a mill, or making a railroad. Here we should have a body of circulating capital turned into a body of fixed capital, i.e., a bridge, a mill or a railroad, which would continue to perform its industrial purpose throughout many years, perhaps generations, and the return to which would be spread over a corresponding period. On the other hand, we might have supposed these stores to have been consumed by laborers engaged in making shovels or axes, which would be worn out by constant use in a few months, perhaps weeks, and which would thus rightly be called circulating capital.

64. Too Rapid Conversion of Circulating into Fixed Capital.—It will appear, from the foregoing, that, while it might not always be easy, or even possible, to say in regard to a given thing, whether it belonged to fixed or to circulating capital, there is, yet, a general distinction to be drawn between masses of capital, as to the length of time over which their usefulness extends. It is, also, true that, the more capital partakes of the fixed character, the nearer it comes to a single and a specific use; whereas, on the other hand, circulating capital can generally be turned, at will, to any one of many industrial purposes. When the railroad has been built, it will do nothing but carry goods and passengers, on land, by a certain track, from one fixed point to another. For any other purpose, it is worthless; whereas the clothes, the hats and shoes, the food, etc., might have been used to build the railroad, as they were, or to build ships which should carry passengers and freight by water, or to put up mills, or to make the looms for the mills, or to raise the wool, the cotton, or the flax to be woven on the looms, or to do any one of a thousand other things.

If, now, too large a part of the capital of a country should, thoughtlessly or under speculative excitement, be put into railroads, the results might be very injurious. There might not be capital enough left to build the ships to carry away the freight which the railroads should bring down to the seaports; there might not be capital enough left to build the mills, and to fill these with machinery and to supply them with materials, and to subsist the weavers and spinners who should make the cloth which should become freight for the railroads. There might not be capital enough left to "improve" and to "stock" the farms of the country, which should furnish grain and cattle for transportation.

Instances of the too rapid conversion of circulating capital into one or another form of fixed capital have been very frequent. These are especially likely to occur among progressive nations. They are always followed by a great waste of labor-power, sometimes by a partial paralysis of industry; sometimes by what is called a "panic," or a "crisis," when the powerful machinery of production goes wrong, and its force, instead of being employed in creating things useful to men, is turned to its own destruction. This danger is a part of the price which highly civilized communities have to pay for the great advantages of the division of labor, the organization of industry, the **invention of machinery.**

CHAPTER IX.

RELATION OF COST OF PRODUCTION TO VALUE.

65. Relation of Labor to Value.—We have defined wealth; and, in the last few chapters, we have shown under what conditions, as to the use of land, labor and capital, the production of wealth, that is, the creation of values, takes place. We are now in a position to take up, for further analysis, the subject of value.

It is often said that labor is the only efficient cause of value; or, that the values of articles are according to the amounts of labor required for their production, severally. It ought to be evident, at the first thought, that this cannot be strictly true, since, for the production of any article, there is required, as we saw, the use of capital, as well as of labor. If, then, of two articles embodying equal amounts of labor, one requires the use of a great deal of capital, and the other very little, the difficulty of attainment is not equal in the two cases. Now, since difficulty of attainment controls supply, the supply of these two articles would soon become unequal, which, assuming that the demand for both had previously been the same, would give a higher value to the former than to the latter.

Clearly, if we were to use the term, cost of production, to express, not only the amount of labor, but also the amount of capital-power, going into any article, it would be much nearer the truth to say that cost of production determines values, than to say that labor determines values.

66. Cost of Production.—But does the cost of production, even as so constituted, determine values? As a matter of fact, value is so often almost the same as the cost of production, and value is so apt to change as the cost of production changes, the one rising and falling with the other, that it is very natural to speak of cost of production as governing value. And, in a general way, this is true; yet it is easy to show that it is not always the case.

For example, we might suppose that a great improvement had taken place in the methods of making cotton or woollen goods of a certain description, or that mines of coal or iron, far richer and more convenient for working than any other before known, had been discovered. In such events, would the cotton cloth or woollen goods, or the coal or iron, now in the market, have their value governed, in any degree, by what it cost to produce them? Not at all. These articles would at once fall to a new value, corresponding to the new cost of producing articles like them. No man would pay four dollars a ton for coal, simply because that coal had cost four dollars a ton, if coal just as good could now be brought in from the mines at three dollars. No man would pay one dollar a yard for a certain kind of woollen cloth, if the new looms could turn out cloth, in every way as good, for eighty cents.

67. Cost of Reproduction.—Is it not, then, the cost of reproduction, rather than the cost of production which determines value? As between the two, is it not nearer the truth to say that it is not what goods did cost, that determines their value, but what they would cost, at the present time? Clearly this is so. No man is going to pay anything for an article, merely because that article did require for its production a certain amount of labor and capital. Speaking generally, what he will give for it will be closely related to what it now costs to produce this article.

But is it, even, the cost of reproduction, i.e., of keeping up the supply, which determines the value of articles? No. While it is generally true that value is close to cost of reproduction, the two are often far apart. Take, for example, the old looms on which the woollen goods, to which we just now referred, were woven. Let us say that these cost, when they were first made, $300, apiece. That, however, as we saw, is no reason now why they should bring $300. Looms of the same pattern could, perhaps, now be made for $250. Will these looms, therefore, bring $250? Not at all. New looms, of a better pattern, having been invented, perhaps manufacturers could not afford to use the old looms unless they were to obtain them at a very low price, say $100. Possibly the new looms might be found so much more efficient that no manufacturer could afford to use the old looms, at any price; and these may therefore bring only their value as old iron. Here we have a case where an article will sell neither for its cost of production nor for the cost of its reproduction.

Again, here is a house, in a once fashionable street, which, twenty years ago, cost $25,000. Yet the house, in fact, could not be sold for more than $15,000 or $17,000. The foregoing are not strange, single cases. A very large part of all the articles in the world, which have value at all, would not sell for what it would cost to produce equally good articles at the present time.

What, then, is the trouble with the statement so frequently made, that cost of production, or, at any rate, the cost of reproduction, governs value? This is the trouble. Cost of production is only another term for difficulty of attainment. Now, we saw (Par. 15) that two elements enter into value: First, difficulty of attainment, which controls supply; second, utility, which creates demand. To assert, then, that cost of production, or cost of reproduction, determines value, is to say that value is composed of one of these elements only, and not of both.

While the distinction we have drawn between the cost of production and the cost of reproduction is one which needs to be kept always in mind by the student of political economy, it is much more convenient to use the former term; and this we shall accordingly do, throughout the remainder of this treatise. But the reader is asked to remember that, when we speak of cost of production, in respect to any article in the market, what we have reference to is, not the past cost of producing that identical article, but the present or immediately prospective cost of producing an article so nearly like it that, for commercial purposes, there will be no difference between them. Past labor, labor already spent, has no control over, or influence upon, value. It is only present labor, or prospective labor, which, in any way, governs value. How far it does this, how far it fails in doing this, we shall see under our next title.

68. Relation of Market Value to Normal Value.—While, for reasons stated in the last paragraph, it is incorrect to say that the cost of production determines actual value—which we shall hereafter call "market value"—we must always keep the idea of the cost of production clearly in mind, when speaking of the exchange of wealth, since it is this which determines "normal value," a phrase we are now to explain.

Market value is, as has been abundantly stated and illustrated, governed solely by supply and demand. Normal value may be represented by a line [though, by no means, a straight line] which market value always tends to approach, or to which it always tends to return after any departure therefrom. If the market value of any article is, at any time, below the cost of its production, some of those who have been engaged in producing that article will probably soon cease to produce it at all; others will certainly produce less of it than before. The supply being, by these means, reduced, the market value will, if the demand remains the same, rise toward, or to, the normal value. If, on the other hand, the market value is above the cost of production, some, perhaps all, who have been producing this article will produce more of it, perhaps much more of it. It is even possible that some persons who have not been previously engaged in producing this article, may now undertake to do so. The supply being, by these means, increased, market value will turn downward, toward, or to, the normal value.

Now, just as changes in demand, due to the tastes or the wants of the community, or changes in supply which cannot be foreseen, due to accidents, to fires, to floods, to short crops and a variety of other causes, are continually drawing market value away from the normal line, so the self-interest of producers is continually working, in the ways above described, to bring market value back to the normal line. But the tendency of market value to go away and stay away from the normal line is greater in the case of some commodities than in the case of others. With some articles, that tendency is very strong and very persistent. With other articles there are incessant slight fluctuations, now on the under, now on the upper, side of the line which represents the cost of production. It is important that we should dwell here, for a moment, upon the chief causes which tend to bring about and to maintain the divergence of market from normal value.

69. Causes which affect Demand.— In the first place, we have the causes which affect demand. There are large classes of articles the need of which is very steady and constant. People always want these articles, and generally want about so much of them. If, from poverty, a person had to pinch himself at any point, he would give up almost anything sooner than any part of what he has been accustomed to have of these articles. The demand for them, consequently, remains very steady, from week to week and from year to year, perhaps through terms of years. At the other end of the scale, there are many classes of articles, the demand for which is very irregular and uncertain. In respect to some of them, fashion enters, requiring incessant changes in form and style and color. That which was the best, last year, is scarcely worth having, this year. Sometimes the changes of fashion go so far as to throw an article very nearly or altogether out of use.

There are still other large classes of articles, regarding which the changes of demand are not due to fashion, but to the varying means of those who purchase them. If people at any time do without them, it is not because they no longer desire them, but from what is called "want of money." These are articles which people give up when they have to give up anything. The desire for them remains the same; but the demand, economically speaking, diminishes or disappears altogether.

Causes which affect Supply.

Let us now consider the causes which tend to make market value differ from normal value, through affecting the supply of articles. There are many of these; but we can deal only with the most important.

70. (I) The Existence of a Stock.—Suppose there were an article which was found in a raw state, near at hand, ready to be cut down, or dug out, or merely brought to market, as required, at one season just as well as at another. In such a case, market value would never go far away, or long stay away, from normal value. If demand fell off, production would fall off accordingly and promptly. About as much as was wanted would be brought in, day by day; and every day's product would have an exchange-power close to its cost.

The conditions we have just described are realized in the case of few commodities. With most it is necessary to have a stock, larger or smaller, on hand, at all times; and the work of production cannot go on uniformly throughout the year. In some cases, articles can be grown, or others brought to market, only in a single season of the year. Maple sugar is produced within a few weeks of alternate thawing and freezing, in the spring. Wood for fuel is generally brought out of the forest when the snow is on the ground, as it is easier to haul it on sleds than in carts. On many rivers, logs can only be floated down to the sawmills, perhaps hundreds of miles below, during a very short season, when the streams are swollen by the melting of the snows. Ice can only be gotten out in the depth of winter. For the production of some articles the heat of mid-summer is required.

Now, if all the year's supply of any article has to be produced or brought to market in one part of the year, the producers can only guess, and perhaps guess vaguely, what the demand will be five or ten months later. In the case of such industries, the supply cannot be readily checked, if the demand falls off; or be quickly increased, should the demand prove greater than was anticipated.

In the case of some important classes of articles, the amount of production must be determined on, not months, but years in advance of the demand. In order that there may be bread, it is only necessary that the baker shall have time to heat his ovens. In order that there may be flour it is only necessary that the miller should have a week's notice. But in order that there should be wheat from which to make the flour, the farmer must have decided, the year before, how much land he would plant in wheat; the soil must have been broken up, the seed sown, and the growing grain cultivated through the summer. In order that there may be a sufficient supply of wool, the sheep-raiser must have begun his work two or three years ago. In order that there may be horses fit for draft or for the cavalry, four or five years, at least, are required.

71. (II) Substitution of One Article for Another in Use.—A second cause which influences the divergence of market value from normal value, is found in the varying degrees in which different articles can be substituted for others, in use, should occasion arise. There are some articles which have almost no substitutes. If the person cannot get the precise thing he wants, he knows of nothing which would take its place. In the case of other articles, there are many possible substitutes, some of which are nearly as good, while some will barely answer the purpose. If, for example, beef is very scarce, people can use other kinds of meat, without any great loss of physical benefit or pleasure. If wheat is scarce, resort will be had increasingly to other kinds of grain. And this substitution will begin at once, and will be made almost unconsciously. People who have been using wheat five days in the week and Indian corn, or rye, two days, will now use Indian corn, or rye, three days in the week, and wheat only four days. In this way the balance will be brought around again, or, at least, wheat will be kept from rising as high as it otherwise would.

On the other hand, for most of the uses of iron there is nothing that can be substituted for that metal, except at very much greater cost. Copper is worth, say, twelve times as much as iron; aluminum, twenty times as much as copper. Consequently, if the supply of iron proves deficient, the value of it may rise higher and higher, through a term of years, without any considerable substitution of other articles. There will, of course, be less iron used, since people will put stone and brick arches and wooden beams into bridges and houses, where, otherwise, they would have used iron. But, in spite of this, there will still be so much need of iron, for a multitude of purposes, that the value of the stock might be doubled before a new supply could be brought in.

72. (III) Organization of Industry.—We have elsewhere shown how the organization of industry increases the possible production of wealth. The same cause, however, tends to put apart, and to keep apart, market value and normal value. Where a community has been organized into a great number of trades and professions, each person being highly expert in his own particular business, or craft, but knowing little or nothing of others, it is far less easy to increase production if the supply be deficient, or to check production if the supply be in excess, than in a community where arts and trades are few and simple, and each man is more capable of turning himself, should occasion arise, to some other kind of work. Self-interest will still enter, to check production or to increase it, according to the "state of the market," i.e., according to demand; but this will be done much less promptly and effectively, for the reason which has been stated. Men will go on working in the business to which they are accustomed, long after the remuneration they receive has, through a decline in demand, fallen below the remuneration of equal exertions and sacrifices in other branches and industries.

73. (IV) Investment of Capital—Existence of Plant.—In the same way, the need of extensive buildings, fixtures, machinery and apparatus, for the production of certain classes of commodities, may prevent a rapid increase in the supply of those commodities, to correspond to a rapid increase of demand, should such take place. Thus it happens that market value, in these lines, may remain a long while above normal value, in spite of all which the principle of self-interest can do towards bringing the two kinds of value together.

On the other hand, the fact that a large body of so-called "plant," i.e., structures, fixtures, etc., suited to the production of certain goods and of no others, is in existence, may retard the movement of market values upward to the normal line. in cases where a great falling-off in demand has lowered the value of such goods below the cost of production. Inasmuch as the plant is there, and can be used for nothing else, manufacturers may go on producing, even though they get almost nothing for the use of the plant, after paying the wages of labor and the **cost of materials**.

It may even happen that the existence of plant, in a large amount, constitutes a sort of necessity to produce. Thus, in the case of work being stopped in a mine, the shafts and galleries might in a few weeks be filled with water, which it would require much time and great expense to pump out when work should be resumed. It might, therefore, happen that a mine owner, rather than allow his mines to fill up, would go on, for a while, producing at a loss, that is, not even getting back all the wages paid and all the materials consumed. In the same way, it not unfrequently happens that an iron manufacturer for a while produces at a loss, rather than allow his furnaces to "go out of blast."

The degree to which the foregoing cause operates differs widely in different industries. In some, the amount of plant required for a certain product is very small; in others it is very large. Even among those industries where the plant is large, there is a great difference as to the length of time required to extend it; as to the amount of "wear and tear" which is involved in its regular daily use; and as to the injury likely to result from a stoppage of the works.

74. (V) Liability to Deterioration of Product.—Still another cause, which, in the case of many articles, has the effect to exaggerate deviations of market value from the normal line, is found in a liability, greater or less, to deterioration of the product. Thus, in a fish market, the price of a fish might have been a shilling when the market opened, eight-pence at ten o'clock, sixpence by noon, while in the afternoon one could have it almost on his own terms. Strawberries and peaches are often sold, at night, at one-half or one-third of the morning price. The necessity of storage, in the case of a postponed sale, has often the same influence on the price of a commodity as liability to deterioration. The dealer, not having the facilities for storing his stock, may let it go at a very low price, rather than keep it over.

75. (VI) Customary Price.—In respect to certain commodities, public opinion dictates that there shall be a certain, stated, well-known price. Thus, people would not tolerate varying and uncertain prices of admission to places of public amusement; varying or uncertain tolls over bridges, or fares in public conveyances; varying and uncertain fees for the performance of necessary services. To have to haggle and bargain at the door of a theatre, over the price of admission; on the brink of a river, as to the sum to be paid for a cast across the stream; in the sick-room, about the fee for a prescription, or the cost of the medicine that should save life or relieve pain, these things would be intolerable. Hence, public opinion generally establishes a price, for all such occasions, which is irrespective alike of the service rendered to the individual buyer, and of the cost, to the seller, of rendering that service in the particular case. For instance, a traveller would give a large sum of money, rather than pass the night in a storm on a river bank; yet he gets a cast across, at the customary price, be that twopence or a shilling. On the other hand, the ferryman or boatman makes a much greater sacrifice in taking the passenger over at night, in a storm, than if it were in the afternoon of a pleasant day; yet public opinion requires him to subject himself to the greater sacrifice, without any higher charge.

Where public opinion cannot be trusted to establish a customary price, in cases like the above, the law generally enters and fixes the rate. Of course, the price paid must be enough, on the whole, to make it worth while to keep up the service, whether of the apothecary, the physician, the ferryman, the actor or the opera singer. But the price to be paid is made independent of the wealth or the poverty, the knowledge or the ignorance, the little or the great need, of the individuals purchasing.

76. (VII) **Habit and Mental Inertia.**—The last of the causes which we shall mention, as resisting the effort of market value to return to the normal line, is found in the force of habit and in the lack of what is called "initiative," on the part of many or most persons.

No human being ever escapes altogether from the force of habit. It is always easier to do what we have done before, than to do what we have never done; to do what we have done twice, than to do what we have done only once; to do what we have done often, than to do what we have done seldom. The degrees, however, in which men are bound by habit, or in which they are indisposed to do what is not familiar to them, differ widely. A capability of taking the initiative in action, mental courage and activity, freedom from apprehension and superstition, a readiness to meet new conditions, and perhaps even a pleasure in encountering risks and odds, are among the fruits of education and experience. They become an inheritance in families, and even a characteristic of nations and races.

The effects of habit upon values are very important. Habit always, in some degree, often in a great degree, resists the economic tendency to a new price. This effect is seen at its height in wages, the price of labor. A day's wages often remain the same through months, sometimes through years, although, in fact, the utility of the service rendered to the employer changes frequently in that time.

Over the prices of goods habit exerts an influence no less real, though not equally powerful. It often keeps prices steady, against an economic reason for change; and, even when movement takes place, it begins later and ceases earlier, by means of this constant resistance.

CHAPTER X.

PRODUCTION AT THE GREATEST DISADVANTAGE.

77. Relation of Cost of Production to Value.—In the last chapter, we undertook to reach the relation between Value and the Cost of Production. What we found was that Cost of Production determines Normal Value, which actual or Market Value continually tends to approach, though frequently drawn away, and often kept long away, by various causes, affecting supply, or demand, or both.

We have now to take another step in the theory of value. We have thus far assumed that all parts of the required production take place under conditions of equal advantage as to cost, so that the normal value of any kind of goods would be the cost of producing any part of the supply. But, in fact, of the four grand agents of production, land, labor, capital and business ability (see par. 55), two, the first and the last named, have, by force of nature, a wide range as to productive power, from which it results that different portions of the required supply of a certain kind of goods may differ widely as to their several costs of production.

78. Equality of Conditions as to Labor and Capital.—To illustrate this rudely, let us suppose a certain district to be divided into a hundred large farms, each farmer employing fifty men, and having at command $10,000 of capital. Now, we may, for the purposes of reasoning, assume the body of laborers and the body of capital upon any one farm to be the exact equivalents of the corresponding bodies upon any other farm. Of course this might not, probably would not, be literally the case, so far as the bodies of laborers are concerned. One set of laborers might, as it happened, be a little poorer than those employed upon a neighboring farm. But there would be nothing in the nature of the case why an inferior set of workmen should be found upon one farm more than upon another. This would be purely one of those accidents which, for the purposes of reasoning, we are bound to set aside.

As to the capital, we have no need to offer any qualification of our assumption that the several sums of $10,000 are the precise equivalents of each other. There would be just as many ploughs and horses, just as many carts and oxen, just as much food and clothing for the subsistence of laborers, just as much money for wages, in one $10,000, as in any other.

79. Inequality of Conditions as to Land.—But if, now, we suppose these equal bodies of labor and capital to be applied to the raising of crops, shall we find that the conditions of production continue equal? By no means. We shall find differences, very considerable differences: and these, not occurring through accidents which we may disregard, as having nothing to do with the reason of the case; but differences due to the very nature of the subject; differences which cause some portions of the supply to be produced at a great advantage, while other portions are produced at a great disadvantage. It is to finding out how these differences in the cost of production affect normal value, that we devote the present chapter.

What is the cause of the differences which we have indicated as certain to arise whenever equal bodies of labor and capital are applied to the raising of crops? That origin is two-fold. In part, it is found in the varying productiveness of the soil. Those variations, if we contemplate any wide field of industry, are not small, but large; they are not accidental, but are in the nature of the case. The fifty laborers working upon, say, farm No. 31, may be assumed to be the equivalent of the fifty laborers working upon farm No. 5, or upon farm No. 64; but farm No. 31 will only yield 15 bushels of wheat, per acre, while No. 5 will yield 18 bushels, and farm No. 64 will yield 24 bushels. These differences in product do not come from the laborers; they come from the soil; and such differences as we have indicated above are not extreme. There are farms, among the hundred, which will yield less than 15 bushels; and there are others which will yield more than 24 bushels.

80. Inequality of Conditions as to Business Ability.— Then, again, were we to suppose that there were certain farms, absolutely equal in their productive power, we might be assured that there would be found differences, very considerable differences, among the farmers occupying and cultivating them, as to the ability to control and direct bodies of labor and of capital for the production of wealth: differences as to the degree of care and foresight, of energy and economy, of commercial prudence and administrative skill. Such differences in the farmers would come out in the crops, were the lands the same, the laborers the same, the capital the same.

It is true that the abler farmers would tend, little by little, to bring into their employment the best laborers; but it is, also, true that, with the very same laborers, they would get a better, some of them a much better, result than the less efficient farmers. It is true that accidents and misfortunes, of one kind or another, would come to all the farmers in the county—floods or droughts or fires or vermin or rust or mildew, or what not; but it is, also, true, that, in the first place, fewer of these calamities would, in the long run, fall upon the far-seeing and painstaking farmer than upon his less diligent and prudent neighbor; secondly, that those which did come would fall with less force; and, thirdly, that the resulting mischief would be more quickly repaired and remedied in the former than in the latter case.

81. Production at the Greatest Disadvantage determines Normal Value.—Now, with differences existing as to the conditions of production, both as regards the fertility of the land and as regards the degree of business ability, what shall determine normal value? I answer:

THE NORMAL VALUE OF ANY KIND OF GOODS IS DETERMINED BY THE COST OF PRODUCTION OF THAT LAST CONSIDERABLE PORTION OF THE NECESSARY SUPPLY WHICH IS PRODUCED AT THE GREATEST DISADVANTAGE.

Let us proceed in this matter by successive illustrations. Wheat is raised upon some lands, in England, at a cost not exceeding two shillings, a bushel. Is this wheat, therefore, sold at two shillings? Does it even tend to be sold at that price? Is there any economic force, whatever, which operates to compel, or to induce, the farmer to sell that wheat at that price, or somewhere near it? All these questions are to be answered by a simple no. The cost of production in this case has absolutely no connection whatever with the price. Did anybody ever, in these days, hear of good wheat being sold in Mark Lane, London, at two shillings a bushel? Yet there are lots of it produced at a cost below two shillings.

Again, there is a vast extent of lands on which wheat is raised at the cost of three shillings a bushel. Is this wheat sold at three shillings, or does it tend to be? Again, no. Still further, there are lands on which wheat is raised at the cost of four shillings, and others, still, on which it is raised at the cost of five shillings; but the product is not sold at a price equal to the cost of production, or in any

way corresponding to it. What, then, does fix the price of what we may call the two-shilling wheat, the three-shilling wheat, the four-shilling wheat, the five-shilling wheat? I answer, it is the cost of raising "*that last considerable portion of the necessary supply which is produced at the greatest disadvantage.*" Let us suppose that there are ten million bushels of the two-shilling wheat, twenty million bushels of the three-shilling wheat, thirty million bushels of the four-shilling wheat, forty million bushels of the five-shilling wheat. We should then have one hundred million bushels produced at the cost of five shillings, or less. But let it be supposed that the demand for wheat exceeds, and tends considerably to exceed, this amount. Just how much the demand shall exceed a hundred million bushels, will, of course, depend upon the price. Let us suppose, for instance, that there are enough people who want wheat, and who want enough wheat, and who want wheat badly enough, to make up an effective demand for a hundred and thirty million bushels, at not exceeding six shillings. If then, the next grade of land, that, viz., which will yield wheat at the cost of six shillings, were extensive enough to produce, if required, fifty million bushels, we should have the normal price of wheat, on these conditions, fixed at six shillings, a bushel. This price would just repay the cost of cultivation on the last grade of soils, yielding no profit.*
That price would equally be paid for all other portions of the supply of wheat, yielding profits which would represent the difference between the cost and the price. To whom this profit shall go, is a question which it would be premature to raise at this point. Only a portion of the six-

---

* I use the word, profit, for the present, in its generic sense. Such profit, in the case of land, will hereafter be specifically called rent.

shilling land would be cultivated. No part of the seven-shilling, or the eight-shilling land would be brought into use.

82. Take Silver Mining as an Illustration.—Silver is produced, in not a few mines, at the cost of twenty-five cents, an ounce, or less; but it is not, on that account, sold for twenty-five cents. If the demand for silver, for use as money or in the arts, be sufficient to fix the price at one dollar, silver will be produced at what we may call the twenty-five cent mines, the fifty-cent mines, the seventy-five-cent mines and the-one dollar mines; but it will all be sold at the same price, namely, one dollar. The last class of mines will yield no profit, but only pay for the working; while the other classes of mines will yield a profit on their product of, respectively, seventy-five, fifty and twenty-five cents, an ounce. Nobody thinks of offering Mr. Mackey or Mr. Haggin twenty-five cents, an ounce, for his silver, merely because it cost only that sum. All the silver produced is sold at the same price in the same market. That price is fixed by the cost of production from *the mines the least rich in their deposits, or the most expensive to operate, which the existing demand requires to be worked in order to secure the necessary supply.* The demand being no greater than it is, the dollar-and-a-quarter mines and the dollar-and-a-half mines, of which there are a great number, will not be worked, any more than will be the two-dollar, the three-dollar and the four-dollar mines, which, between them, contain an immense amount of silver, very much scattered.

In like manner, we might go over the whole ground of the articles known to the market, finding, in every case, that normal price is fixed by the habitual average cost of producing "that last considerable portion of the supply which is produced at the greatest disadvantage;" while, in every case, likewise, all other portions of the supply are sold at the same price, whatever their individual cost of production, yielding a profit, the disposition of which we shall have occasion to investigate when we reach the subject of the Distribution of Wealth.

83. Varying Productiveness as to Business Ability.—We have thus far shown the effect, upon normal value, of varying productiveness in the lands under cultivation for the supply of the market. We are now to consider the effect, upon normal value, of varying productiveness in the persons engaged in the direction and control of labor and capital.

In doing so, let us proceed, as before, by illustration. Let us take the case of the manufacture of cotton goods.

We may suppose that the present price of the staple is ten cents, which, throwing transportation out of sight, represents the cost of its production at the greatest disadvantage, that is, on the least fertile lands devoted to this crop. Portions of the cotton may, indeed, have paid a profit (rent) of one cent, or two cents, or three, or four, a pound, to the owners of rich lands; but of this the manufacturers of cotton goods know nothing, and for this they care nothing. The only fact with which they, as manufacturers, are concerned, is that, the demand for cotton being what it is, cultivation has, to satisfy that demand, been carried downward to a certain grade of soils, *cost of production upon which* has determined the price, ten cents, which they find ruling in the market. This price all manufacturers, capable or incapable, are equally obliged to pay, so that all start on an equality as regards the cost of their materials. In the cost, to them, of the labor requisite to production, they are also substantially on an equality. We have, also, a right to assume them to stand on the same footing as regards the loan of capital and the price to be paid for its use, namely, interest.

If, now, we contemplate a body of manufacturers, fifty, or a hundred, in number, supplying the same market, what is to determine the normal price of that kind of goods? According to the principle we have already ascertained, it must be the cost of production of that last considerable portion of the necessary supply which is produced at the greatest disadvantage. But how should there be any such thing as advantage or disadvantage, in respect to production, since all stand on a level as regards the prices of materials, the rate of interest, the wages of labor? I answer, differences will be developed, from the very earliest beginnings, in respect to the degree of business ability with which these forces will, by these manufacturers, be applied to these materials, for the production of this kind of wealth; and those differences will be large, and, except for the operation of accident or fraud, will be measurably constant. In any body of twenty, fifty, or one hundred manufacturers, there will be some who will produce more; others who will produce much more; still others who will produce very much more, of wealth, in the form of cotton goods, than certain members of that body who employ the same amount of labor and capital.

84. How one Manufacturer Produces More of Values than Another.—This excess of values produced by certain manufacturers over those produced by others, less successful, in the same line of business, may be brought about in many and various ways. It may be through greater care of materials, from the day of purchase, through the time of storage and through all the successive processes of production, down to the day the goods are sold. It may be, by more of organizing and energizing power, enabling certain manufacturers to select always the right man for the place; to correlate all the parts of the service and subordinate everything to the supreme end in view; to create and maintain throughout their entire force a spirit of earnest, enthusiastic work. It may be, through ingenuity in devising expedients and meeting exigencies of a mechanical nature. It may be, through skill and taste in producing better designs or a higher finish of goods. It may be, through a sound judgment regarding the present and prospective demands of the market, and a sort of prescience in anticipating great and sudden changes of condition. It may be through an instinctive sense of character, governing the decision, to what persons goods shall be sold, and on what times and terms of credit. By one, or several, or all combined, of these and other ways of reaching the result in view, viz., the largest possible creation of values by the use of a given amount of labor and of capital, it will inevitably come about that the members of any considerable body of producers in the same line, under external conditions substantially the same, will be stretched out over a very wide scale.

85. Production by the Least Competent Employers Determines Normal Value.—In such a state of things, what constitutes production at the greatest disadvantage? I answer, it is production by the least competent employers. It is the cost of their production, therefore, which determines the normal value of that kind of goods, at that time, for that market. The demand is such, by the very statement of the case, as to require production by all these manufacturers : otherwise the least successful of them would already have ceased, or would speedily cease, to produce. Since the demand, however, is sufficient to keep them all producing, that demand must determine a price for those goods which will repay the cost of production at the greatest disadvantage, that is, by the least competent producers.

Demand will not, however, under ordinary conditions, that is, normally (which is the state of which we are speaking] fix a price which will more than repay this cost of production at the greatest disadvantage. Exceptional circumstances may indeed, arise, under which demand will be so highly stimulated as to raise the price to a point where all producers, highest and lowest, shall, for the time, obtain, by the sale of their goods, a surplus over the cost of production, that is, profits. If, however, this state of things lasts long, or promises to become permanent, other persons will be tempted to come into the business, or those already in the business will as quickly as possible enlarge their plant, to take advantage of the situation. There will thus be a constant tendency [which is what we mean when we speak of what is normal, in production or trade], to bring value down to the cost of production at the greatest disadvantage, that is, production by the least competent producers actually contributing to the supply of the market.

CHAPTER XI.

MONEY: THE MEDIUM OF EXCHANGE.

86. Difficulties of Barter.—We have thus far spoken of the exchange of wealth, as if the different producers exchanged their products directly with each other: carpenters, blacksmiths, masons, tailors, now working for each other, now working for fishermen, hunters, or tillers of the soil, and receiving from them, in return, fish, flesh, grain, or fruits. Such a direct exchange of services or of products does, indeed, take place in a primitive community; and, even in the most advanced communities, it continues to take place to a certain extent. But this direct exchange, which we call barter, or truck, is effected with much difficulty, even in primitive communities; and that difficulty increases very rapidly as occupations become multiplied and as the services or products to be exchanged increase in variety.

87. Double Coincidence of Wants and of Possessions.—The difficulty referred to is the difficulty of securing a double coincidence of wants and of possessions. The phrase just used is a long one; but the thing itself is easily understood. Where the division of labor has gone a great way, a producer will wish to consume, or personally enjoy, only a part, and that a very small part, of what he himself produces. The rest of his product he expects to see consumed by others, from whom, in turn, he looks to receive the particular things which he desires to consume or enjoy. So far, the conditions of an exchange are met. But when any producer actually goes about to make those exchanges, he may have to spend a great deal of time and walk a great way, in order to find a person *who both has what he wants, and wants what he has*. He may find many who have what he wants, but do not want what he has, and many more persons who want what he has, but who have not, also, that which he wants, before he will find one person between whom and himself exists that "double coincidence of wants and of possessions" of which we spoke. This difficulty might often be found so great as to compel a man to expend more time and effort in exchanging his product than in making it.

88. Difficulty of "Making Change."—Another obstacle which is encountered in direct exchange, or barter, in the case of many articles, arises from the difficulty, or even the impossibility, of so dividing products as to make a fair exchange. If three hats be worth five bushels of wheat, an exchange will be easy enough, provided the man who has hats wants wheat, and the man who has wheat wants a hat. A hat will be given for one bushel, two pecks and about five quarts of wheat; and both parties will be satisfied. But if three hats are worth four pairs of shoes, an exchange will be impossible, unless one party takes more hats, and the other party more shoes, than he needs. This difficulty, again, would often go so far as to render direct exchange impossible.

89. Need of a Common Denominator of Values.—A third obstacle to barter would be found in the difficulty which producers would experience in finding out for how much of the various products of others a certain quantity of their own product ought to exchange.

This obstacle to barter is not a fanciful one. In a community where direct exchang was the rule, each article in the market would have to be quoted in terms of every other,* or, else, every producer would be obliged to work out a long "rule of three" sum, to tell for how much of his own product a certain amount of any other man's product ought to exchange.

Let us take a simple case, a very simple case, an almost impossibly simple case. Let it be supposed that a man, who wishes to exchange sugar for tacks, finds out, by inquiry in the market, that one pound of tobacco has that day been exchanged for four pounds of flour; one pound of flour for half a pound of tacks; one pound of sugar for two pounds of rice; three pounds of rice for one pound of tobacco. At what rate, then, shall he exchange his tacks for sugar? The problem here is a very easy one, almost too easy to occur in practice, since the commodities we have taken are very few, and the numbers are all factors of twenty-four. Let us work it out. If one pound of tobacco is worth four pounds of flour, and a pound of tacks is worth two pounds of flour, tacks are worth half tobacco, by weight. If one pound of sugar is worth two pounds of rice, and a pound of tobacco is worth three pounds of rice, sugar is worth two-thirds tobacco, by weight. If, then, tacks are worth half tobacco, and sugar is worth two-thirds tobacco, tacks are worth three-fourths sugar, by weight; that is four pounds of tacks should buy three pounds of sugar.†

90. Wanted: A Medium of Exchange.—Such are the obstacles to direct exchange, or barter. The sense of these difficulties early drove the world to the means of avoiding direct exchange. This was effected by the use of some

---

* Using figures to represent different articles, such as wheat, cotton, wool, iron, sugar, tobacco, coffee, etc., the teacher might here place upon the blackboard tables which should show the difficulty of quoting each article in the market in terms of every other.

† In the illustration given above, it is assumed that tacks are worth 6 cents; sugar, 8; tobacco, 12; flour, 3; rice, 4.

article, which, either by law or by general agreement, all producers should receive for anything which they had to sell, being made willing to do so by the assurance that all other producers would receive this article from them, whenever they, in turn, wished to buy. Any article, so used in any community, becomes the general medium, or means, of exchange; and to it the people of our race apply the name, money.

Now, let us see how this instrument, or means, or medium, of exchange works in practice. Let it be supposed that, in a given community, wheat has come to be so generally used as money that every producer knows and feels perfectly assured that, with wheat, he can buy, at any time, in any place, from any person, whatever he may desire to consume. This being so, he will himself prefer to sell his own product for wheat rather than for anything else. In such a state of things, the problem of exchange becomes a very simple one. A producer has no longer to find out for how much of this or that, among twenty or fifty or a hundred articles, a certain amount of his own kind of goods is selling for. He has only to find out how much wheat that kind of goods is selling for; and this he can readily do by a single inquiry. Having ascertained this, he is no longer obliged to find the men who want the goods he has and also have the particular goods he wants; but the moment he finds a man who wants his goods and also has wheat (and every one who has any wealth at all now keeps wheat on hand, for this purpose) he can close the bargain at once. Finally, the great difficulty about "making change" is avoided. If it is an ox he has to sell, he gets for it, say, a wagon-load of wheat; and of this he gives half a peck for a pound of sugar, a bushel for a keg of nails, two bushels for a hat, four bushels for a gun, six bushels for a roll of cloth, and so on, to the extent of his wants and his means. No matter how small the value of the thing he wishes to buy, he can always take out a quantity of wheat which will be of about the same value.

91. The Money Function.—Let us now recapitulate the ways in which money performs its great office as a medium of exchange.

First, it dispenses with the double coincidence of wants and possessions, which is involved in barter.

Second, it promotes the making of change, as between articles which cannot themselves be divided without destroying or impairing their value.

Third, it furnishes a "price current" of all the articles in the market, through giving a common denominator for the value of each and every article, by turns.

92. Definition of Money.—Having described the money function, we are now able to define money. In other words, having seen what money does, we can tell what money is. Everything which does the work which has been indicated above, is money, no matter what it is made of, no matter what its size, weight, shape or color. To parody an old proverb,* money is that money does. The following is our formal definition of money. Like our definition of value (par. 3) it is necessarily long and much involved ; but nothing less than this will convey the whole truth, so that it cannot be misunderstood.

Money is that which passes freely from hand to hand throughout the community, in final discharge of debts and full payment for commodities, being accepted equally without reference to the character (or credit) of the person who offers it, and without any intention on the part of the receiver to consume it, or enjoy it, or apply it to any other use than, in turn, to tender it to others, in discharge of debts or in payment for commodities.

---

* "Handsome is that handsome does."

93. An Historical Illustration.—Let us take an illustration from the history of Virginia. Tobacco early became the chief export of that colony. Since tobacco was always in demand for shipment, it was readily taken at the country store. Every planter brought his tobacco thither, knowing that it would be taken, as a matter of course. Every week, or every month, the trader loaded up his teams and sent his stock of tobacco to the sea-shore, where, in the chief towns, it was exchanged for West India goods, dry goods, hardware, etc., imported from abroad. With these the teams returned loaded; and the planters took the molasses, the cloth, the boots or the tools they wanted, to the value of the tobacco which the trader had received from them.

Even such an extensive use of tobacco, in exchange, did not, however, make it money. The transactions which have been described were merely instances of barter. But the fact that tobacco was thus freely taken at the country store soon gave an extension to its use in exchange which did make it money. Since tobacco was taken at the store, in exchange for goods of every kind, it came to be taken between man and man, throughout the community. The lawyer and the physician were glad to receive their pay in tobacco, because this was always good for groceries and dry goods; while the fact that tobacco was taken, not only by the store-keeper, but also by the lawyer and the physician, made the farmer who raised corn willing to take it in exchange for his product.

And, so, tobacco became money in Virginia. It was not, however, until every one took it, and took it as a matter of course, that it was properly to be called money. So long as men accepted it with any degree of uncertainty as to finding persons who would in turn accept it from them; so long as men took it with the feeling that it was something which they were buying, and which they would have to sell over again, something for which they must needs hunt up a purchaser, tobacco was not money.

94. Universal Acceptability Essential to Money.—No article becomes money until it has acceptance so nearly universal that practically every person who has any service or product to dispose of, will freely, gladly take it, in preference to seeking, at the time, the specific products or services which he may require from others. He takes it from any man, whenever he has anything to sell, because he knows that any other man will take it from him, whenever he may wish, in his turn, to buy. When an article reaches this degree of acceptability, it becomes money, no matter what it is made of, and no matter why people want it. If, as a matter of fact, people do want it, that suffices for all the purposes of a true money.

The reader should fix his mind strongly on this central idea of a Medium of Exchange. Money is always a medium; an intermediate thing; not an end, but a means to an end. Men take it, not for its own sake, but for what it will bring them. They hold it, not to enjoy it, but to be ready for the moment when they shall part with it, in purchasing those things which they desire to enjoy.

95. Price.—We have thus far, in this treatise, spoken much of Value, and shall continue to do so; but the time has now come to introduce a new term, viz., Price. Value is power in exchange: price is power in exchange for money. The price of an article is its money-value. The value of a horse, for example, represents the power which the horse confers upon its owner to command, in exchange for itself, the labor of other persons, or many and various products, at will, corn, cotton, iron, or what not. The price of a horse represents the power which the horse confers upon its owner to command, in exchange for itself, the money of the country.

Price is, thus, value in terms of money. Now, value, as we saw, depends always upon the relations of demand and supply. Price, therefore, being a species of value, must depend always upon the relations of demand and supply. Increase the quantity of money in the country, the number of horses and the demand for horses remaining the same, and the price of horses will rise: that is, it will require more money, more coins, say, of gold or silver, to purchase a horse. Increase the number of horses, the demand for horses remaining the same, and the amount of money being unchanged, the price of horses will fall: that is, fewer coins of gold or silver will purchase a horse.

CHAPTER XII.

PRIMITIVE FORMS OF MONEY.

96. The Cereals as Money.—We have told what money does, and what money is; and we have, in illustration, spoken of one article, tobacco, which has actually served as money, through a considerable time and over a considerable extent of territory. Let us now consider other historical forms of money.

Wheat, corn, and rye have extensively performed this office. It is manifest that the cereals have two important qualifications for use as money.

First, they are in universal request, for personal consumption as food.

Second, the value of a day's labor, in cereals, comprises many separate grains. Consequently, you can take out of such a mass of wheat, or corn, or rye, the price of the smallest and cheapest article. There is no difficulty in making change with this kind of money.

On the other hand, the cereals, as money, are subject to two drawbacks: first, in the great weight and bulk of the quantity which represents a day's labor; and, secondly, in their liability to injury, through rust, insects, damp, overheating, or from the mere passage of time.

97. Cattle and Sheep as Money.—Cattle have also extensively performed this office. Oxen were used as money among the Greeks of the Homeric period. Sheep served the Italians, at a later period, as the common medium of exchange. Even after the abandonment of Britain by the Romans, we find the inhabitants, in the scarcity of coin, returning to the use of "living money," especially in Scotland and Wales. "It is very possible," says Sir Henry Maine, "that kine were first exclusively valued for their flesh and milk; but it is clear that in very early times a distinct and special importance belonged to them as the instrument or medium of exchange."

Cattle or sheep may be either a good money or an inconvenient money, according to the circumstances of the community. In a pastoral state, they present many advantages for this use. They carry themselves; and thus avoid the principal objection to the use of grain as money. On all sides are fields and plains, over which the animals may graze; while every member of the society is familiar with the methods of guarding and tending them.

On the other hand, cattle and sheep have two serious drawbacks to such use. The first is that each animal has too high a value to be used for single, daily purchases. Even the calves and lambs will scarcely answer all the requirements of small change. The second drawback to the use of cattle and sheep, as money, is the difference in quality which exists among them. Even in a picked herd or flock, there is great room for choice; while it is amazing how small and lean cattle can be, if they are to be used for paying debts or taxes. In the early days of the Massachusetts colony, citizens were allowed to pay their taxes in this way; and it is related that the cattle which came into the hands of the town treasurers were something wonderful to behold.

But while cattle and sheep have been found by many tribes and peoples, in a pastoral state, and even when advanced a certain way in agriculture, to be tolerably good money, in spite of these objections, it is evident that the very possibility of answering this requirement fails in all highly civilized states. The cost of feeding animals, and the risk and trouble of keeping them, become so great as absolutely to preclude their use as money.

In addition to cereals, and to cattle and sheep, a great variety of articles have, at one time or another, in one country or another, been used in this way. Rice was so used along the Coromandel shore; cocoa, among the aboriginal Mexicans; olive-oil, by the inhabitants of the Ionian Islands; blocks of rock salt, by the Abyssinians; strings of wampum, with bullets for small change, by the early New-Englanders; small cubes of compressed tea were used as money in the famous Russian fairs; dried dates in the African oases; beaver skins and seal skins, in many countries.

98. The Metals as Money.—One large class of substances have a great importance in the history of money, having been used as the medium of exchange in the earliest times, and among a wide circle of nations. The metals, especially seven of them, have been found to possess in a very high degree the material properties required for this purpose.

Iron, lead, tin or copper, one or all, early became the money of almost every country whose history we know. The numerous uses of these metals made them universally acceptable; while, the art of mining being in those days very rude, a small body of metal represented the labor of days, and thus contained a high purchasing power.

Metal money was, in certain respects, better than any other form of money known to barbarous communities:

(*a*) The metals, though subject in some degree to loss through exposure to the air, suffer almost indefinitely less from fire or other forms of accident than most kinds of wealth that are not metallic.

(b) Bodies of these metals can, with comparative ease, be divided or reunited, as may be required; they may be melted down and cast into any shape; they may be alloyed or purified, with comparatively little labor or loss of substance.

It is through its failure in the last respect, that still another metal, besides those named, has not been used as money. This is platinum: a noble metal; in some respects the best of all. In 1828, the Emperor of Russia undertook to use platinum as a money metal, but, after about twenty years, the effort was abandoned, owing to the extreme difficulty of rendering platinum from ingots into coin and from coin back again into ingots, as might be needed.

As the art of mining improved, iron, lead, and tin, one by one, became too cheap to be conveniently used as money. In all other respects, the metals were just as well qualified for this use as ever; but the great weight of the quantity of any one of them which could be produced by a day's labor, made such coins in an increasing degree inconvenient. Copper longest held its own; but even this, after a while, ceased to be used as money in highly civilized countries, except as small change. Among barbarous or semi-barbarous nations, however, copper still remains the chief money.

99. The Precious Metals.—Two of the metals have enjoyed a preëminence in the history of money which has earned for them the proud title, the Precious Metals.

Not that gold and silver are the most costly of all. Several metals are more valuable even than gold; but these are found in extremely small quantities, far below what would be required to furnish all the coins needed for use in any one considerable country.

Of the two so-called precious metals, silver first came into use as money. We hear of it in early Hebrew history. It was long coined by the Greeks and Romans, while gold remained merely treasure in palaces and temples, or was used for extremely precious ornaments. The great Philip of Macedon, in the early part of his reign, was wont, when he retired to rest, to place under his pillow the small and only cup of gold he possessed.

The extreme beauty of silver, brightest of all the metals, together with its many uses in the economy of life, make it an object of admiration and desire among all peoples, in every stage of social advancement. Easily fusible, highly ductile, practically imperishable, silver would have filled our highest conception of a money metal, had not the earth yielded one transcendent product, in comparison with which even silver fades from desire.

So great is the difficulty of obtaining gold, that a vast amount of purchasing power is concentrated, whether for conveyance or for concealment, in very small bulk. Humboldt, in one of his memoirs, states that, at then existing prices, one kilogram of gold would purchase 1611 kilograms of copper, 9700 of iron, 20,974 of wheat, or 31,717 of barley.

But while gold is thus precious, it is found in many countries, and in sufficient quantity to allow of its convenient use as an every-day medium of exchange by wealthy nations. Were gold as scarce as vanadium, the piece in which a workman received his day's wages would require to be handled with delicate pincers, like the parts of a watch, and would be liable to be blown away and lost by an unexpected sneeze.

The durability of gold, its fusibility, ductility and malleability, form a group of properties of the highest importance for the purposes of coinage and circulation; while they add greatly to its uses in the industrial and decorative arts. One cubic inch of gold may be beaten out to cover millions of square inches. Gold may be alloyed and refined, united and divided with the greatest ease, and with absolutely no loss of the pure metal.

CHAPTER XIII.

CREDIT: THE STANDARD OF DEFERRED PAYMENTS: THE TABULAR STANDARD: BIMETALLISM.

100. The Growth of Credit.—What we have thus far said concerning capital would be nearly all true, were every portion of capital in the hands of its owner, to be used by him in production or trade. And, indeed, in that primitive state of industrial society of which we have spoken so much, capital generally remains in the hands of its proper owner. Of course, even here capital is sometimes loaned by its owners to other persons, upon promise of repayment, at a definite time, or upon demand, which promise is generally supported by a pledge or mortgage of lands or of some form of wealth. Frequently, the body or the personal liberty of the borrower is pledged for the repayment of the loan, so that if he fail to pay at the proper time, the lender, the person who has given credit, the creditor, has the right, under the law, to seize his person, either to make him work as a slave, or to shut him up in prison. But, in such a state of society, the total amount of capital is very small, and of this only a very small proportion is loaned. The great majority of those who have capital are both desirous and able themselves to employ it in business, in the simple agriculture, or in the small manufactures, or in the petty neighborhood trade, then carried on.

As, however, communities grow older and advance in the

industrial arts, the amount of capital rapidly increases; and of this larger amount a continually larger share is let out to others than the owners. The reason for this last fact is twofold:

(*a*) There is a continually increasing number of persons who do not have occasion to employ their own savings in their own business. Take the case of a small farmer. When, perhaps, the grandfather first acquired the farm, he was put to great straits to find capital enough to properly improve it. He was obliged all his life to pinch himself and his family to get the means to purchase animals and tools, to build fences and sheds and barns and a poor sort of house. His son, finding much of this done, was not obliged to live quite so meanly: but still he, too, continued, through his life, to put all he could possibly save into various kinds of improvements, including deeper ditches, higher walls, larger barns and, perhaps, a better house. The grandson, coming into possession of a well-improved farm, has a much less urgent need for whatever wealth he can save out of his earnings; and, if he does not choose to enlarge his farm, he has every year something left over which he can lend to any one who desires to build a little mill on a neighboring stream, or to set up a small shop or store in the village. The further the division of labor is carried, the larger will be the number of those who have capital to lend.

(*b*) There is another cause which works to the same end. The larger the operations of business and the more complicated the organization of industry, the smaller, relatively, becomes the number of those who can safely and successfully undertake production and trade. Very many who have capital, in large amounts or in small, fear that, should they undertake to use it in business for themselves, they would lose it in part or in whole, and hence they prefer to entrust it to others whom they deem more capable, who are already in business and can use this additional capital to do more of the same kind of work.

101. Modern Credit.—This movement, for the loan of capital, which we have seen beginning in a very early stage of industrial society, goes on at a continually accelerated ratio until, in such communities as those to which we belong, a very large part, sometimes by far the larger part, of all the capital in existence is in the hands of those who do not own it, but borrow it from the owners, upon various conditions and terms of repayment. While this is going on, the laws regarding the treatment of the debtor, in case he should fail to make payment according to his contract, are continually growing milder. Those which made the unfortunate debtor a slave to his creditor are first repealed. Then imprisonment for debt, where no fraud is suspected, is first mitigated and finally abolished. At last, so-called bankruptcy laws are passed, so that a man who has borrowed money which he cannot repay, and who can satisfy the judge that he has done his best, in good faith, has his debt wiped out, and is permitted to begin his work in life over again.

These gradual changes in the law relating to debt are not due wholly to a better sense of justice or to greater humanity. They are largely due to policy, for, if production and trade are to be greatly, and even mainly, carried on with borrowed capital, as is absolutely necessary in such a state of society, then the borrowing of capital must be made easy and safe, and the old, cruel laws must be abolished.

102. The Creditor Class.—I have shown how, in an early stage of society, the cultivator of a well-improved farm may have capital to lend to the man who wishes to set up a mill or a shop. In a long-settled country, like England, the amount so loaned by the agricultural interest, for building up manufactures and extending trade, becomes enormous. Then, as one branch of manufactures becomes rich and strong, it is able to loan capital to those who are starting new branches of manufacture. Moreover, the professional classes, so called, become lenders to a large amount. A lawyer or physician, who has accumulated twenty or fifty thousand dollars, in the course of his practice, has no occasion to use his capital in his own business; and is therefore glad to lend it, upon good security, to some one who will employ it in business and give him a part of the profits. Even the laboring classes become lenders; and, though the amount that each has to loan is small, the aggregate amount which hundreds of thousands, or millions, of laborers may have to loan, if they are both industrious and frugal, is very great. Finally, there is an increasing number of those who, having inherited money from their fathers or others, are not disposed to employ it productively themselves, but, either through fear of losing their capital or from a desire to take life easily, prefer to have others manage it for them. This is one of those things of which we say that they acquire force by their own motion. The further the "credit system" is carried, the greater the inducements to lend capital to persons who have peculiar opportunities for employing it advantageously, until it may come about, in any country, that but a small part of those who have capital use it in business for themselves.

The Standard of Deferred Payments.

103. Money as the Standard of Deferred Payments.—The introduction of credit into trade and industry makes a new demand upon money, viz., that it shall act as the standard of deferred payments. If a man parts with the good she has produced, upon the condition that he is only to be paid for them at the end of some months, or if the owner of capital lends it to another to be repaid, perhaps, years after, it is evident that a good money must be something more than a convenient medium of exchange. It must also possess a reasonable degree of stability in value, so that the creditor may receive back, at the time of repayment, that which shall be worth as nearly as possible what he parted with.

104. Wheat as the Standard of Deferred Payments.—The articles which have been historically used as money differ very widely in this last respect. Some, which have been excellent mediums of exchange, have proved to be very poor standards for deferred payments. Wheat, as we have seen, has been used as money in many ages and in many countries, and has served the purposes of a medium of exchange tolerably well. As a standard for payments deferred for a few years, however, wheat may act very badly. It may happen that the crop of one year will be only three-quarters or two-thirds of that of the year preceding; and, wheat being something which everybody wants, and wants very much, its value may, in consequence of such scarcity, rise to double what it was. In such a case, the man who has loaned capital, in the form of wheat, will, on being paid back in wheat, during a year of scarcity, receive back double what he lent. This is a great wrong to the debtor, and may ruin him entirely; while the creditor, though he receives much more than his due, will derive therefrom no corresponding benefit. *All history teaches that unearned gains do not help menas much as undeserved losses hurt men.* Light come: light go. Industry and frugality, hopefulness and cheerfulness in labor, the feeling of justice between man and man, the willingness to loan capital to others, all these are seriously impaired and sometimes fatally injured by such unearned gains to one party, such undeserved losses to the other.

105. Gold and Silver as the Standard of Deferred Payments.—On the other hand, the metals have a considerable stability of value, within a short term of years. Especially is this true of gold and silver: Being practically imperishable, and being mainly used as money, any one year's production, or any two or five years' production, bears a very small proportion to the total stock in existence. If we suppose the total amount of gold and silver in the hands of men to be ten thousand millions of dollars (American money), and the annual average production to be a hundred millions, it will be seen that, should the annual production fall off to fifty millions, for one year, or three, or five, the value of the precious metals would be very little affected thereby. In the same way, should the annual production rise to one hundred and fifty millions, for the same time, the value of silver and gold would not be much reduced, in consequence.

But, while gold and silver have thus a high degree of stability of value, as compared with wheat, within a brief term of years, they tend to change much more than wheat during long periods, such as fifty or one hundred years. While one crop of wheat may be large, or may be small, as compared with another, and while we may even have two or three bad years, followed by as many good years, the cost of producing wheat does not vary greatly from age to age. On the other hand, after fifty years of a rapid production of gold and silver, the principal mines supplying the market may be found almost completely worked out; and a long period may ensue, during which the value of gold and silver may steadily rise, before new mines or new mining countries shall be discovered, perhaps ages after. This has been the experience of the world many times in human history. Unfortunate as this condition is, nothing has yet been hit upon to remedy the evils resulting. The spasmodic and intermittent production of the precious metals has always constituted a grave obstacle to industrial and social progress, although it was not until recently that the effects of this cause were clearly perceived and fully appreciated by historians and statesmen.

A Tabular Standard.

106. A Tabular Standard for Deferred Payments.—A strong sense of the inconvenience and the injustice resulting from the use of any single article, as money, has led certain economists to propose the introduction of a standard for deferred payments which shall be different from the money used in buying and selling where payment is to be made at the time. The standard they propose is to be formed, not of any one article, but of several, even of many, articles, joined together for this purpose. The idea underlying the plan is that, if a number of articles be taken, some will rise, to be sure, but others will fall; and that, if enough articles be selected, nearly as many will rise as will fall, and thus the average value of the whole will not greatly change.

Those who thus propose what is called a tabular standard of value, i.e., a standard made up from a table, or list, of many different things, do not intend that money shall be dispensed with, in ordinary buying or selling; or even that money shall be dispensed with in making deferred payments. The tabular standard is only to be used to determine *how much money* shall be paid, at the end of a period of credit.

Let us illustrate the working of such a system. A sells a house to B for $5000. B is to pay for the house at the end of three years. Now, with the use of money, it is probable that B, at the end of three years, will pay to A what will be worth either more or less than what $5000 would have bought at the time of the sale. It may be considerably less; it may be considerably more. The least likely supposition will be that the $5000 will then be worth just what they are now. Either A or B is almost certain to lose something, without any fault of his, which the other will gain, without having done anything to deserve it.

But let us suppose that Government had, according to this scheme, established a tabular standard of value. This could have been done by a law, which should declare that certain quantities of coal, of cotton, of iron, of wool and of other articles, twenty or thirty in number, should constitute "the standard of deferred payments;" and that certain government officers should every day publish in the newspapers the cost of such a bill of goods, according to the prices of the day before. Now let us suppose, that, on the day when A sold the house to B, the value of the tabular standard was $25: that is to say, $25 would, the day before, have bought all those goods, in the quantities fixed by the law. A and B, therefore, covenant that B shall, at the end of the three years, pay, not $5000, but (200 × $25 = $5000) 200 units of the tabular standard. At the end of the term of credit, three years, A and B find that the value of the tabular standard, as proclaimed by the commissioners, is only $20; and B, therefore, pays to A $4000, in money. Now, it is true that A has received only $4000, instead of $5000 which the house was worth at the time of the sale; but, with the $4000 he thus receives, A can go into the market, and buy just as many goods as he could have done, with the price of the house, three years before. B is thus saved from losing $1000. Credit has been given and taken, without either party gaining or losing through the change in the value of money in the mean time.

That the use of a tabular standard would prevent a great deal of injustice and industrial injury cannot be questioned. It is, however, a serious question, whether people will ever take the trouble to establish this system and maintain it. That trouble would not be very great; but most people are averse to taking the least trouble in the matter of buying and selling. So far, mankind have put up with all the evils attendant upon the use of money, which rises and falls in value from time to time. It is probable that they will continue to do so, although the scheme we have stated is perfectly practicable, should people care enough about it to take a little pains for the sake of the good it would do.

BI-METALLISM.

107. Fluctuations in the Relative Value of Gold and Silver.—Reference has been made, in the last few paragraphs, to the fact that the production of the precious metals has, through long periods of time, been highly spasmodic and intermittent, vast amounts of these metals being produced in one period, while, in another, production has greatly fallen off. While this is true of the two metals taken together, it is true in a much higher degree when either metal is taken alone. At times, silver has been produced in large quantities, while the production of gold has almost ceased. Then, again, the production of gold would spring up rapidly, while the amount of silver taken from the mines fell off. It has seldom happened that periods of great gold-production have coincided with periods of great silver-production.

Looking at this fact, many economists and statesmen have thought that, if gold and silver could somehow be joined together, in their use as money, there would be far less tendency to a violent rise or fall in the value of the compound mass, than in either, taken alone. One method, which has been proposed for effecting this object, has been to make each coin contain a certain amount of gold and a certain amount of silver, so that every person who uses coins should have to use both gold and silver. A scheme, more highly thought of, and one which has actually been put in operation, by many governments, at different times, is that to which the name, Bi-metallism, is usually applied.

108. French Bi-metallism.—We shall perhaps get the best idea of what might possibly be done in this way, by referring to the law which was enacted in France, in 1803. At that time, the value of gold was assumed to be $15\frac{1}{2}$ times that of silver. The law of 1803 decreed that every debtor should have the right to pay his obligations in coins containing the stipulated amount of gold, or in coins containing $15\frac{1}{2}$ times that amount of silver, at his own choice. The idea underlying this law was that, should gold thereafter tend to become more than $15\frac{1}{2}$ times as valuable as silver, all debtors would naturally prefer to pay their debts in coins of silver, the cheaper metal. This would make silver more sought for: i.e., it would increase the demand for silver. Now, to increase the demand for an article, other things equal, is to raise its price. Thus, a force would be set at work to counteract the force which was tending to lower the value of silver, as compared with gold. On the other hand, since no debtor desired coins of gold, the demand for this metal would at once be reduced. Now, to reduce the demand for any article is, other things being equal, to lower its price; and thus, in the instance given, a force would be set at work to counteract the force tending to raise the price of gold, as compared with silver.

In the opposite case, that is, should silver become more scarce, and hence tend to rise in comparison with gold, the same principle would apply; but the forces would work in an exactly opposite direction. Since every debtor would seek to pay his obligations in coins of the cheaper metal, i.e., gold, the demand for this metal would, by that fact, be enhanced, while the demand for silver, to pay debts with, would fall off. Thus, again, forces would be set at work to counteract those which were tending to make $15\frac{1}{2}$ ounces of silver worth more than an ounce of gold.

109. The Latin Union.—Such was the French scheme. At dates subsequent to 1803, other countries, viz., Italy, Belgium, and Switzerland, joined with France in this measure, forming the league known as the Latin Union. The operation of the French law proved extraordinarily favorable to the stability of "the ratio" between the two metals, viz. $15\frac{1}{2}$ to 1, fixed in 1803. Shortly after that date, occurred a series of fierce revolts and revolutions in the Spanish states of South America, then the principal seat of silver mining; mining machinery was destroyed; mining populations were scattered; the mines themselves filled up or fell in. There was, thus, a very strong tendency to raise the price of silver, relatively to gold. But the force which the French law had set in operation was found sufficient to counteract this cause. About 1830, important gold mines were discovered in Russia, and again the two metals tended to fall apart from the fixed ratio; but again the operation of the French law served to keep gold and silver close to the established ratio, not only in France, but all over Europe and in America, as well. In 1848, gold mines of extraordinary richness were discovered in California, and, only three years later, in Australia, also. Then came the great strain on the bi-metallic system.

It really seemed as though the force which the French law brought into operation could not possibly counteract the force with which the floods of new gold were seeking to tear the two money-metals apart from each other. Within twelve or fifteen years, as much gold was produced in California and Australia as had existed in 1848 through all the world. The wisest and bravest of the French statesmen and financiers were alarmed. Apparently, nothing could prevent gold from falling, under the enormous increase of supply, until it should be worth only ten, or even only seven, times as much as silver. But France, although everything seemed so black and threatening, held firmly on to the principle of the law of 1803; and sure enough, the storm passed over, and the bi-metallic system was not uprooted. Although the ablest financiers had predicted that gold would fall fifty per cent., it, in fact, fell only one or two per cent., and very soon recovered from even that loss.

It would be too long a story to tell, here, how France, in 1873, suspended, although she did not repeal, the law of 1803, which had done so much to preserve the stability of value between silver and gold. The writer believes that this measure was unnecessary; and that, had the statesmen of that period possessed as much moral courage as those of 1850–57, the French system would again have weathered the gale, and the world would now be in the enjoyment of all its advantages. Whether the Latin Union, with or without the co-operation of other nations, like England, Germany, and the United States, will ever again put the law of 1803 in operation, is a question which it would be idle to discuss here.

The reader should understand that the subject of which we have been speaking is one regarding which there is a great difference of opinion among economists, some holding that the bi-metallic system can never be made to work successfully and permanently. The writers who entertain this opinion are entitled to great respect; but it is perfectly fair to say that many, very many, who once held this view have, within the past few years, come over to the side of bi-metallism, and that this movement is still in active operation.

CHAPTER XIV.

BANKS AND BANK-MONEY.

110. The Origin of Banks.—We have spoken of the growth of the credit system. We are now to speak of the most important agency for carrying on and extending that system, viz., the Bank.

But, while the management of credit is the great and the true function of the Bank, banks have, in fact, had their origin in many different sources. In Italy, where the first banks of modern times appeared, the banks were finance companies, which negotiated loans for the king or prince; but came afterwards to exercise the true banking function. In Amsterdam, in 1609, a very important bank was formed, which had for its principal purpose the melting down and assaying of the vast and varied mass of coins from many countries, of every degree of impurity,* often much worn and clipped, which the trade of that great commercial city brought into the hands of its merchants. After these coins had been melted down and assayed, each merchant was given credit on the books of the Bank, to the amount of pure gold, or silver, found in the mass of coins received from him. These bank credits soon became a kind of money, merchants paying for goods by orders, or checks, upon the Bank. It will be seen that this Bank was really a kind of mint. It did a vast deal for the trade of Amsterdam, in competition with commercial cities which

---

* That is, containing very different proportions of "base metal," or alloy, such as copper or lead.

had no such means of ascertaining the real value of the coins received by their merchants from other countries.

111. Origin of English Banks.—In England, banks had two different origins. The country banks grew out of the business of the shop-keepers and local traders. As these had occasion to send money frequently to London and the chief sea-ports, in payment for merchandise, they got into the way of taking money from the people around them who had to pay debts or make purchases in the city or in the coast towns, doing this either as a favor or for a small commission. Those traders who did this work most promptly and satisfactorily, and in whom people had the most confidence, finally became known as bankers, and had this for their principal or their sole business, out of which they made a profit, besides rendering a public service.

In London, on the other hand, it was the goldsmiths and silversmiths who became bankers. These, having large amounts of the precious metals always on hand, for the purpose of making "plate" or ornaments, had their shops strongly fortified, with armed men on guard, to beat off robbers. As other people had no such means of security, and as the streets were ill lighted, or not lighted at all, at night, and as there were few policemen in those days, while there were many bold and ruffianly persons abroad, people got in the way of leaving their money and other valuables with the goldsmiths, who gave notes, or receipts, for the amounts deposited. These notes, or receipts, were finally made transferable by indorsement. It was in this way that Lombard Street, on which the London goldsmiths had their shops in the sixteenth and seventeenth centuries, came to be the greatest banking street in the world.

112. Origin of American Banks.—In the United States, again, banks had still another origin. They were generally first set up as shops, or factories, for making paper-money, of the kind which we know as bank-money. The process was as follows: A bank was chartered by the State to do business in each city or smart town: that is to say, the legislature passed a law, authorizing certain persons, named therein, to establish a bank at such or such a place. The persons named, with others whom they chose to associate with themselves, met together, paid in a little money, generally very little; chose directors, who, in turn, chose a president; and at once began to issue notes, each bearing the signature of the bank officers and promising to pay a certain sum of money, one dollar or two dollars, or five dollars, upon demand, in specie, that is, in gold or silver coins made by the United States government.

113. Bank-money.—The idea underlying this issue of bank-notes was as follows: Merchants, manufacturers, farmers or others, who desired to purchase supplies or labor, would come to the bank with their notes of hand, which the bank would discount: that is, the banks would accept the notes-of-hand, paying the face value in their own bills, first taking out the interest for the three months, the six months, or the year, for which these notes-of-hand were to "run." The persons whose notes-of-hand had thus been discounted, paid the bank-notes, or "bank-bills," out to their laborers or to others from whom they had purchased supplies or materials, expecting that, at the maturity of their notes-of-hand, they would be able, out of the proceeds of their business, to pay the bank in full, either in its own notes, or in the notes of other banks, near by. Meanwhile the issuing bank was to receive interest on the paper-money it had thus manufactured and put into circulation.

This interest, however, was not all clear profit to the bank. There was the cost of making the paper-money, which, to be sure, was not very great, involving the engraving of a plate and the printing of the notes therefrom.

Then there were the current expenses of the business, including the rental of an office, the salary of a cashier and of a clerk or clerks, stationery, postage, etc. Then, again, there was the cost of the "specie-reserve."

114. The Specie-reserve.—This last term requires to be explained. It was always possible that some persons, holding the notes of the bank, should come in and demand the specie which the notes promised. They might do this, either because they actually wanted the gold or silver for some purpose; or from enmity to the bank, hoping to "break" it, by an unexpected demand; or because the banks had issued so many notes as to create a "premium on gold," a phrase for the explanation of which we must refer the reader to the next chapter (par. 143). Now, in order to meet such a possible demand, the bank must be actually in possession of some specie.

How large this "reserve" should be, depends much upon circumstances. If the notes of a bank are scattered over a territory of ten thousand square miles, it is plain that a much smaller number are liable to be presented for payment, at any one time, than if the notes were nearly all held in the city where the bank has its office. A great many other things, on which there is not time to dwell, enter to affect the question, how large the specie reserve of any given bank should be.

The profit of the bank, through the manufacture and issue of paper-money, is, then, the interest on its circulating notes, after deduction of the following items, viz.:

1st. The cost of manufacturing the notes.

2d. The current expenses of the business, that is, the cost of putting the notes out and keeping them out.

3d. The loss of interest on the amount held as a reserve in specie.

115. Wildcat Banking.—It was the profit on "the circulation" which constituted the main, and often the sole, motive force, in the establishment of banks, in the early history of the United States. And so urgent was the desire for increasing that profit, that the specie-reserve was often cut down in the most reckless manner. In some of the new States, the phrase "Wildcat Banks" was not inappropriately applied to many of the institutions brought into existence at this time. The amount of specie held by them was often so small as to have been ludicrous, were it not for the constant peril to the business interests and to the private happiness of the community, which this criminal recklessness involved. A reservoir with an unsafe dam is hardly a greater danger to the village situated upon the stream below, than is a bank with an inadequate reserve. The amount of suffering inflicted upon the innocent and helpless, the destruction of accumulated wealth, the paralysis of productive energies, caused by the breaking of rotten banks, could never be expressed in words. If the State has any duties, at all, beyond merely keeping people from picking each other's pockets and cutting each other's throats, the first of those duties is to provide adequate securities against the abuse of paper-money banking. Indeed, as a means of picking other people's pockets, bad banking can scarcely be surpassed by any other human agency.

116. The Banking Functions.—We have seen in what various ways banks have actually grown up in different countries and in different times. But, however any individual bank, or the banks of any country as a whole, may have originated, banks all tend to come, in time, to do about the same things. Nearly all of them act more or less as places of "safe deposit." Nearly all of them, at one time or another, take-on the character of finance compa-

nies, helping to "place" government loans, or selling the
bonds of great industrial corporations. Very largely, also,
banks make and issue paper-money, although in some
countries this privilege is restricted to certain favored
banks, or to a single bank which is largely controlled by,
and perhaps partly owned by, the State.

But, however banks originate, and whatever they do, in
one or another of the foregoing ways, one thing they all
come to have in common. This is the management of
commercial credit (par. 110). Commerce may be carried on
to a considerable extent without banks, at least without any
institutions known by that name; but, wherever banks
have been, for one purpose or another, established, they
immediately begin to draw-in to themselves nearly the
whole business of conducting and managing the credit
system of the community in which they are placed.

To illustrate the operation of this principle, let us take
the case of a bank founded in one of the small Western
cities of the United States, say about 1850. The only
force which caused this bank to be established was the anticipated profit of the issue of bank-notes (pars. 112–114).
But no sooner was it established than people who had
money to lend, and people who desired to borrow money,
alike began to resort to its counter. Those who did not
feel themselves shrewd enough to loan their savings to advantage, that is, at once profitably and safely, brought
them to the bank. The officers of the bank, making this
their principal business, giving their minds to it, and having ample means for ascertaining the "standing" of the
various persons in the community who might wish to borrow, could loan the capital so placed at their disposal on
the very best terms, viz., at the highest rate of interest consistent with good security.

The means which the bank officers had for obtaining information were not always such as were open to others. Reputable merchants, who knew their business to be in a sound state, and wished to borrow capital to increase that business, would lay their account-books open, in confidence, to the officers of the bank; while, on the other hand, in the case of would-be borrowers who were of a more doubtful character, the bank-officers would institute private inquiries as to their personal habits, their mode of living, their punctuality in dealings.

By such and other means, the officers of the bank we are describing were enabled to loan all the capital which the members of the community desired to entrust to them, at the very highest rate of interest which was consistent with good security. Of this interest, the larger part went to the owners of the capital; while the bank made a handsome profit through a small commission on a very large amount loaned. There were, however, a few long-headed, shrewd, able men of wealth in the community who did not feel that they had any occasion for the services of the bank in this respect, deeming themselves perfectly competent to make their own loans; and in some cases these men were eminently successful, looking after their loans with a carefulness and intentness born of the thought that it was their own hard-earned savings which were at stake.

The vast majority, however, welcomed this means of giving and taking credit; and, in general, the capital loaned under this system was both more profitably and more safely employed than it would have been had each one of its thousand owners undertaken to conduct the loan of his share for himself. While the amount of wealth which many of these persons actually had to lend was very small, the aggregate amount thus brought into the bank was very large; and from this great reservoir of capital streams were made to flow, in proper times and in proper amounts, to water the whole field of industry. Whatever of good a merchant or a manufacturer may claim to do for the community in which he lives and conducts his business, it is certainly true that a banker, who is both able and honorable, performs an even more useful work. The fields of industry which, but for him, would now be baking from drought, and now be flooded and devastated by tempestuous torrents, are, through the judicious operations of banking, kept evenly and equably irrigated by a steady flow of commercial credit.

117. How Capital Comes into a Bank.—We have spoken of a bank as the intermediary between those who wish to lend and those who wish to borrow. It must not, however, be supposed that men bring carts and oxen and tools and food and clothing into the bank, and that those who wish to use such things in production or trade go to the bank for them. Capital comes into the possession of a bank always in the form of "rights," or credits. Thus, a man who has sold his crops or his manufactured goods, and received therefor notes-of-hand, promising payment, either upon demand or at some future, fixed, date, takes these notes-of-hand to the bank and there " indorses them:" that is, by a writing upon the back he makes them payable to the bank itself. For this the bank becomes a debtor to him, while it becomes the creditor of the persons who gave these notes. These persons, therefore, it can order to pay money, in the amounts and at the times stated on the face of the notes, severally. This power it makes use of in lending capital to those who wish to borrow and who can satisfy the officers of the bank of their financial soundness.

Sometimes the amount of rights, or credits, which the bank has thus had placed at its disposal, for the purpose of discounting notes, is many times its own capital. It is the certain reward of prudence and integrity in the management of a bank, that people continually increase the amount they have on deposit, until, in time, a good old bank comes to have a really enormous body of wealth at its disposal. This includes, not only the sums which are brought to the bank for the specific purpose of being loaned out, but also the "reserves" of merchants, on which no interest is expected. Some merchants have, almost habitually, five, ten, or twenty thousand dollars deposited in the banks in which they do business. This is because it is both more convenient and more safe for the merchant that the bank, with its vaults and its barred windows and its armed watchmen, should take care of this property, than that it should remain in his own hands.

Of course, if only one merchant should thus leave a sum on deposit at the bank, the officers could not safely loan any part of it, since the owner might, any day or any hour, call for the whole. But, if one hundred merchants, say, should leave on deposit an average of ten thousand dollars each, the bank could safely loan a considerable part of the million dollars, since it would be practically impossible that all the merchants should call for their money at the same time. The bank might safely lend four hundred thousand dollars on mortgage of real estate; lend three hundred thousand on "short time" business paper, that is, on notes-of-hand, given by merchants or manufacturers, payable in a few weeks, or a few days, or even "on call;" and hold two hundred thousand, more, in "governments," or other stocks or bonds, which could be sold almost at a moment's notice. The remaining one hundred thousand dollars, out of the million, it might keep in the form of specie or bank-notes, ready for any call which might be made upon it. It will thus appear that, out of a million of dollars of commercial deposits, the owners of which expect no interest the bank might properly and safely use nine hundred thousand dollars, receiving a handsome income therefrom.

118. Banking Economizes the Use of Money.—Besides economizing the use of capital, in the way we have just shown, banks greatly economize the use of actual money. If there were no banks, each merchant, each private citizen of means, would have to keep by him, in his pockets or in a chest, a considerable amount of "ready money," for daily uses or to meet sudden demands. If, however, the members of the community, alike the very rich and the merely well-to-do, form a habit of keeping their money in bank, there will be a great saving in the amount of money required, on the whole. Twenty thousand dollars, perhaps only ten thousand dollars, in bank, will go as far towards meeting the needs of the community, as fifty thousand dollars in private hands. The days on which one man wants to use money will not be the same as the days on which his neighbor has occasion to use it; and the bank, holding the money for all, will be able to make a much smaller amount do a much larger work in effecting exchanges. Hence it follows that countries where the banking system is highly developed, as in England and the United States, require very much less of actual money than countries like France and Germany, where there are comparatively few banks, and where the great majority of the people keep their funds in their own shops or houses.

119. Banks Economize Time, Labor and Risk, in Paying Debts.—Besides economizing the use of money, banks effect an enormous saving in the time, the labor and the risk, involved in the daily payment of the debts incurred in the ordinary course of business. In every large city, there are every day to be paid, and to be received, hundreds of thousands, or even millions, of dollars; and this great work is performed by the bank with infinitely less of effort than would be required if the same work were to be done by individuals, each for himself. Let us suppose that in a certain city there are one thousand merchants or traders, and that each one of these has, on the average, to make twenty payments a day. Think of the amount of time and labor that would be expended in sending trusty clerks or messengers all over that city, at the end of the day, to make those twenty thousand payments! Think also of the risk involved in sending such sums of money through the streets: risk arising both from the danger of robbery * and also from the possible dishonesty of clerks and messengers! But when these payments are to be made into the bank, and that generally by checks, drawn upon deposits already in the bank, the time, labor and risk involved become reduced to a minimum.

120. The Cancellation of Indebtedness.—The foregoing would hold true, were the times in which merchants have to make payments not generally the same as those in which they have to receive payments. But, since merchants are all the while both buying and selling, the payments to be made, and to be received, on the same day, largely cancel each other. One day a merchant may have two thousand dollars to pay, and twenty-five hundred to receive. In this case, the bank "sets off" the one sum against the other, so that the merchant's debtors have only to provide five hundred dollars to meet the difference. On the next day, perhaps, he has fifteen hundred dollars to receive, and two thousand dollars to pay. In this case, he sends his bank a

---

* At one time there was known in New York a class of men called Butcher-cart Thieves, who lay in wait for messengers carrying bags of specie or parcels of bank-bills. After snatching a bag, the thief, or highwayman, would jump into a butcher's cart, drawn by a fleet horse, with a confederate at the reins, and, in the surprise and confusion, would often escape pursuit.

check for five hundred dollars, drawn on his own deposit in the bank, or, else, some one else's check, which he had purchased for the purpose; and, again, all accounts, so far as he is concerned, are balanced.

The cancellation of indebtedness, of which we are here speaking, is carried to an inconceivable extent in modern commerce. The bank, through the almost universal practice of "depositing" commercial paper, becomes, by turns, *creditor to all debtors*, in the community, and *debtor to all creditors;* and, having thus in its hands nearly all notes and bills maturing, day by day, it is able to offset one by another, so that only a very small fraction requires to be paid in money.

121. The Clearing-house.—We have thus far written as if there were but one bank in any community, however large. In a great city, however, many banks may be required to do all the business of all the merchants. In the city of Boston there are more than forty banks in operation. Each bank carries on the cancellation of indebtedness within itself, so far as possible; and, at the end of each business day, sends a clerk to a Clearing-house, or bankers' bank, with a statement of the amount due from it to every other bank in the city, and of the amount due to it from every other bank, together with the money necessary to make up the difference, if the balance be against the bank in question. If, on the other hand, the balance be in favor of the bank in question, the clerk is authorized to receive the difference.

122. Banking Promotes Punctuality in Payments.—Besides effecting a great economy in the use of capital; a great economy in the use of money; a great economy in the time, labor and risk involved in making payments, banks bring into commercial life a principle of much importance to industry and trade. This is the principle of punctuality in making payments. This may be said to be almost wholly a product of the banking system. Wherever payments are due from one person to another, even when the debtor is well-to-do, there is always great uncertainty, and generally not a little delay, as to the time of payment. If rents are due on the first of the month, a few tenants pay on that day; others, on the second; some, on the third, fourth and fifth; others, not until the tenth; others, still, only after being "dunned" again and again. If payments are due on account of groceries or meats or clothes purchased, those payments generally dribble along, over weeks and even months. Such is the uniform experience of all communities in the matter of paying debts, whenever the transactions are "between man and man."

In respect, however, to all payments which are to be made into a bank, the rule of absolute punctuality is universally enforced, without fear or favor. If a note is due on a certain day, and the payment is not made before the close of banking hours, say three o'clock in the afternoon, the note "goes to protest:" that is, an officer of the bank goes before a notary public and makes oath that payment has been demanded and has not been made. The delinquent is notified of this, and is informed that, unless he immediately makes payment, together with "costs," * he will be proceeded against at law. It does not matter who the man is or how rich he is. It is needless to say that a protest is always a source of intense mortification to a merchant or a banker. Indeed, it is, except to a man of great wealth and high credit, almost fatal. The announcement, in the newspapers, that such or such a firm has allowed a note to go to protest, is generally accepted as meaning that the firm is bankrupt. Consequently, every business man or business house takes every precaution; and, in case of

---

* That is, the cost of protest, including the notary's fee.

financial embarrassment, strains every nerve and makes every sacrifice, to avoid such a calamity.

Now, this punctuality in payments which the bank demands and enforces, is of the highest advantage to production and trade. Indeed, it may be said to be absolutely essential to the vast operations of modern industry. Retail trade has necessarily to submit to all the inconveniences and losses that are involved in the lack of punctuality which we have noted; but the great production, the great trade, could not be carried on unless the manufacturer or the wholesale merchant knew how much he could rely upon certainly receiving each day, to meet the obligations due from him on that day. It is, therefore, a service of inestimable importance which banks render to society by enforcing the rule of absolute punctuality in payments.

But, it will be asked, is not this advantage to society, as a whole, obtained at the cost of much hardship and suffering on the part of individuals? I answer that, here and there, now and then, inconvenience and even injury may result to persons from the severe and unrelenting enforcement of this rule; but that, in the vast majority of cases, the requirement of punctuality not only does no injustice, but is of actual benefit, even to the debtors themselves. Speaking broadly, procrastination always and greatly increases the burden of debt. If railroad trains, instead of leaving the station on the minute, so far as possible, as they now undertake to do, were to adopt the policy of waiting for people, it is probable that a great many more persons would lose their trains than do where the rule of punctuality is enforced. To hold men sharply and sternly up to their duty, may require measures which seem harsh; but there can be no doubt that it is, on the whole, a great kindness. Duties are never so easy to perform as on the very day when they ought to be performed. Debts are never so light as on the day when they first come due.

123. Banking Promotes Commercial Integrity. — But there is more to be said on this point. The banking system, by its requirement of punctuality in payments, has done more to promote commercial integrity than any other cause, perhaps than all other causes put together. Procrastination not only increases the burden of debts; it insensibly but surely generates dishonest feelings regarding them. A man who has again and again put off the payment of a debt at last comes to feel that that debt is somehow a great wrong to him, and is only too ready to take advantage of any means of escaping payment, however shabby or shameful. Delay of payment always means doubt regarding payment; doubt regarding payment always sets evil thoughts at work in the brain, to find the way of avoiding payment altogether.

That kind, or that degree, of honesty which keeps men from actual robbery or theft, comes at a much earlier stage of society than that kind, or that degree, of honesty which makes men cheerfully willing to pay the debts they have fairly and openly contracted. For one man, in our present social state, who would steal, twenty will do that which is no better than stealing, in order to escape the payment of honest debts.

When banks have long existed in any community, the instincts of commercial honesty become developed in a really remarkable degree. Men, knowing that they have got to pay their debts, and to pay them on the very day they are due, take it as a matter of course. What men take as a matter of course they take easily. In such a community, the mind of the merchant does not begin to dwell on the dangerous thought of first postponing and then escaping payment. The way to evasion is almost always through procrastination. If the door to procrastination be barred, evasion will be less and less resorted to, less and less thought of.

124. Foreign Exchange.—We have spoken of the cancellation of indebtedness among the merchants of a city. The same principle is largely carried out to cities, states and nations. For example, there are a great many merchants in New York who, every month or every day, have sums to pay to merchants in Chicago, for corn and wheat, beef and pork. There are, also, a great many merchants in Chicago who have sums to pay, in the same times, to merchants in New York, for dry-goods, groceries, and hardware. If, now, the debtor merchants in New York had to send to Chicago all the money necessary to discharge their obligations, and the debtor merchants in Chicago had to do the same thing towards New York, there would be an enormous amount of money always going backward and forward between the two cities, at great cost, great risk and much loss of time. Instead of this, there is a mutual cancellation of indebtedness, just as far as this can be carried. A dry-goods merchant of Chicago, who has to pay a hundred thousand dollars in New York, goes to a wheat merchant, on the next street, and buys from him a draft, or order, upon a New York wheat exporter, for that sum. This he sends, by mail, to his own creditor in New York, who calls upon the wheat exporter for the money. Thus two large debts have been paid, without any money whatever passing between Chicago and New York. Of course, it will not always happen that the amount of debts due to a city, in a certain time, is equal to the amounts of debts due from that city in that time. Where there is a failure of coincidence as to the amount of indebtedness between two cities, money must be sent, by one of them, to make up the difference.

Whenever the principle of the cancellation of indebtedness is carried out to cities and states and nations, we use the term Exchange, or Foreign Exchange. The term, foreign exchange, is only properly used where different nations are concerned.

125. Par of Exchange.—We have assumed the case of a merchant in Chicago who has one hundred thousand dollars to pay in New York, and who, instead of sending the money to New York, purchases the right of another Chicago merchant, probably in another branch of business, to receive that amount of money in New York; and in this way pays his debt. But at what rate shall the first merchant purchase this right? Shall he pay for it a hundred thousand dollars, or more, or less? That will depend on whether "exchange on New York" is "at par," or "above par," or "below par." Let us illustrate the meaning of these terms.

Suppose that, at the time in question, Chicago merchants had twenty-five millions of dollars to pay in New York, while New York merchants had only twenty million dollars to pay in Chicago. It is evident that *all* the Chicago merchants who had money to pay in New York could not find merchants in their own city who had the right to receive money in New York. Competition would then begin for the rights which were to be purchased. The Chicago merchants would be obliged to pay something more than a thousand dollars for the right to receive a thousand dollars in New York. If, on the other hand, the amount to be paid by New York to Chicago exceeded the amount to be paid, in the same time, by Chicago to New York, competition would set in among the "sellers of exchange" in Chicago. Each of these would be willing to let his right to receive a thousand dollars in New York go for something less than a thousand dollars, since, otherwise, he would be obliged either to bring the money actually to Chicago, at some expense, or else to leave the money idle in New York.

Exchange is said to be "at par" between two places, when a man, by paying in a certain sum of money in one of these places, can purchase the right to receive an equal amount of money in the other place. Exchange is said to be "above par," when a man is obliged to pay in more money in the place where he does business than the amount that he can thereby purchase the amount to receive in the other place. Exchange is said to be "below par," when a man can purchase the right to receive money in the other place by paying in a smaller amount in his own town or city.

126. The Limits of Exchange.—What are the limits of exchange: that is, how far may exchange rise above par; how far may it fall below par? I answer, that the limits of exchange between two places are fixed by the cost of transporting money between those places. If "exchange on New York" rises above par in Chicago, it can go no higher than the cost of sending money on from Chicago to New York, because, rather than pay more than this, Chicago merchants will actually send the money. For a similar reason, exchange cannot fall below par by more than the cost of bringing-on the money.

Of course, the reader will see that the fact of exchange being above par, or being below par, constitutes a certain, small, disadvantage, or advantage, as the case may be, to the trade of a city or a country. If I, as a merchant in New York, sell certain goods to a merchant in Liverpool for one thousand dollars, but have to sell my right to receive that sum for nine hundred and seventy-five dollars, it is, to me, the same as if I had sold the goods for nine hundred and seventy-five dollars. If, on the other hand,

I could have sold my right to receive the money, at a premium of twenty-five dollars, it would have been the same to me as if I had sold the goods for one thousand and twenty-five dollars.

127. Three-cornered Exchange. — We have thus far spoken as if the cancellation of indebtedness, by means of so-called exchange, were carried on between two cities or two countries only. As a matter of fact, three cities or three countries may take part in effecting this cancellation of indebtedness. The United States, for example, sells to England much more than it buys from England; and, therefore, so far as these two countries are concerned, there would be a great stream of money constantly flowing from England to the United States. But the United States buys much more from China than it sells to China; while, on the contrary, England sells much more to China than she buys from that country. The merchants of the United States, consequently, pay their debts to China by "exchange on London." Having the right to receive large sums in London, they sell these rights to Chinese merchants, who are glad to obtain them in order to pay the indebtedness of China to England. In this way, it will be seen, the amount of indebtedness which is cancelled through the operations of "exchange" is greatly increased, and the amount of money to be actually sent from country to country is correspondingly diminished.

We have spoken of three-cornered exchange; but, in reality, foreign exchange is a many-sided figure. What we have represented the United States, England and China as doing, all nations do, so far as they can, each using every favorable balance with another nation to offset some portion of their indebtedness to still other countries.

The operations of exchange are largely carried on through banks, although a special class of "dealers in exchange" arises in all cities where this business is especially important. The chief centre of exchange-operations is London. To this great clearing-house are sent "bills of exchange" from every quarter of the globe. No matter in what city, upon what continent, a man may wish to pay a debt, he can almost always find in London some one who has a "credit" on that city, that is, a right to receive money there. By purchasing this right, or credit, and sending it to that city, he can pay his debt there without sending the money.

128. The Banking Agencies.—Such, as clearly as I can describe them in this short space, are the Banking Functions. The banking agencies may be classed as four:

1st. State, or government, banks.
2d. Joint-stock banks.
3d. Private banks.
4th. Bill-brokers and individual dealers in exchange.

The banking agency which has been chiefly employed in the United States, is the joint-stock bank. The vast majority of all the banking work in the history of this country has been performed by banks of this character, although private banks are not unknown, and the profession of bill-broker has always been extensively followed. In the early part of this century a very large proportion of the banking work of England was done by private banks; but during the last fifty years the proportion of private banks has been constantly diminishing, and their work has been more and more taken up by joint-stock banks.

In the United States down to 1865, joint-stock banks were generally created, or "chartered," by general or special acts of the legislatures of the several States. Since that date, however, most of the banks of this country have been brought under the National Banking Law; and their issues of bank-notes are regulated by the Treasury Department at Washington. Formerly the bank-money of the United States was of the most heterogeneous character. The banks of some States made very bad money, while the banks of other States made very good money, and the banks of other States made money neither very bad nor very good. Now, all the bank issues of the United States are homogeneous; and no man cares whether the bank-notes he has in his pocket come from Massachusetts, from Michigan, or from Missouri.

CHAPTER XV.

POLITICAL MONEY: INFLATION.

129. The Essence of Political Money.—We have thus far spoken of two kinds of money. The first might perhaps be called natural money. It is sometimes, though not quite correctly, called "value-money." In the United States, it is often called "hard money." This is money of which it may be said that, no matter what it is made of, the supply is naturally limited by the cost of production. Take metal money, for instance, whether of copper, of silver, or of gold. The reason why the supply is no greater than it is, is because the cost of production is no less than it is. Diminish the cost of production, and the supply might and probably would be correspondingly increased; but, so long as the cost of production remains the same, the supply cannot be greatly or rapidly increased. To raise two hundred thousand ounces of gold from the crust of the earth requires twice as much labor as to raise one hundred thousand ounces.

The second kind of money, viz., bank-money, is not subject to natural limitations of supply. The cost of the materials out of which such money is made, viz., paper, an engraver's plate and printer's ink, bears a very small proportion to the value for which the notes are expected to pass in circulation. The cost of making a one-dollar bank-bill may perhaps be one cent. The cost of making a ten-dollar bank-bill is no greater: hence, the additional nine dollars of this money cost nothing. We may, therefore, say that bank-money has no natural limitation of supply. It is as easy to make ten millions of it as to make one million.

But, while bank-money has no *natural* limitation of supply, there is a more or less stringent *commercial* limitation, found in the fact that the bank is by law obliged to give specie, dollar for dollar, for all its own bills which may be presented to it. If, then, bank-money be put out in excess, there will (for reasons which will be shown in pars. 140–1), at once or at an early date, begin a movement which will bring the bills back to the bank, for redemption in coin. The bank, therefore, in order to avoid "suspension of specie payments," which is failure, or bankruptcy, is bound to be careful not to put out its notes in excess, and to be always provided with ample reserves of specie. This necessity constitutes what I have called the commercial limitation upon the supply of this kind of money.*

The movement of bank-notes back to the bank, for redemption in coin, is called the Reflux. Most economists hold that the reflux takes place so promptly that bank-money can never be issued in excess, to any degree or for any period of time. There are some economists who hold that the reflux does not begin so promptly but that excess may occur, in some degree, and be continued for some time. All, however, are agreed that, if the laws punishing banks

---

* I am here speaking of bank-money, in communities where the principles of sound banking are known and respected. In the early history of the United States, much of the paper put out by the banks (see par. 115) was strictly inconvertible paper-money—just as much so, as if redemption had never been promised, for redemption was never intended and was not provided for. Neither law nor public opinion enforced the obligation of the bank to pay specie on demand. Banks were allowed to continue in business after they had failed to redeem their notes; and even declared dividends out of the profits of money which they withheld from their lawful creditors.

for insolvency are severe and are strictly enforced, excess can never be carried to a great extent, or be continued through long periods of time, owing to the reflux. We may, therefore, safely say that this kind of money is subject, in a very high degree if not altogether, to a commercial limitation of supply.

Of the third kind of money, that of which we are about to speak, it may be said that it is subject to neither natural nor commercial limitations of supply. Like bank-money, it has no appreciable cost of production, since it is as easy, or almost as easy, to make twenty millions of it as to make ten millions, or one. Unlike bank-money, it is not subject to reflux, because the government which issues it is not bound to redeem it, dollar for dollar, in coin.

130. Political Money Described.—What we here call political money is sometimes called government paper-money, or "Fiat" money. It consists of bills, or notes, or scrip, issued from the treasury of the government itself. Payment in coin may or may not be promised upon the face of the notes; but, inasmuch as the government cannot be sued by its subjects, or citizens, and inasmuch as the government can never, by its own courts, be declared bankrupt and sent into insolvency, such money must be considered as all practically irredeemable, or "inconvertible," as it is more commonly called. If government chooses to redeem its notes, it can do so; if it does not choose to redeem its notes, it cannot be compelled to do it. One month the treasury may redeem in gold all its own notes brought to it; another month it may refuse to redeem any. All the time the money is inconvertible, because redemption is at the pleasure of the government, not a matter of right on the part of the holder of the notes.

131. Is it Good Money or Bad Money?—The question whether political money acts well or ill, for the trade and industry of the country, has been much discussed, and widely different opinions are entertained regarding it. It may, however, fairly be said that the most learned economists, the soundest financiers, the greatest statesmen, in all countries, are nearly unanimous in their opposition to it. I believe that the reason why many generally intelligent persons favor this kind of money is because they see only a part of the case. Let us inquire what is to be said for and against political money.

132. Is Political Money Cheap?—In the first place, it is alleged that political money has the great advantage of superior cheapness, over either of the two kinds of money previously described. Let us suppose that a country has used bank-money, to the amount of four hundred millions of dollars, the banks all the while holding a hundred and fifty millions, in coin or bullion, as a basis for their circulation. If, now, the bank-notes were all to be withdrawn, and the government were to issue, in their stead, four hundred millions of its own notes, or bills, the hundred and fifty millions of specie could be sent abroad, to other countries, which still used gold or silver, and one hundred and fifty million dollars' worth of iron for railroads, of machinery for mills, of wool for making cloth, or of silk goods or wines, could be brought back. It is a perfectly proper instinct of mankind to choose the shorter of two equally good ways of reaching an object; the cheaper of two equally good instruments for doing a piece of work. Money is nothing but an instrument of exchange: and, if political money does its work as well as any other kind of money, and is also cheaper, it is altogether to be preferred. On the other hand, the work which money performs, in any state of industrial society, is so vastly, so vitally, important, that no money can be said to be really cheap which does that work poorly. A rotten bridge, a leaky dam, may possibly be cheap, but bad money cannot be. Let us then inquire how political money does its work, whether well or ill.

133. Political Money as the Medium of Exchange.— We saw (par. 91) that money performs its great office, as a medium of exchange,

1st. By dispensing with the double coincidence of wants and of possessions which is involved in barter;

2d. By promoting the making of "change";

3d. By acting as the common denominator of values, for all the articles in the market.

All of these things political money can do just as well as any other kind of money. History abundantly shows that, if a strong and well-ordered government undertakes to furnish its own people with money, by issuing notes from its treasury, in amounts no greater, or not much greater, than the amount of gold, or silver, or bank-notes, previously circulating, and if the government, in so doing, makes its notes (1st) receivable for taxes or public dues, and (2d) "legal tender" for debts due from one citizen, or subject, to another, such notes will pass easily into circulation throughout the community, without objection or distrust, and will thereafter act as the common medium of exchange, as a matter of course. Every person, in his place in the industrial order, be that high or low, will be just as eager to obtain these government notes as he formerly was to obtain bank-notes, or gold and silver. No one will resort to barter, or curtail or modify his production of wealth, as a means of escaping the use of such money. Such money, being thus used as a general medium of exchange, becomes, by virtue of that fact alone, the common denominator of values. If three articles exchange severally for eight, four and two pieces of paper, of a certain color and bearing certain words and figures, we learn the relative values of these three articles just as readily and just as exactly as if they exchanged, severally, for eight, four and two coins, of a certain size and bearing certain devices.

134. Political Money as the Standard of Deferred Payments.—Now, since political money will do all this, why is it not a good money? I answer, because, as we saw in paragraph 103, the money of a highly organized industrial state has to act, not only as a medium of exchange, but, also, as a standard for deferred payments. Now, since political money is subject to neither a natural nor a commercial limitation of supply, having itself no cost of production, it is possible, it is always, socially speaking, highly probable, that the amount of such money may be made to vary so greatly as to make it a very unsatisfactory standard. Those variations of amount may easily be carried to such extremes as to work the grossest injustice, as between debtor and creditor, and inflict the greatest injury upon production and trade.

We have seen (par. 105) that even metallic money is subject to considerable variations of amount, from age to age; but here the injury that may be done is not of man's devising, and hence is without that sting of injustice which accompanies injuries that are done of a purpose. Moreover, it would be a very extraordinary condition of things (although such a condition of things has existed) which should allow the amount of precious metals to be doubled in twenty-five years, or to be diminished one-half in a hundred years. The amount of government paper-money, however, may readily be doubled or quadrupled in a few months. Not only is this physically possible, but as much as this, and even a great deal more, has actually occurred. Congress, during our Revolutionary war, issued twenty times as much money, of this character, as there had been of metallic money (silver) in the Colonies. The French revolutionary government, a few years later, issued probably fifty times as much paper-money as there had been of metallic money in France, when they began.

135. The Inherent Tendencies of Political Money.—But it is not a sufficient reason for rejecting any instrument, which might be of use to society, that it may conceivably be grossly abused, or even that it has actually been so abused, under circumstances not favorable to its proper working. To reject a social instrument, or agency, on such an account, would be as foolish as to accept it merely because it might conceivably be used to advantage. The question is, always, of *the tendencies* of social agencies and instruments. Human nature being what it is, are they *likely* to do more harm than good? If they are, it would be inexpressibly foolish to adopt them, even though it could be shown that, if properly used, they might effect a great saving of labor, or yield a great gain of power.

Now, regarding political money, it can, without any prejudice, be said that it is subject to two evil tendencies, both of which are very strong; both of which operate continuously; both of which are liable, at special times, to become aggravated to such a degree that they can scarcely be resisted.

136. The Fiscal Motive to Excessive Issues.—The needs of the public treasury constitute the most formidable of the two dangers which beset government paper-money. Any government, no matter how strong and prosperous the people, is liable, now and then, to find its revenues, even in time of peace, fall short of its necessary expenses. If a government, in such a strait, has already large amounts of paper-money outstanding, the pressure upon the treasury, or upon the parliament or the congress, to increase those issues of paper, to meet the exigency, will be very strong. History abundantly shows the weakness of governments under such a temptation, even where solemn public promises had been given that no such increase of issues should be made. Political virtue is seldom sufficient to resist this temptation, provided the government and the people have once become accustomed to the idea of government paper-money. Time is no safeguard in this respect. The liability to over-issue does not diminish with the lapse of years. Moderation in the use of such money does not form a political habit, which becomes a security against abuse. On the contrary, the more familiar a people become with such money, the less strenuous will be their opposition to over-ssues. I deem it perfectly fair to say this.

137. Paper-money in War.—But it is on the occurrence of war, that the greatest dangers from that source arise. A government which already has this kind of money in circulation is almost certain to resort to its excessive and destructive use, should war break out. The needs of the treasury, for the means to raise and equip armies and navies, become at once enormously increased. It is so much more easy to supply these needs by pouring out a great volume of paper-money, in payment for goods and services, than to do this by enhanced taxation or by government loans, that it would be unreasonable to expect the government not to resort to that means. The moral courage, the political wisdom, which would be required to restrain rulers and legislators from such a course, are seldom found.

Yet the resort to issues of paper-money, at the outbreak of war, is always delusive and often destructive. The reason is as follows : The treasury issues the paper-money mainly for the purchase of military stores and supplies, including provisions and clothing for troops. Yet the prices of these articles are at once raised by such issues. The prices of all things do not rise equally. When the volume of money is increased, houses and lands, perhaps, do not rise at all, at the beginning ; but articles immediately merchantable, i.e., goods in shops and warehouses, rise in price very rapidly. Now, it is these articles, especially, which the government goes into the market to purchase. Consequently, the treasury, with a larger nominal amount of money, finds its purchasing power diminished, and feels itself poorer than ever.

The next step is a fatally easy one. The poorer the government becomes, the more paper-money it emits; the more paper-money it emits, the poorer it becomes. The most probable end is a weltering chaos, involving the utter bankruptcy of the treasury and the prostration of industry and trade, with untold injury to the community, and the highest injustice as between man and man. This was the end actually reached in the American Revolution and in the French Revolution, during the last century. In the war of Secession, Congress had the unusual courage to stop, when the "greenbacks" had reached four hundred million dollars, and thereafter to raise all the means required, by loans or taxes. Enormous evils, however, had already been incurred, and the cost of the war vastly increased.

It is one of the cowardly maxims of current politics, that a great war cannot be successfully carried on, by a free people, without the issue of government paper-money, to "make the war popular," to "raise prices," to "float loans," etc. · Such a maxim is as false as it is cowardly. Paper-money adds nothing to the real resources of a nation; while the political virtue of any generous people will, if properly appealed to, be found sufficient to command all their energies in any war which is waged for national independence or national honor or in defence of important rights. The effect of paper-money upon the public body is much like the effect of alcohol upon the individual: it stimulates, it excites, it too often bewilders and crazes; it can never add anything to the strength available for a severe and protracted contest. If there is ever a time when a nation needs its full, collected, vigor, with a steady pulse, a calm outlook, a firm hand, a brain undisturbed by the fumes of this alcohol of commerce—paper-money—it is when called to do battle for its life against superior force.

138. Scaling Down Debts.—In all free governments, or governments much subject to popular impulses, a second danger of over-issue arises from the appetite which is engendered for further emissions, to "scale down debts," or to "make trade good." After a people have once felt the intoxicating effects of excessive paper-issues, in enabling them to pay their debts in money which is worth less, perhaps much less, than that in which the debts were contracted, there is aroused a strong and urgent appetite, sometimes a ferocious passion, for new emissions, which shall still further reduce the value of money and still further rob the creditor class. Beneath the smooth and respectable surface of human society, in its ordinary moods, lie passions of the most violent and destructive nature. It is the task of the statesman to keep these from breaking forth and devastating society, while he trusts to the insensible operation of moral forces gradually to impair their strength and ultimately to supplant them by virtuous and beneficent motives. Scarcely any cause so breaks-up the restraints under which the bad impulses of human nature are held in check, and lets loose upon society such a horde of villainous passions, as does the issue of paper-money, when it has once passed the bounds of prudence.

Few communities known to history possessed more of sterling virtue than the early colonies of New England; yet these people, once infatuated and intoxicated by bad money, fairly rioted in dishonesty, in the treatment of public and private creditors. It required an immense effort of public virtue to finally turn the scale in favor of honesty; but this was accomplished, and, by an act of wise statesmanship, the very roots of this poisonous plant were dug out.* Ever since that time, the commercial credit and the financial honor of New England have been nobly maintained; and the reward has been found in flourishing trade and expanding manufactures. If it is the true task of statesmanship to so order society, to so dispose its forces, to so organize its forms, as to hold the bad impulses of human nature in check, while giving full scope and free play to those motives which seek at once individual happiness and the public welfare, then it may boldly be said that there is no act so unstatesmanlike as to institute the *régime* of government paper-money.

139. Political Money at its Best.—We have shown two grave dangers which beset political money, and from which it cannot hope to escape. We have seen that the danger of over-issue never ceases to threaten such a money. Its path winds all the way along the edge of a precipice.

Let us now inquire what could be claimed for political money, at its best. Would it be a good money, even were the danger of over-issue, arising from the two causes indicated, to be altogether removed? I answer, such a money could never be a good money, because it has no automatic regulation of its amount, to keep it on a level, as to value, with the money of other countries. It has been said that government paper-money has no cost of production. We are now to note that its circulation is limited to the country in which it is issued. In common phrase, it is non-export-

---

* The period of New England history above referred to, is comprised between the second disastrous expedition against Canada, 1710, and the Revolutionary war. Massachusetts rid itself of paper-money in 1747, under the enlightened leadership of Governor Hutchinson.

able. To see the full bearings of this fact, we need to go back to metal-money, and inquire how its total volume is distributed among the several countries which take part in the commerce of the world.

140. The Geographical Distribution of Metal-money.—It would be a very difficult question to answer, how much money a given nation requires. Even were the amount of its annual production known, and the amount of its annual trade, we should not have the means of answering this question. The amount of money required to do a certain amount of trade depends upon the extent to which the banking system is organized (par. 118); upon the degree to which cancellation of indebtedness (par. 120) is carried; and also upon the "rapidity of circulation." The last point is of great importance. In some communities, a dollar will be used to pay debts or make purchases, as many times in the course of one week, as in the course of a month in other communities. "The nimble sixpence does the work of the slow shilling." To say that a country needs so much money because it has so much trade, would be like saying that a railroad needs so many cars to transport ten millions of bushels of grain from one place to another, without knowing how often the cars will be able to make the round-trip.

Fortunately, it is not necessary that any one should know how much metal money any particular country requires. If one country has a larger share of the metal money of the world than is for its own good and for the good of others, the excess will be drained away insensibly, and without any one taking care concerning it. A country should, for its own good and for the good of others, have in circulation money enough to keep its prices on a level (cost of transportation being taken into account) with prices in other countries. Any excess above this amount is called Inflation. Now, if the money of a country be inflated, prices must rise. If prices rise, that country becomes a bad country to buy from, since all persons naturally desire to buy in the cheapest market. For the same reason, that country will be a good country to sell to, since all persons are moved to send their goods to the dearest market. Since, therefore, the country is both a bad country to buy from and a good country to sell to, its imports will increase and its exports diminish. As the immediate consequence of this, metal-money will have to be sent out of the country, to pay the difference between the value of the goods it has sold and the value of the goods it has bought.

This process will begin even before the shrewdest banker, or financier, or statistician, could have told that the money of that country was in excess. You have seen a carpenter or mason lay a spirit-level upon a beam, or upon a wall. If the surface is not exactly horizontal, the little bubble under the glass runs out of sight, although the departure from the horizontal be so slight that no eye, however trained, could detect it. So, in the case of a country having metallic money in excess, the exportation of gold, or silver, begins before the wisest man in the land could have told that there was inflation. This process continues just as long as the excess remains; and it ceases, of itself, just as soon as the excess is removed.

It is by such a process that metal-money preserves its level, the world over. No man has occasion to take care for it. There is no need of setting up machinery to do this work. There is no danger of any mistake about it, either in doing too much or in doing too little, either in beginning too early or too late. The highest good of each country requires that it should have just that amount of money which will be brought to it, and kept in it, by the operation which we have described. To have more money, would make that country a bad market to buy in. To have less money, would retard and embarrass the exchanges which the people of that country have need to make. And what is thus for the good of each country, by turns, is for the advantage of all countries, as a whole, enabling the required exchanges to be made with the greatest ease and confidence.

141. The Regulation of Bank-money.—We have shown, in the preceding paragraph, that the geographical distribution of metal-money, among the several countries of the world, is affected insensibly, automatically and surely. But how is it with countries having bank-money? Can bank-money be exported, in case of excess? I answer, no. Bank-money is not subject to export. It is true that a few Bank of England notes are occasionally carried to the continent of Europe. This, however, is not because such notes are in excess at home; but because a few travellers choose to take a portion of their funds with them in that shape, knowing that the bankers in the largest cities of the Continent are always glad to have some Bank of England notes on hand. Such an exception we may safely disregard; and say that bank-notes are non-exportable. How, then, it will be asked, can bank-money be subject to automatic regulation of amount?

The process is as follows: If bank-notes be issued in excess, prices will rise, and that country will consequently become a bad country to buy from and a good country to sell to. Exports being, by this cause, diminished, while imports are increased, money will have to be sent out of the country, to pay the balance. Since the bank-notes cannot go, a draft will be made upon the specie in the "reserves" of the banks. In other words, there will be a "drain" of gold, or silver. If the law, as is sometimes the case, forbids a bank to keep-out more than a certain proportion of notes, or bills, to the gold, or silver, in its vaults, the loss of the specie will require the banks to "contract their circulation," accordingly, and thus the excess of notes will be removed. If, on the other hand, the law makes no such requirement, the bank-officers will be obliged, in the exercise of ordinary prudence, not to send back into circulation the notes that are first paid into the bank, in the course of business. These notes the bank-officers will prefer to lay away in their vaults, until the specie they have lost shall come back again.

Of course, it will be seen that this action requires the exercise of ordinary prudence on the part of the bank-officers. If these are reckless, they may wait until they get a second warning, in the form of still another "drain" upon their reserves. Speaking broadly, however, we may say that, if the banking system of the country is in good hands, the amount of bank-money is almost as surely and quickly subject to regulation as is money of gold or silver.

142. Political Money not Subject to Automatic Regulation of Amount.—On the other hand, political money is not subject, in any degree, to automatic regulation of supply. Such money, it is true, is never likely to be deficient in amount. The needs of the treasury and the clamors of the trading, and especially of the speculative, class, may be trusted to prevent that result. The danger is all on the other side, viz., that such money will be issued and maintained in excess, since, if, from any cause, at any time, too much of such money be put out from the treasury, there is no natural or commercial drainage, by which the excess shall be removed. A country which has such a money is like an interior district which has no outlet through the rivers and thence to the ocean. If too much water falls upon such a district, it turns to swamps or quicksands, according to the nature of the soil. A country where an excess of government paper-money has been issued becomes a swamp or a quicksand, commercially and industrially speaking. It becomes at once a bad country to buy from, a good country to sell to, because prices are high there; but this fact does not tend to remove the excess, because such money is not available for export, to pay balances.

How, then, can such a country pay the balances due to its unfavorable trade? Why, by gold, which it purchases, for this purpose, from other nations. As soon as any paper-money country is driven into this strait, we have the phenomenon of a Premium on Gold.* This is an almost inevitable accompaniment of government paper-money. Since some gold must be had, for the purpose of paying foreign balances or for use in the arts, gold, which in that country has ceased to be money, is bought and sold, like any other commodity; and its price (in paper-money) rises and falls like the prices of other commodities. The premium on gold may be high or it may be low; but some premium, greater or less, is almost certain to exist wherever government paper-money is the sole money of the people.

143. The Present Situation in the United States.—The last phrase of the preceding paragraph intimates a qualification that must be made, whenever government paper-money is spoken of. At the present time we have, in the United States, government paper-money, popularly known as "greenbacks." Why, then, is there not a Premium on Gold? I answer, because the amount of such money has been fixed by law at a point far below the amount of money which the people of the United States require. In addition to the greenbacks, we have

1st. Bank money, in large amount;

---

* Or on silver, if that be the money in which foreign balances are paid, as, for instance, in the East Indian or Chinese trade. For convenience, we speak, here, only of gold.

2d. Gold and silver, coined and uncoined, in the hands of brokers and dealers in bullion;

3d. "Gold certificates" and "silver certificates," in vast amount, which the Treasury has issued, and for which it holds the actual gold and silver, dollar for dollar, in the "sub-treasuries" at New York, Boston, Baltimore, New Orleans, San Francisco, and other places, ready to be paid out to whoever may present the "certificates."

If, now, the aggregate amount of all these kinds of money should come, at any time, to be in excess, the "drain" would come either upon the gold and silver in the hands of brokers and bullion dealers, or else upon the gold and silver held by the government for the redemption of the "certificates." Long before the drain should get down to the government paper-money, any excess in the aggregate amount of money within the United States would have been corrected.

What, then, it may be asked, can be the objection to government issuing a certain, limited, amount of this political money? I answer, that, if the amount to be so issued is fixed far below the lowest point to which the money of the country could ever be reduced, even at its lowest ebb, the only objection to its issue is found in the possible danger that, when both government and people have become thoroughly accustomed to this kind of money, its amount will readily be increased, in case of financial disaster or upon the occurrence of war. A country which has such a money is very likely to be drawn into the abuse of it. A country which has not such a money is not likely to resort to it, except in a great exigency.

144. Effects of a Gold Premium upon Trade.—Let us now return to the case of a country, the government of which has undertaken to furnish its people with all the money they require, in the form of inconvertible paper.

Let it, for the sake of argument, be assumed that war will not occur, to drive the government to over-issues; and that, in time of peace, both government and people are so wise, so honest, and so brave, that they will not purposely inflate this paper-money under any temptation. Upon this series of favorable assumptions, what would be the effect of such money upon trade?

It has been said that such a money is not likely to be deficient in supply. Both the needs of the Treasury and the demands of the trading, and especially of the speculating, class, will be certain to prevent this. But why should such a money become excessive, if neither the government nor the people desire over-issue? I answer, because there is no man, and no body of men, wise enough to tell just how much money, no more and no less, the trade of a nation requires, at any given time. Metal money is in a continual state of flux, now flowing in this direction, now in that, according to the needs of trade. One time, the West requires a larger share of the nation's money; at another time, it is the East. For weeks, every steamer which leaves New York takes more or less gold to Liverpool; then, again, it is the incoming steamers which carry gold. It is by the incessant movements of money, that trade remains steady. If money is to become stagnant, trade must take up the fluctuation; and, by the inevitable influence of speculation, that fluctuation becomes excessive, extravagant, pernicious.

If we were to suppose that, upon any given day, the amount of inconvertible paper-money in the country were exactly what the good of trade required, that is, exactly the amount of metal-money which would be in circulation, it would be, in the highest degree, probable that, in a very short time, a few weeks, perhaps a few days, that amount would become excessive. If it were metal-money, the excess would be insensibly and automatically drained away, as we have seen. Since paper-money cannot be regulated in this way, a premium on gold will at once appear. *The moment a premium on gold appears, gold becomes the subject of speculative dealing.* That speculative dealing early becomes intense and furious. The whole amount of gold in the country is perhaps sold over and over again* during a single week, or a single day. Under the influence of this cause, the premium on gold soon ceases to afford any measure of the excess of paper-money. The premium goes up and down, like a small boat on a tempestuous sea. Now the "bulls" have it; now the "bears."†

What effects upon trade are produced by the fluctuations of the gold premium? We shall best show this by illustration. A merchant in New York sells goods to Liverpool, on sixty days' credit. Those goods the merchant has bought with paper-money: he is to be paid in gold. Perhaps at the time the sale takes place the premium on gold is twenty per cent. When the sixty days have expired, the premium on gold may be thirty per cent. or it may be only ten. In the one case, the merchant has realized a great gain, which he has done nothing to deserve; in the other case, he suffers a large loss, through no fault of his own. It has already been stated (par. 104) that unearned gains do not help men as much as undeserved losses hurt

---

* Not sold and *delivered;* but sold speculatively, perhaps by men who have no gold, to men who want no gold. Such buying and selling is called speculative. Those who buy and sell in this way, being neither producers, traders, nor consumers, are simply engaged in gambling. They bet upon the future price of the article in which they deal.

† In the phrase of the market, the "bulls" are those dealers who are working for a rise in prices, so that they can sell to advantage; the "bears," those who are working for a fall of prices, so that they can buy to advantage.

them. If human history teaches anything, it teaches this, unmistakably.

Moreover, in such a state of things, not only is trade subject to unearned gains and undeserved losses, but the whole trading community becomes animated by a highly speculative spirit. Merchants, instead of confining themselves to prudent, careful dealings, trying to save a little here, and make a little there, buying judiciously and selling judiciously, remaining content with a reasonable profit, and studying patiently the real demands of consumers, launch out into enterprises of a grand and startling character; become indifferent to little savings, contemptuous of small gains; and operate rather with reference to the anticipated fluctuations of the gold premium, than with reference to supplying the actual, current wants of consumers. Soon, "combines" and "corners" come in to produce great waves in the markets for produce, which swallow up the frail barks of petty dealers, and wreck the small fortunes which have been accumulated through years of patient toil. All trade, is in its nature, more or less speculative, even with a good money; but bad money and a fluctuating gold premium make trade little better than gambling.

145. The Effects upon Industry.—A nation might perhaps put up with the unfavorable effects of paper-money upon the trading class, were it not for the inevitable effects which are produced upon industry. Manufacturing, under such impulses from trade, also becomes highly speculative; production gathers itself into great waves; producers become dissatisfied with the proper fruits of care and pains and labor, and fix their eyes upon the glittering prizes which are awarded to lucky "hits" and momentary successes.

146. The Effects upon the Consumption of Wealth.— Light come: light go. Those who, in such a state of industry and trade, reap large gains, too often spend them foolishly, recklessly, perhaps wantonly; while those who have suffered from the injustice which the régime of paper-money always causes, in so great a degree, eat their scanty bread, made bitter by the sense of wrong and undeserved hardship. A period of paper-money inflation always sees great changes in the consumption of a people; and those changes are almost all away from what is wholesome, moderate, and temperate, toward what is extravagant, foolish, or pernicious.

In such a state of industrial society, it is always the poorest and the humblest, those who have least to spare, those who are farthest away from the sources of power, who suffer most, and who have least the opportunity for repairing the wrongs done to them. Rightly did Daniel Webster call such money "the most effectual of inventions to fertilize the rich man's field by the sweat of the poor man's brow."

CHAPTER XVI.

PROTECTION OR FREE TRADE.

147. The Territorial Division of Labor.—In Chapter VII, we showed how the division of labor comes about, and indicated some of its more important advantages. The same principle which divides the population of a village or a small district into hunters and herdsmen, sailors and fishermen, grain growers and fruit growers, carpenters and blacksmiths, butchers and bakers, peddlers and shopkeepers, lawyers and doctors, is carried out, in greater or less degree, to large districts, states and nations. Some districts, some states, give themselves mainly to agriculture, in one or another branch; some resort chiefly to fishing, shipbuilding and navigation; some, to mining and to the manufacture of metals from the ores; some, to textile manufactures or to the production of pottery or porcelain from clays.

148. Soil and Climate.—There are three principal sets of forces in the territorial division of labor. These are

(1) Soil and climate.

(2) The industrial adaptations of the people.

(3) The accumulation of capital.

The chief controlling force is found in soil and climate, including all those elements which may be called geographical.

Soil and climate have always a powerful influence upon the occupations of any community, although that influence is much greater in respect to certain classes of occupations than in respect to others. It is in the mining industries that the force of this cause reaches its maximum. Nature here fixes the limits within which alone industry can be prosecuted; although men may or may not take advantage of the opportunities offered. Generally speaking, also, it may be said that in mining districts there is seldom any considerable variety of occupations. Neither manufactures nor agriculture are likely to grow up, on any considerable scale, in connection with mining, on account of the rugged and inaccessible, and often sterile, nature of the regions concerned.

Agriculture comes next to mining, in the degree to which the constraints of nature are felt. In regard to some crops the lines are drawn so strictly that man has little choice given him, except only the choice of not producing at all. In certain narrow districts along our southern coast, rice is raised, and nowhere else in the United States. This crop can only be cultivated on lands which are periodically flooded by water, either naturally or by artificial means. The temperature of the growing season must, also, be high. In New Jersey and in certain other Northern States, are small districts which are almost wholly given up to the raising of cranberries for the market. The crop is a profitable one; but it can only be raised under peculiar conditions as to soil and water. There is a well-defined honey-producing district in California.

Hops are raised to a great extent in certain districts of New York and Wisconsin. Cotton is raised almost wholly south of a certain parallel of latitude, because this plant requires both heat and moisture, in an exceptional degree, for its cultivation. Yet the human will and the progress of the agricultural art have something to do with determining the seats of cotton cultivation. Cotton is now largely raised on high lands in South Carolina and Georgia, where, before the War of Secession, no one thought of planting it, except in small patches. Tobacco can be raised either at the North or at the South, in Connecticut as in Kentucky, and this plant has no very clear relations to the amount of moisture; yet certain districts are found, upon extensive trial, to be so much better suited than others to the production of a proper quality and quantity of this plant, that the tobacco region of the United States may be said to be fairly well defined. Here, as in the case of hops, we have a crop which fluctuates greatly in price from year to year. Such a crop is likely to be less widely spread, for the same quantity of product, than a crop which is steadier in price. Wheat is grown almost wholly north of the thirty-sixth degree of latitude; while Indian corn, or maize, can be cultivated through a much wider range of country, giving the inhabitants, therefore, a larger choice as to the fields which shall be sown for this crop.

When we come to manufactures we reach a department of production where, it might be supposed, the human will was almost supreme, as regards the points of location; yet, even here, the influence of geographical conditions is very strong. For example, it is to the remarkable groups of water-powers afforded by its rivers, that New England owes much of its development in manufactures. Those rivers, falling down from the mountains at the north, make their way to the sea over a succession of irregular terraces. Whenever a stream plunges from one terrace to another, it places an enormous force at the disposal of men, for manufacturing purposes; and, inasmuch as the rocks of this region are very hard, the water-fall is subject to but little change from age to age. Sometimes, the river takes its last plunge straight down into tide-water, so that vessels can load the grain or the lumber or the cotton cloth almost from the mills.

On the other hand, there are extensive parts of the

United States which are so generally level that the rivers flowing to the sea create almost no water-powers; while, even in some elevated regions, the underlying rock is so soft as to be speedily worn away by the action of the water, producing, instead of a few sharp falls, a succession of rapids and shoals. Some of these rivers, too, take their last plunge at a distance of one hundred, two hundred or even three hundred miles from the shore, so that, if mills were to be erected there, the vessels which were to bring away the produce, or carry up the materials, would have a long and tedious voyage to make.

Climate, moreover, has not a little to do with success in certain branches of manufactures. There are parts of France which are supposed to have a great superiority in the production of silk goods of brilliant colors and delicate shades, by reason of their prevailing climate. Some districts, as in England, have just about that degree of moisture in the air, throughout the year, which is most favorable to the spinning of cotton. In still other regions, the highly electrical condition of the atmosphere is unfavorable to mill-work.

Upon all out-door mechanical employments, the comparative severity or mildness of the weather has a great influence. In some countries, a stone or brick mason can perform his task, with but little interruption, through the entire year; in other countries, the building season is practically limited to eight months; in others, to six months or even five.

While the soil has little direct influence upon manufactures, it has yet an important secondary influence, as producing, or not producing, the materials of manufacture. A region in which cotton is grown has a certain advantage, other things equal, in the production of cotton goods. The manufacture of porcelain and pottery is usually carried on where the clays suitable for this industry are found most freely and of the best quality. Ores are generally smelted at or near the mine. The existence of coal in any district is an enormous aid to manufacturing industry.

The foregoing conditions, however, are subject, in a high degree, to the will of man and to the progress of the industrial arts. England imports cotton from America, from Egypt and from India, and makes it into cloth which she sends back to the very countries from which the staple came. In many instances, ores of iron are carried hundreds, and ores of copper even thousands, of miles, to be smelted. Districts which are destitute alike of natural water-power and of coal, have, notwithstanding, achieved great success in manufactures.

149. Industrial Adaptations of the People.—Far less conspicuous to the sight, but, in the case of many industries, of greater influence, are industrial adaptations, either inherited or acquired by education. Strong as are the constraints of geographical conditions, there is that in the spirit and mind of man which can make the wilderness blossom like the rose, which can redeem a land from the sea, which can cut paths for commerce where nature has interposed the mightiest barriers, which can build up manufactures in remote and desolate places. Some of the greatest achievements of industry have been made under circumstances the most forbidding and with means the most inadequate. Any land, however sterile, which possesses an energetic, skilful and enterprising people, will, in the course of a few generations, be richer than any other country, however bounteously endowed by nature, whose people are thriftless, ignorant and inert.

But it is something more than this which we mean when we speak of the industrial adaptations of a nation. Of two highly enterprising, intelligent and skilful peoples, each will have, by reason of something in its past, certain special adaptations, of an industrial character, which the other has not. One nation, like France, will easily achieve a remarkable success in the production of goods which have grace of form, beauty of color and elegance of finish. Another nation, like England, will be unsurpassed in the production of goods where durability and substantial service are prime requisites. Another nation, still, like the United States, will instinctively turn itself to the production of articles demanding great ingenuity, mechanical insight, and a ready comprehension of the relation of parts to a whole. The agricultural machines, the locks and safes, the musical instruments, the sewing-machines, the rifles and pistols, the scales and balances, of such a nation, will be sent to the ends of the earth. Some peoples, again, have, in a high degree, the patience, the foresight, the carefulness and the delight in animal life, which give them a remarkable success in breeding, raising and tending cattle and sheep, swine and poultry, and, consequently, in producing those forms of wealth which are derived from such sources.

The industrial adaptations of a people sometimes become very special, indeed. Partly from inherited instincts, partly through secret processes handed down by their forefathers, the people of a certain city may have a marvellous skill and taste in producing a certain, single kind of goods, be it sword-blades that can be bent double without breaking, or toys of infinite delicacy and variety, or carpets and shawls whose patterns and dyes are the admiration of the world.

150. The Accumulation of Capital.—In addition to the foregoing forces, which control or influence the distribution of industries, an important force is found in the accumulation of capital. Given, two peoples exactly alike in all their qualities and characteristics, occupying countries similarly endowed by nature, but one of them older in settlement, and richer in accumulated wealth than the other, there will inevitably be important differences in the avocations of those peoples. They will have much in common; there will be much that is peculiar to each. The greater capital of the older country will not merely enable its people to produce more of the same kind of things; it will enable and almost require its people to produce things of a different kind. There are certain industries which almost wholly belong to long-settled countries.

Moreover, the accumulation of capital tends strongly to the local concentration of certain kinds of manufactures. The rule, "to him that hath shall be given," applies greatly to manufacturing industry. There is a curious tendency, in some branches of business, for producers to herd together. This is even seen in trade. If you go to a large city, you will find the leather dealers, the wool merchants, the sellers of sewing-machines, or musical instruments, close together. One might suppose that the contrary would be the case: that a merchant would prefer not to have his competitors and rivals near him, and would place himself at a distance from them. This is so, to a large extent, in retail trade; but in wholesale trade the rule is the other way. So it is with the great manufactures: long experience has shown that one derives a benefit from the presence of others. This is partly due (1) to the fact that individual manufacturers can, in this way, acquire an earlier and more exact knowledge of what is going on in their lines of production; in part, (2) to the concentration, within a limited area, of the laborers skilled in that kind of work, so that any manufacturer can readily increase his laboring force; in part, (3) to the fact that the shops which supply the materials for that kind of manufacture, and the works which make its peculiar machinery, come to be located near by; in part, and perhaps the greater part, (4) to the fact, that when a region contains many factories of a certain kind, it comes to be known as the centre, or "headquarters," of that manufacture; merchants and agents visit it in large numbers; and the goods produced there acquire a special name and reputation.

The force of the foregoing cause is very great: so much so that, with regard to certain manufactures, it may be said, it is not worth while for a country or a region to produce at all, unless it is to produce a great deal: to have any factories of that sort, unless it is to have many.

151. Neighborhood Industries.—Precisely the opposite is true of certain industries which we call "neighborhood industries." It is of the very nature of these, that they should be scattered widely over the country.

Among these industries may be reckoned most of the ordinary mechanical trades. The carpenter, the blacksmith, the plumber, the house painter, the paperer, the glazier, the brick and stone mason, must do their work on the spot where the product is to be used or consumed; and these trades, taken together, comprise a large part of the mechanical labor of even the greatest industrial nations. There are more carpenters in the United States than persons engaged in the iron manufacture, or in the cotton manufacture, or in the woollen manufacture. Again, the building of roads, canals, and railroads, and largely, also, the construction of bridges, must be performed on the spot. A railroad cannot be built in one country and exported to another for use. The skilled and unskilled labor required for the operation of a railroad, has to be employed in the place where the service is to be enjoyed. Locomotives and cars may, indeed, be built at a distance; but a vast amount of repairs is constantly to be done near to the track upon which the locomotives and cars are used. There are, also, some branches of manufactures, proper, which strongly tend to be scattered over the face of the country, such as the making of heavy wagons, coarse furniture, and plain brick.

Such industries as those we have enumerated, constitute an important exception to the rule that manufacturing industries tend to local concentration. When, for example, we say that a country or a large region, possessing a rich soil and favorable climate, is mainly agricultural, we must bear in mind that this country or region will still have, in the forms above mentioned, a great deal of mechanical industry.

And it is also to be noted, as a most important consideration, that, out of these primitive mechanical industries, the higher, the finer, the more complicated branches of manufacture tend to grow up, just as fast as the necessary skill and capital are attained. The machine shop follows the blacksmith's shop, in natural order; the factory that has been turning out rude farmers' and pioneers' wagons and carts, comes, in time, to make the coach and the gentleman's drag; shops which were built only to repair articles brought from a distance, at last undertake, slowly and cautiously, to make those articles themselves. In these and similar ways, the "neighborhood industries" become "plantations" of the great manufactures, just as single trees, set down here and there over a region, tend to form, first, groups of trees, of their own kind, then groves, then forests.

152. Advantages of the Territorial Divison of Labor.— We have, thus far in the present chapter, undertaken to describe, of course very rudely, the process by which the territorial division of labor takes place. The economic advantages resulting therefrom are so clear that they scarcely need to be mentioned. Each country, devoting its energies to those forms of production for which it is best fitted, alike by its geographical endowment and by the skill, tastes, and habits of its people, at once does that which is best for itself and best for mankind. The good of each serves the good of all. While each nation develops its industry along the line of its own peculiar powers and adaptations, international trade brings all the nations together, in exchanges which are mutually beneficial. Each, doing that which it can do best, thereby contributes in the highest degree to the welfare of others; and in its turn, through a fair exchange, receives back articles of necessity, of comfort, or of luxury, which it could not have produced except through a greater, perhaps a vastly greater, outlay of labor and capital. Freedom of production within the nations, and freedom of trade between the nations, is the proper general condition of human industry.

153. "The Encouragement of Manufactures."—It has, however, been strongly held, by many persons, that, in a new country, having as yet but small capital, something may properly be done by law, to encourage the growth of manufactures, instead of leaving this altogether to the interest and the "initiative" of individual producers. It has been held, that, by imposing "customs duties" upon foreign articles, in certain lines, "a start" might be given to the production of these articles, which, after a brief term of such "protection," would be produced to advantage. It is alleged, in support of this opinion, that, in such a country as has been described, conditions might, in general, be favorable to the production of certain articles, and yet, on account of timidity or want of foresight on the part of capitalists and manufacturers, their production might be long delayed; whereas, a little impulse from the government, a brief term of protection, might suffice to bring such industries into being and to support them through the time of trial, experiment, and large, initial, outlay for plant and machinery.

Such an opinion is perfectly rational. Capitalists and manufacturers are often timid, often mistaken, often blind to their own true interests. It is conceivable that a country, in which capital was at the best scarce,* might be on the verge of a successful career in a certain line of production, and yet not enter upon it, for the reasons indicated. A law which imposed duties upon articles, in this line, might furnish the impulse needed. While many of the results of so-called protection are subject to doubt and dispute, I believe that instances of the successful application of this policy are to be found in our own history and in that of other countries.

154. The Possible Disadvantages of the Protective System.—Against whatever advantages may be deemed likely to result from the successful introduction of certain branches of manufacture, at a date earlier than that at which they would have appeared, but for protection, are to be set two things.

(*a*) The instances of failure. If capitalists and manufacturers are fallible, so also are governors and legislators. If capitalists and manufacturers are selfish, governors and legislators are likely to be moved strongly by sectional or partisan interests. The history of protection abounds in gross mistakes and grave misadventures, in the attempt to set-up industries artificially by force of law. The silk duties in England and the hemp duties in the United States are striking examples of such failures. It is, of course, impossible to put into figures the mischief done, whenever the policy of encouraging manufactures is

---

* This is an essential point. When capital is abundant, capitalists are almost too ready to try new things.

wrongly applied. Even where the failure is not total and final, i.e., where at last the industry becomes established, it may still be true that its premature establishment has cost more, in waste of labor and capital, than the industry will ever be worth to the people of the country.

(*b*) The undue continuance of protective duties. Perhaps the greatest objection to the putting-on of protective duties is the difficulty of taking them off. At the outset, whenever protection is asked for an " infant industry," it is invariably asserted that this will be required for but a short time. Such has been the theory upon which almost every one of the protected industries of the United States has been started. As a matter of fact, however, the time seldom comes when those who represent a protected industry are willing to admit that governmental assistance is no longer needed. On the contrary, it has been the experience of the United States, with but few exceptions, that the protected industries have from time to time demanded higher and still higher protection, and that with increasing urgency; while against any proposed reduction of duties, all concerned struggle with the utmost vehemence, filling the public press with their outcries, arousing sectional prejudice and passion, and producing apprehensions and alarms which are exceedingly injurious to production and trade.

155. The Balance of Advantage and Disadvantage.—We have seen what is the possible advantage of a protective policy, at its best, in promoting the introduction of certain branches of manufacture into countries which are ripe for them, at an earlier date than that at which they would otherwise have appeared. We have noted, also, the possible disadvantages of a protective system, first, through the mistakes of legislators and governors in making choice of the industries to be protected; secondly, through the passionate resistance offered by the protected industries to a removal or reduction of duties. The question, on which side the balance of advantage and disadvantage lies, is one which every citizen must decide for himself. It is not a matter for either mathematical or moral proof. One man will, according to his way of thinking, his education, his business interests, or the section of country in which he lives, take a very large view of the benefits of protection, and treat its possible disadvantages slightingly. Another man will, according to his cast of mind and various conditions, think it of small importance whether certain branches of industry come a little earlier or a little later, but deem it an enormous evil that industries should be forced into being for which a country is not fitted, or that protective duties should be continued upon industries which have passed the time when they ought to "go alone."

The question is one which, as I have said, each one must decide for himself; and, in doing so, it is inevitable that he will be profoundly influenced by local and personal considerations, as well as by inherited opinions and the force of education. If he is a wool manufacturer, he will be likely to think that wool ought to be free, so that he may get his material at a low price. If he is a wool grower, he will be likely to think that foreign wool ought to be taxed, so that he may sell his crop at a high price. If, on the other hand, he is a cotton planter, he will be likely to think that both raw cotton and cotton goods should be free of duty; first, because most of his crop is going to Europe, anyhow, and hence its price will not be affected by any duties which the United States Government can impose*; secondly, because he and his family and his "hands" will have to use a great deal of cotton cloth, which he naturally desires should be as cheap as possible.

---

* By the Constitution, Congress is prohibited from imposing any duties on exports.

If a man is engaged in iron mining, he is likely to think that foreign ore should be heavily taxed. The pig-iron manufacturer, on the other hand, is likely to think that foreign ores should be free, but that English, Scotch, and Swedish iron should be taxed. The manufacturer of bar iron and boiler plate, on the other hand, desires to buy his pig-iron at the lowest price, no matter where made; but would be glad to be relieved from foreign competition as to his own product.

The formation of a tariff thus becomes a struggle of conflicting interests. How bitter that struggle may be, how disgraceful the methods which may be resorted to by the contestants, how ready men of good repute may be to sacrifice general to sectional or local interests, can only be learned by a careful study of the tariff history of the United States.* The American Congress is, alike by its membership, its organization, and its traditional opinions and sentiments, peculiarly ill-fitted to deal with so difficult and delicate a matter as the decision, what industries shall be protected; how much protection each of these shall receive; how long that protection shall be continued.

(*a*) By its membership, because it is composed of men, chiefly lawyers, who have had little training in political economy and finance, and, on the other hand, know little, practically, of industry and trade.

(*b*) By its organization, because its committees are too small in numbers and command too little respect for their work, so that the most carefully digested bill, when brought upon the floor of the House, is at once torn to pieces, in a furious rush of all the parties interested.

(*c*) By its traditional opinions and sentiments, because

---

* The history of the tariff of 1828 is peculiarly instructive in this respect.

"log-rolling,"* instead of being considered a grave political crime, is too often regarded as a proper legislative method: many members holding themselves justified in voting for items in which other members are interested, upon condition of receiving the votes of those members for the items in which they or their constituents are concerned.

156. The "Pauper Labor" Argument for Protection.— In addition to the argument in favor of so-called protective duties, for the promotion of manufacturing industry, as a temporary policy, there is known to our political literature an argument in favor of a protective system, as a permanent policy, by which a prosperous country, in which wages are high and in which laborers are skilful and intelligent, shall be cut off from trade with countries in which wages are low and in which the body of laborers are ignorant, degraded, and spiritless, with a low standard of living and without industrial ambitions. Those who advocate this permanent system of protection, and support it by what is called "the pauper-labor argument," hold, in effect, that, in trade, a sort of economic virus passes from the less fortunate to the more fortunate country, poisoning the industrial system of that country. In this view, low wages constitute a disease which is communicated through the goods produced by the laborers who receive such wages, just as the plague or the cholera is sometimes imported into European countries in rags from Smyrna or Alexandria. This "pauper-labor" argument for protection, as a permanent policy, is one which we shall not be prepared to discuss until we have discovered the principles which govern the distribution of wealth, to which we now pass.

---

* You help me roll my log, and I will help you roll yours. There are frequent instances of several "interests," in a legislative body, uniting their forces and carrying through each measure by turns.

PART II.

DISTRIBUTION AND CONSUMPTION.

CHAPTER XVII.

THE PROBLEM OF DISTRIBUTION.

157. Distribution Defined.—We have defined wealth; have seen in what its Production consists; have considered the natural conditions as to land, labor and capital, under which that production takes place; and have sought for the laws which govern the Exchange of the wealth thus produced. We are now to speak of the Distribution of wealth. This term we must carefully define, because it is often subject to misapprehension.

In private conversation, and even by some intelligent writers, the distribution of wealth has been spoken of as if it were a geographical distribution: the sending of commodities, over land and over sea, from producers to consumers. It is not in this sense that we use the term. The distribution of wealth means *the division of wealth among those persons and classes of persons who have taken part in its production.* The geographical element has nothing to do with this. It does not matter whether the persons among whom a body of wealth is to be distributed, live closely together or are widely separated. What we inquire about, is the nature of the forces, and the mode of the operation of those forces, by which the product is divided among those who have taken part in its production.

158. Distribution in Primitive Society.—The complexity and the difficulty of the problem of distribution vary according to the stage which industrial society has reached. When four hunters go out in company, thinking that thereby they can best surround and capture their game, the question of the division of the spoils is an easy one. Probably they agree to take each a fourth share. If, however, there is among them one hunter so experienced and so skilled that the others know their chances of great game will be vastly better by reason of his being of the party, it is likely that this man will claim, and the others will readily concede, a larger share. But if, again, there is of the party one who is young and inexperienced, he must be content to receive the small share which the others are willing to allow him. In this case there would be three grades of remuneration : a large share, for the chief ; moderate shares, for the two trained hunters ; a small, perhaps a very small, share for the novice.

The determination of these several shares would, however, not be a matter of much difficulty. Prone as men are to quarrel, it is remarkable how readily, with how little of jealousy, of friction or of complaint, working men, of all races, in all ages, in all occupations, have accepted differences of remuneration, based upon manifest differences of strength, skill, experience or general intelligence. Whatever difficulties, whatever perplexities, attend the distribution of the product of industry, very little of this is due to those who furnish the labor power.

If, again, we were to suppose a number of fishermen to unite in a venture, we should have the same question raised concerning the share of each, according to the degree in which he deemed himself, and was by his comrades deemed, capable of contributing to a successful result. We should, moreover, have the additional difficulty of deciding how much of the catch should go to the owner of the boat : that is, the question would arise as to the amount to be paid, as interest, for the use of certain body of capital (par. 57). But, even so, the problem of distribution would not be a very difficult one, in an industry so primitive as fishing out of a sea which nobody owns.

If, however, these fishermen were to go into a bay, which some other person, not even of their tribe, controlled, the question would become not a little complicated. The demand for rent, for the right of fishing in the bay, would probably arouse more envy and anger than any demand previously made. If that demand could not be resisted, it would probably be sought to be evaded, in every way possible. Perhaps not one of the fishermen would think of stealing a boat from a neighbor at night, to do the fishing in; while every one of them, perhaps, would be ready to go secretly into the bay, under cover of darkness, in order to escape the payment of the required rent.

Moreover, if there were some great chief, at a distance, who claimed a part of the fish taken upon that shore, it is probable that all the fishermen would agree to smuggle the fish back into their huts, if they could manage to do so, without paying this tithe or tax. I mention these last two elements of the case, because it needs to be borne in mind, not only that the problem of distribution increases in difficulty and perplexity, as more and more parties are introduced; but also that there are certain shares respecting which the great majority of uninstructed men entertain feelings very different from those with which they regard other shares. We have said that there is seldom any difficulty among the laboring class as to the division, between themselves, of the total amount which is to go to them as a body. There are, however, other shares of the product, regarding which a great deal of prejudice exists, and sometimes a great deal of passion is aroused.

159. Distribution in Modern Industrial Society.—The most complicated case which we could conceive in regard to a primitive community, whether of fishermen or of huntsmen or of agriculturists, would be plain and simple, as compared with those which habitually arise in communities like our own. Take the case of a cotton factory, producing, in a given time, a million yards of cloth. Here we have the following claimants for shares of the product:

First, those who furnish the labor power required for this production;

Second, the owner of the land on which the mill stands;

Third, the owner of the water power;

Fourth, the owner of the mill;

Fifth, the owner of the machinery, of the stock of materials, and of the working capital used in these operations;

Sixth, the employer, who furnishes the business ability to carry on production successfully; who takes the risk of making nothing and the chance of making much for himself; who conducts the negotiations with the various parties, and organizes all these persons and agents into a productive body; with whom, finally, it rests to say, what shall be produced and how it shall be produced; of what materials, in what forms and styles, to what amount; to whom, at what prices, on what terms of credit, the product shall be sold.

It is true that more than one of the parts enumerated above may be found in the same person. The owner of the mill may be also the owner of the water-power; but then, again, he may not be. Very commonly the owners of mills do not own the water-power they employ; but lease it, at a certain price, from others. What determines that price? The owner of the land may also be the owner of the mill; but this is not necessarily so. Indeed, it is in some countries usual to erect buildings upon leased land. The employer, again, may or may not be the owner of the mill and the machinery; but even if he be, the share he receives, as owner of the mill and the machinery, is just as truly distinct from the share he receives as employer, as it would be were these different persons.

We have enumerated six claimants upon the product of the mill; but, in fact, one of these is not a person but a class, composed of the most heterogeneous subjects, who will be, among themselves, in very different positions as to the claims they can individually make and enforce for portions of the cotton cloth. There are the superintendent, the overseers or foremen, and the clerks and cashiers in the office of the mill, all of whom are just as truly laborers as the spinners and weavers; there are machinists and highly skilled operatives; there are porters, doing mere heavy work, and operatives of little skill and experience; there are men and there are women; there are adults and there are children.

From the foregoing statements, it will appear that the problem, how this great web of a million yards of cloth shall be cut up and distributed among these hundreds of persons, of such different degrees of skill, strength, and intelligence, performing parts so various in the general work, is not likely to be a simple and easy one. Yet he who would write on the distribution of wealth must undertake to show at least the general principles which govern the remuneration of each one of these hundreds of persons, in turn: how much the employer shall receive, and why he shall receive no more and no less; how much the owner of the water-power is to receive, and why he is to receive no more or no less; how much the owner of the land, the able bodied and skilled operatives, the "heavy porter," the woman spinner, the nine-year-old "half timer," is each to receive; and why that remuneration neither will nor can be either greater or smaller.

160. Price as Affecting Distribution.—But we have not yet got to the bottom of the difficulties and perplexities which attend the problem of distribution. We have thus far spoken as if there were only one factory producing cotton cloth, or, else, as if, of several or many factories producing such goods, all were on a perfect equality as regards the conditions of production. But since no two factories are really on an equality as regards certain conditions of production, and since any inequality in these respects must, as we shall show, importantly affect the distribution of the product, it becomes necessary to introduce the notion of price (par. 95). Instead, therefore, of supposing the great web of cloth to be cut into pieces, corresponding to the shares of the several persons who have taken part in its production, we must suppose the cloth to be sold, at such a price as shall be fixed by the competition of other factories, differently situated in some respects; and the proceeds of the sale to be divided among the claimants.

161. Production at the Greatest Disadvantage.—This way of approaching the question of distribution, viz., through Price, requires us to review the principle which governs Normal Price. In Chapter X we saw that the Normal Price of any kind of goods is determined by the cost of "that last considerable portion of supply which is produced at the greatest disadvantage." This principle is of vital importance to the theory of the distribution of wealth. The reader should, at this point, carefully review that chapter, until he is sure that he holds its subject-matter strongly and clearly in his mind.

162. The Assumption of Perfect Competition.—Throughout the next few chapters, we shall speak of the parties to the distribution of wealth and of their several shares, as if competition were perfect. We shall assume that every producer of wealth, in every capacity, every claimant upon the product, on whatever ground he bases that claim, thoroughly understands his own true, permanent, economic interest;

that he clearly sees whatever is necessary to secure for him the largest practicable share of the product to which he has contributed; and that he will not fail at any point or at any time to pursue those means, peacefully and honestly, to be sure, but also firmly, consistently, and courageously, allowing nothing to turn him aside from his purpose.

Of course, this assumption will not correspond to the facts in any human community. Men are always something less than perfectly wise, perfectly brave, perfectly consistent and true to themselves. They are, alas! generally found far, very far, below the standard we have set up. They often mistake their interests; they as often neglect their interests, even when they rightly discern them. Notwithstanding this, it will be profitable and expedient for us to go over the whole ground of the distribution of wealth, upon the assumption which I have made; and thus to see what would happen if all men clearly understood their true economic interests and unfalteringly pursued them. We shall, then, in subsequent chapters, inquire into the effects of imperfect competition: who will lose and who gain; why one should lose and another gain, in case men do, in any considerable degree, fail to see and to seek their true economic interests.

163. The main Parties to the Distribution of Wealth.— In par. 159 we saw that, in the case of a cotton mill, there were six claimants (persons or classes of persons), who were to receive shares, greater or smaller, of the mighty web of cloth, woven in the mill. It is not, however, necessary that, in proceeding to consider the general principles regulating the distribution of wealth, we should carry all these along with us. The main parties to the distribution of wealth are four in number.

Thus, to recur to the instance of the cotton-mill, it is true that the share received by the owner of the water-power, as such, is distinguishable in theory, and may also be distinct in fact, from the share received by the owner of the land on which the factory is built. Nevertheless, both cases come under a certain general law, which we shall call the Law of Rent; and, for all the purposes of an elementary treatise, it will suffice to show the general law, leaving special cases under it to be worked out by the scholar, or explained by the teacher.

In the same way, the share received by the owner of the mill, as such, is distinguishable in theory, and may be also distinct in fact, from the share received by the owner of the machinery, the materials and the working capital. Different persons may actually receive these two shares. And yet, although the mill is fixed capital, and the machinery and materials are circulating capital (par. 63), one general law, which we call the Law of Interest, governs both species. It will answer all our purposes to ascertain what this law is.

The four main parties to the distribution of wealth are, then, the following:

1. The Landlord,—furnishing land power, and receiving Rent.

2. The Employer,—furnishing business ability, and receiving Profits.

3. The Capitalist,—furnishing capital, and receiving Interest.

4. The Laborer,—furnishing labor power, and receiving Wages.

CHAPTER XVIII.

RENT.

164. The Surplus above Cost of Production.—In Chapter X we showed that "the normal price of any kind of goods is determined by the cost of that last (considerable) portion of the necessary supply which is produced at the greatest disadvantage."

Further inquiring how there could be any such thing as advantage or disadvantage, in regard to different portions of the supply, we saw that, in regard to two of the four principal agents of production, there is not, necessarily, any such thing as advantage or disadvantage between different portions of the supply; but that, in regard to the two remaining agents, there is, in the nature of the case, certain to be differences of productive power, which will cause portions of the supply to be produced at an advantage, relatively to other portions.

The two productive agents which do not necessarily vary in their efficiency, as between different portions of the supply, are capital and labor power (par. 78). The two elements which, in the nature of the case, do vary with different portions of the supply, are land power and business ability (pars. 79 and 80).

We further saw that, while different portions of the supply are produced at different, perhaps very different, costs, all parts of the supply are sold at the same price, in the same market. If the price of silver be a dollar, an ounce, that price is received by the owner of the mine at which silver is produced at twenty-five cents, an ounce, just as surely as by the owner of the mines at which silver is produced at a dollar. If the price of wheat be six shillings, a bushel, the farmer whose wheat has cost but three shillings receives the full price. An able and skilful manufacturer does not sell his goods for what they cost him, but at the price which has been fixed for that kind of goods,* by the cost of producing them on the part of the least competent and efficient manufacturers contributing to the supply of the market, in this line.

It thus appears that, upon a large part of the wealth produced (upon *all*, indeed, except "that last considerable portion of the supply which is produced at the greatest disadvantage"), there is A SURPLUS above the cost of production. This is a fact of tremendous consequence in the distribution of wealth. It is the fact with which we must begin our inquiry, for we cannot with advantage take a step forward, before we have found out to whom this surplus is to go.

165. To Whom shall the Surplus Go?—We have seen that, while different portions of the supply are produced at different costs, all are yet sold at the same price. This price, we have further seen, must be high enough to maintain production in the places and under the conditions where it is actually carried on "at the greatest disadvantage." That disadvantage, we saw, relates to the land

---

* It will be remembered that we are here speaking of normal price. Market price may, for a time, by the operation of supply and demand, fall below normal price; and thus the less successful manufacturers may realize a certain loss upon their goods. This state of things, however, cannot continue indefinitely. It is not normal; and the operation of the principle of self-interest tends steadily and strongly to bring the market back to the point where the least successful producers will sell their goods for the cost of their production, but for no more.

power and the business ability employed in production, not at all to the labor power or the capital, so employed. *It is, then, those who own the more productive land and who possess the higher business ability, who will carry off the entire surplus over the cost of production.* No part of this will go to reward labor or capital. Labor and capital will only get what they can produce "at the greatest disadvantage." All that is produced in excess of this will go either to the landlord, as rent, or to the employer, as profits.

We see, then, that all the wealth produced annually, or in any given time, is divided into two great parts. One of these is equal to that amount of wealth which *would have been produced,* had all the labor and the capital been employed under conditions (as to land power and business ability) as disadvantageous as those under which any (considerable) amount of labor and of capital was actually employed. All this wealth is divided, clear, between the laborer and the capitalist. The landlord and the employer get none of it; but they do get all of the product which is over and above this.

Which, then, of these two great parts of the wealth-product shall we take up first for consideration? Shall we take up that part which represents the cost of production (labor and capital), or shall we take up that part which consists of the surplus above the cost of production? I answer, clearly, the latter. Rent and Profits should be treated before Wages and Interest. Many economists have, by reversing this order, fallen into serious confusion, which we may hope to avoid.

166. Rent.—I have said that the entire excess of price over cost is divided between the landlord and the employer. We shall first take up the landlord's share, to which we have already, by anticipation, applied the term Rent. For the purpose of greater clearness and simplicity, we shall, throughout this and the next succeeding chapter, write as if there were no profits. We shall see, when we come to Chapter XIX, that there would be no profits, were there no "production at disadvantage," in respect to business ability,* i.e., were all employers equally able and competent to conduct business. Such a state of things we now, for the purposes of argument, assume to exist, leaving it to a later period to consider how profits actually arise, and by what forces they are limited.

167. The Origin of Rent.—To get a fair start, let us go back to the case which we assumed in paragraph 81. We there supposed that the people of a certain district or country wanted enough wheat, and wanted wheat badly enough, to make up an effective demand for a hundred and thirty million bushels, at the price of six shillings, a bushel. We further assumed that portions of this supply were produced at different costs, as follows, only a part of tract No. 5 being cultivated:

Tract.	Amount produced, in bushels.	Cost, per bushel.	Surplus of price over cost, per bushel.	Surplus of price over cost, for the whole crop.
No. 1	10,000,000	2 shillings	4 shillings	40,000,000 shillings
" 2	20,000,000	3 "	3 "	60,000,000 "
" 3	30,000,000	4 "	2 "	60,000,000 "
" 4	40,000,000	5 "	1 "	40,000,000 "
" 5	30,000,000	6 "	0 "	....
	130,000,000			200,000,000 shillings

Now, since the whole crop is sold at six shillings, it will bring 780,000,000 shillings. How much of this total amount will go to Rent, on the one hand; how much to

---

* Indeed, in pars. 54 and 55, it has been stated that, in a primitive condition of industrial society, there are no profits, or at least none worth bringing into account.

Labor and to Capital, on the other? The answer is given above. The total surplus over cost of production, on the entire crop, will be two hundred million shillings. This amount, then, will go, entire, to the owners of the land, as rent. The remainder, five hundred and eighty million shillings, will go to the laborers and the capitalists who took part in the production of the wheat. How that amount will be divided between these: how much will become Wages, and how much will become Interest, is a question which we shall be called to discuss in subsequent chapters. For the present, it is sufficient to note that the laborers and capitalists have a common interest as against the land-owning class. They can only divide between themselves what the latter do not claim and receive, as the surplus above cost of production.

168. The Margin of Cultivation.—To bring out this last point clearly, let us make another series of assumptions regarding the community in question. We will suppose that each of the four better kinds of land is half as large again as we first assumed it, so that fifteen million bushels can be raised on the two-shilling tract; thirty million bushels on the three-shilling tract; forty-five million bushels on the four-shilling tract; sixty million bushels on the five-shilling tract. The four tracts taken together are, thus, capable of producing one hundred and fifty million bushels, none of it at a cost above five shillings. We will, further, assume that, at this lower price for wheat, the community are able and glad to consume a hundred and fifty million bushels. The entire crop will then sell for seven hundred and fifty million shillings. The community will have the pleasure and the physiological benefit of consuming twenty million more bushels of wheat, while paying thirty million shillings less for wheat than they formerly did. It is not needful to say that this would be a great advantage to the community.

But let us see how the account now stands between the land-owning class, on the one side, and the capitalists and laborers, on the other:

Tract.	Amount produced, in bushels.	Cost, per bushel.	Surplus of price over cost, per bushel.	Surplus of cost over price, for the whole crop.
No. 1	15,000,000	2 shillings	3 shillings	45,000,000 shillings
" 2	30,000,000	3 "	2 "	60,000,000 "
" 3	45,000,000	4 "	1 "	45,000,000 "
" 4	60,000,000	5 "	0 "	....
	150,000,000			150,000,000 shillings

We see that, in this case, the land-owning class will receive but one hundred and fifty million shillings, as rent, or just one-fifth of the price of the crop, whereas, formerly, they received more than one-fourth. Dividing the aggregate rent by the aggregate crop, we find that the landlord class now receive only one shilling, rent, to each bushel of the crop; whereas, in the previous case (par. 167), they received a shilling and a half.

To still further illustrate the operation of this force, let us make a new series of assumptions. Let us suppose that the several better tracts of land are so large that the two-shilling tract can produce thirty million bushels; the three-shilling tract, sixty millions; the four-shilling tract, ninety millions. The three tracts, taken together, then, will be capable of producing one hundred and eighty million bushels, none of it at a cost above four shillings, which, consequently, will become the price of wheat. Let it further be supposed that, at this price, the members of the community are glad to extend their consumption to one hundred and eighty million bushels, enjoying, thus, both the pleasure and the physiological benefit of being better nourished than ever before, while paying less for the larger than they formerly did for the smaller amount. Let us again see how the account stands between the land-owning class, on the one hand, and the laborers and the capitalists, on the other.

Tract.	Amount produced, in bushels.	Cost, per bushel.	Surplus of price over cost, per bushel.	Surplus of price over cost, for the whole crop.
No. 1	30,000,000	2 shillings	2 shillings	60,000,000 shillings.
" 2	60,000,000	3 "	1 "	60,000,000 "
" 3	90,000,000	4 "	0 "	
	180,000,000			120,000,000 shillings.

The reader sees that, in this case, the land-owning class will receive, as rent, only one hundred and twenty million shillings, which is but one-sixth the price of the crop. Dividing, again, the aggregate rent by the aggregate crop, we find that the landlord class now receive, as rent, but two-thirds of a shilling for each bushel of the crop, instead of a shilling, as by the last supposition.

The moral of this is clear, and is of immense and almost illimitable consequence to mankind. Of course, the community, as a whole, is interested in having its labor and its capital applied to good instead of to poor lands: there is no need to say that. But we, also, see, from the above illustrations, that, wholly in addition to their interest as members of the community, laborers and capitalists have a special interest (opposed to the interest of the land-owning class) in not having the "margin of cultivation" lowered, i.e., in not having cultivation forced down to poorer soils. Every time the necessity of meeting the demand for vegetable or animal produce, for food or for clothing, forces cultivation to descend to a poorer grade of land, the land-owning class will receive, not only a larger absolute amount of the produce, but also *a larger share of the produce*.

169. The Increase of Population.—We see, then, at what a cost population increases, after the point of Diminishing Returns has been reached. Not only is there, as we showed in Chapter V, a smaller proportional return to cultivation, but, of that return, a diminishing share goes to those who perform the labor or furnish the capital. As was said (par. 28), all mankind dwell, and must forever dwell, under the shadow of this condition. If a community is led to take up an inferior grade of soils because its labor power and capital power have been enormously increased by the invention of machinery and the introduction of useful arts, the disadvantage of resorting to poorer soils may be more than compensated by the opportunity to apply that increased power to some soils, even if poorer. But, wherever the reason for a resort to inferior land is found, not in greater skill and larger capital and improved arts, but in the primary wants of an ignorant and helpless population, increasing in numbers without advancing in industrial power or in social ambition, the results are miserable, indeed. A large part of all the wretchedness of mankind can clearly be traced to this source.

170. Transportation.—We have thus far compared different parcels of land, as to their productive powers, just as if they lay side by side, equally near to the market where the produce was to be sold. Of course, the reader will see for himself that, if two tracts lie at unequal distances from the market, the several costs of transporting produce must be taken into account, in making out their comparative costs of production. If the price of wheat, in a certain market, is five shillings, a tract of land upon which wheat can be raised at a cost, upon the ground, of two shillings, but which is at such a distance that the transportation to the market costs a shilling, a bushel, will bring a rent not of three shillings, a bushel, but of two. The cost of production of that wheat is three shillings: two shillings for the labor and capital employed on the land; one shilling for the labor and capital engaged in transportation.

Wheat may be raised in parts of Dakota, at a cost of, say, fifty cents, a bushel; but if it costs fifty cents additional to get that wheat to London, and if wheat be selling there at a dollar and twenty-five cents, the Dakota land will only yield a rent of twenty-five cents, per bushel, although that land is just as good as land in Kent which pays seventy-five cents, a bushel, rent.

During the last ten or twenty years, there has been a marvellous reduction in the cost of transporting grain and other agricultural produce from the United States to England. Cheaper steel rails and more powerful locomotives have enabled the crops of the Great West to be hauled to the sea-board at a much less expenditure of labor and capital; at the ports, steam " elevators " have taken the grain from the cars and discharged it into the hold of the vessels, at a tenth part of the cost formerly involved in handling the grain in baskets or bags; while gigantic steamships, with "compound engines," which carry the grain across the sea in ten or twelve days, have replaced the small and slow sailing-vessels, which in the old days did this service.

As a consequence, rents have fallen sharply in England and in Ireland; the lands on which wheat was formerly produced for the British market " at the greatest disadvantage " have been thrown out of cultivation, their place being taken by the wheat-fields of Minnesota and Dakota. This " raising of the margin of cultivation" has acted upon British rents in the way illustrated in par. 168. In the first place, the British public have had the benefit of a lower price for wheat, and hence of a freer consumption of that necessary of life. In the second place, the British labor and British capital still applied to the cultivation of British lands receive a larger share of the total product, while the land-owning class receive a smaller share, than formerly.

171. Land Improvements.—In speaking of rent, the political economist finds it necessary to make a distinction, which the reader must carefully observe, between that portion of the yield of land which is due to the natural powers of the soil, and that portion which is due to so-called improvements. Those improvements embrace everything which is done upon the land, or for its benefit, above what is involved in the mere cultivation of the soil for the annual crop, such as the erection of barns and sheds, fencing, ditching, clearing the ground of brush and timber, or opening roads through it. All such improvements constitute Investments of Capital; and the return which is made to them, through increased crops or diminished cost of production, is a return to capital, and is, therefore, Interest, of which we shall have to speak hereafter. Rent only embraces the return which is made to the owners of land, considered as unimproved.

The foregoing distinction is an exceedingly important one. It is the less likely to be duly observed because, in common speech, the whole return, on the one account as well as on the other, is called Rent. Thus, I might take a lease of an estate, at a rental of three thousand dollars a year. Of that sum, two thousand dollars might really be on account of the native powers of the soil, and one thousand, on account of useful improvements upon it, either enabling the land to produce a greater crop with the same expenditure of labor and capital, or enabling it to produce the same crop with a smaller expenditure of labor and capital. But, neither in the written lease of the estate, nor in the talk of the landlord or myself or my neighbors about it, is this distinction observed. The whole three thousand dollars is called rent. The political economist, however, is bound to observe this distinction, since, as we shall see, the Law of Interest differs very widely from the Law of Rent.

The proportion, in which what is popularly called rent is divided between real rent and interest, varies in the case of different farms, and varies, often very widely, in the case of different regions or countries. A farm in Illinois, which produces, with a certain application of labor and capital, sixteen bushels of wheat to the acre, may be just as good land, naturally, as a farm in England which produces twenty-four bushels to the acre. The farm in Illinois has had comparatively little capital expended upon it; the farm in England has had a great deal of capital expended upon it, of which the additional eight bushels, per acre, is the reward; and is, therefore, interest.

In some parts of the United States, through considerable portions of their history, very little capital has been so applied. Occupiers have been so eager to take as much as possible from the land, each year, that they have applied all the labor and capital they could command to increasing the immediate crop, without doing anything for the permanent improvement of the soil. At the South, indeed, the cultivation of cotton and of tobacco was formerly pursued so eagerly that the lands declined in fertility.

Generally speaking, it is impossible to say how much of the crop of any field is due to the native properties of the soil, and how much to investments of capital. Most of the improvements made in agriculture are made little by little; and no account is kept of them. Moreover, many of these improvements are made in seasons of the year, or in hours of the day, when the labor of the farmer and his sons and his hands would not otherwise have been employed at all; and it is difficult to say how much that labor was worth.

172. The "Cost" of Producing Farms.—Some statisticians and economists have even undertaken to prove that all the value of even the best land is due entirely to improvements, and not at all to the native properties of the soil. These efforts have failed, first, because, as shown above, it is impossible to ascertain what the improvements made upon the land have actually cost, and, secondly, because that proposition is so clearly contrary to reason. We know that some land, in its native state, will yield a handsome crop, on its first year's cultivation; while other land would not return to its cultivators enough to keep them alive. Then, the former lands must have a higher value, as compared with the latter.

We know, moreover, that some land has a larger capability of responding to investments of capital than other land. Very well, then, the former land must have a higher value, as compared with the latter. Suppose two entire Counties were to-day to be "discovered," in Illinois: would that land have no value? On the contrary, it would at once be worth from twenty to thirty dollars an acre, although not a dollar's worth of capital had ever been applied to it. The furious rush made by tens of thousands of persons, from every part of the United States, to Oklahoma, during the present year, when that territory was first declared "open to settlement," is testimony, that cannot be misunderstood, to the fact that land, in its native state, may have value, even a very high value.

All through the history of the United States, men have been seen by thousands, and by hundreds of thousands, exiling themselves from home and taking up their march across the continent, to occupy new lands at the West. If the value of land is entirely due to improvements, why was not all this labor and capital expended upon the lands at home, near to the seats of manufacture, and upon the rivers which flow to the Atlantic? That it was not, but that, on the contrary, large tracts of land were here left altogether uncultivated, while population poured westward, over ten, twenty and thirty degrees of longitude, is evidence, which surely no one ought to mistake, that lands, as they are found in a state of nature, differ widely as to their immediate productiveness, and widely, also, as to their capability of responding to improvements.

173. The No-Rent Lands.—It will have been observed that, in speaking of the origin of rent, in par. 167, we assumed that the lowest grade of lands under cultivation, at any given time, pay no rent. This is a point on which the reader should fix his attention. The whole theory of Rent depends upon the existence of No-Rent lands. Of course, in speaking of certain lands as bearing no-rent, we mean, either, literally no rent at all, or else a rent so small that, with reference to the magnitude of the other interests involved, it may properly, in economic reasoning, be called no rent.* One of the first lessons which the social or the economic philosopher has to learn is that there is a point beyond which he must cease to regard an element or a factor. Even the mathematician carries his computations out only to a certain decimal place.

---

* Until recently, any citizen of the United States could, by law, freely take up excellent land, of a high degree of fertility, at the government price of $1.25 per acre. Now, the interest upon the purchase-price of this land, would, at seven per cent, be nine cents, an acre, per year. Yet, in raising a crop from the land, from eight to twelve dollars' worth of labor and capital would be applied to each acre. Clearly, where rent falls to one per cent upon the cost of cultivation, we may speak of it as no-rent.

Even were it true that no piece of land was ever cultivated without paying some rent, in some degree, however small, this would not in the least affect the validity of our principle. Whenever the rent of land becomes so small that it is less than the value of the hay or the grain which the farmer leaves upon the field, neglecting to glean it, this may certainly be called no rent, for all the purposes of economic reasoning; and rent no larger than this is paid, to-day, for large bodies of grazing and even of cultivated land.

174. The Law of Rent.—We are now in a position to formulate the law of Rent. We have seen what is the origin of Rent. Rent arises out of the differences which exist in the productiveness of the different soils which are under cultivation, at the same time, for the supply of the same market.

Such is the *origin* of Rent. What is the *measure* of Rent? I answer, the amount of Rent is determined by the degree of the differences which has just been referred to. The normal rent of any piece of land is fixed by the difference between its annual yield and that of the least productive land actually cultivated for the supply of the same market. To recur to the illustration previously given, if the six-shilling land is on "the margin of cultivation," and thus, itself, bears no rent, the two-shilling land will bear rent of four shillings, per bushel. Any man may just as well pay such a rent for the privilege of cultivating this land, as cultivate a tract of the six-shilling land, for nothing. But if the margin of cultivation should rise, so that the five-shilling land should be the poorest cultivated, then the rent of the two-shilling land would sink to three shillings, a bushel. In every case, rents are measured upwards from the no-rent line.

175. Rent Does Not Form a Part of the Price of Agricultural Produce.—From the principles we have already established, we are able to deduce a conclusion which may, at first, be startling to the reader, viz., that rent forms no part of the price of agricultural produce. This surely is a "hard saying;" but it can be demonstrated as strictly as any theorem in geometry. We know that rent forms no part of the price of agricultural produce because that price is determined by the cost of raising it upon lands which pay no rent. How, then, can rent be an element in that price? If the price of wheat is six shillings, this is because, in order to raise the required amount of wheat, cultivation has to be carried down to the six-shilling land. In a word, *the price of produce is not high because rent is paid; but rent is paid because the price of produce is high.* If there were enough of the two-shilling land to raise all the wheat required, and more, the price of wheat would then be two shillings, and no wheat-land would pay any rent.

176. Rent Is Not Obtained by Deduction from Wages.—We are now to announce another proposition, which may prove not less startling than the last. It is that rent is not obtained by deduction from wages. If wages are low, this is not because rents are paid for the better lands, but because the cultivators of the poorer lands can pay no more wages with any hope of getting them back in the price of their produce.

Only a certain amount of labor could be profitably employed on the two-shilling land. This would leave a large amount of labor unemployed. Even the added cultivation of the three-shilling land would not take up all the labor "in the market." It will, perhaps, not be until the four-shilling, the five-shilling, and the six-shilling land have all been brought under cultivation, that the entire amount of labor will find employment. Now, the last tract of land being as poor as it is, and the price of wheat being only six shillings, the cultivator of that tract can only pay a certain rate of wages. Were he to undertake to pay more, he could not get it back in the price of his produce ; and would, therefore, soon be obliged to suspend production.

The rate of wages being thus fixed by the capabilities of the six-shilling land, this rate will be paid for labor on all the higher grades of land. There will be no economic force to compel the cultivators of the better lands to pay higher wages; nor would it do any good to the laborers, were they to undertake to do so. For, in that case, the laborers would abandon the poorer lands and all rush to get employment on the better lands. Since, however, these lands could only profitably employ a certain amount of labor, this would leave a portion of the laborers unemployed, and a portion of the fields actually required for supplying the community with wheat, uncultivated.

CHAPTER XIX.

RENT, CONTINUED. THE OWNERSHIP OF LAND.

177. The Tenure of Land.—We have now, so far as seems practicable in an elementary treatise, laid down the general principles which govern the rent of land. We have seen where rent originates, and what is its measure, or limit. We have seen that, by the operation of purely economic forces, all the excess of price over cost must go to the owner of the land.

But, it may be asked, *who is this owner of the land?* and why should he be in a position to demand and obtain this large share of the annual produce of industry? Why should not some one else have the whole or a part of the wealth thus appropriated? These are questions which it is perfectly fair to ask; which many people, in many countries, are now asking with great earnestness.

178. How about the Consumer of Agricultural Produce? —In the first place, as a step towards answering these questions, let us ask what other person or persons could reasonably make claim to that portion of the produce which the land-owner receives, as rent? Is it the consumer of agricultural produce? Does he suffer any wrong by the present system? Nay, would it even be possible to confer any benefit upon him by a change of system?

Of course, the consumer desires to obtain his produce at the lowest price possible. Of course, it would be better for him if the price were lower than it is. But we have seen that the price of produce is not higher by reason of rent being paid. The price of wheat is what it is because the cost of producing wheat on the poorest lands under cultivation is what it is. Somebody has got to eat the wheat grown on the six-shilling land; and consequently has got to pay six shillings for it. Who is the man that has the right, in preference to all others, to eat the wheat grown on the two-shilling land and pay only two shillings for it? What gives him that right? How is he any better than the men who are to eat the wheat grown on the poorer lands and are to pay the cost of raising it?

No! Not the faintest claim can be set up, on behalf of the consumers of agricultural produce, that they should receive any part of that which now goes to the landlord, as rent. It is perfectly right and just that what one man pays in the market for wheat, every other man should pay.

179. How about the Agricultural Laborer?—Is it the laborer, who can put forward a claim to this share of the produce? I answer, no. The laborer who works upon the six-shilling land, which pays no rent, is just as deserving as the laborer who works upon the two-shilling land, and is entitled to just as high remuneration. To allow the laborers upon the better grades of land to divide among themselves the whole or any part of that which the land-owners receive, as rent, would be the grossest injustice. We have already seen that it would be socially impracticable, since such a scheme would lead to a mad rush of all the laborers to the best lands; to the abandonment of tracts required to supply the community with food; to turmoil, violence and bloodshed, in the struggle for employment upon the highest grade of land, upon which, alone, any laborer would consent to work.

180. How about the Capitalist?—We have, remaining, only one person, or class of persons, whom we can conceive as making a demand for rent, or for any part of it. This is the capitalist. Could he reasonably put forward such a claim? I answer, such a claim would be just as sound on his part as on the part of the laborer, and no more. The capitalist who lends horses and carts and implements and food and clothing, to be used in the cultivation of the two-shilling tract, is entitled to no higher remuneration than the capitalist who lends similar things to be used in the cultivation of the six-shilling tract. Justice, as between capitalist and capitalist, will only be realized when each receives for an equal service an equal return.

181. How about the Community?—I have said that there is no other person, or class of persons, regarding whom we could raise a question in this connection. Is, then, the right of the land-owner, to receive rent, beyond any challenge? I answer, no. While no person and no class of persons, other than the land-owner, can put forward a reasonable claim to rent, or to any part of it, there is, yet, a claim to be considered. It is the claim of THE COMMUNITY, to which the land-owner belongs, to which the laborer belongs, to which the capitalist belongs, and in which they all have rights and interests.

182. The Nationalization of the Land.—The claim that the community, or the State, should receive all the excess of price above cost, has been put forward, at various times, without attracting much public interest. Within the last ten years, however, this claim has again been put forward, and has, this time, been urged with so much enthusiasm and eloquence as to attract public attention very widely and to arouse an intense interest in many minds. The agitation of the subject is not unlikely to proceed even further; and those who are now in school will probably be called upon to express their views and to take their positions, as members of the public body, with reference thereto. I, therefore, proceed to speak of the project to which the term, Nationalization of the Land, is applied.

There can be no question, I think, that if the community chooses to claim rent, it has a clear and a full right to it. Of course, when I speak of rent, in this way, I mean true economic rent. That part of rent, popularly so called, which is due to improvements made in the land (par. 170), is not embraced in the foregoing statement. Moreover, the statement made above assumes that the community, or State, will respect and save all those rights which have been vested in individuals by its own acts and laws. No matter how strong the claim of the State upon rent may be deemed to be, if the State has allowed and encouraged me to purchase with my own earnings a piece of land, in the reasonable expectation and the then legal assurance that I am to receive the rent of that land, the State becomes simply a robber, neither more nor less, if it proceeds to take that land away from me, or to take from me the right to receive its full proper rental, without compensation.* The State has the right, however, at any time to give public notice that thereafter it will claim and collect for itself all future increase in the rental or the selling price of all lands within its jurisdiction.

183. The Equities of Rent.—Subject to the foregoing

---

* It is greatly to be regretted that just that which in the text is denounced, in terms which I have not been careful to measure, is proposed by Mr. Henry George, in his famous work, "Progress and Poverty," and in his subsequent writings and addresses. Mr. George distinctly repudiates the idea of giving compensation to the owners of land which the State may take away from them, notwithstanding that they have acquired their properties under the sanction and encouragement of the State, itself, and even though the State itself may have sold the land and put its price into the treasury. Such a proposition is simply infamous, and does not deserve discussion by any honest person.

qualifications, viz., (1st) that the right of the owner of the land to the full value of his "improvements" be recognized, and (2d) that compensation be given for the full value of the land, at the time the system of land nationalization should go into effect, there could be no objection, on the ground of public justice, to the adoption of such a system. It certainly is true, as claimed by the advocates of this policy, that any increase in the rental value or selling value of land (aside from investments of capital, already spoken of), is due, not to the exertions and sacrifices of the owners of the land, but to the exertions and sacrifices of the community. It is certainly true, as claimed by the advocates of land nationalization, that economic rent tends to increase with the growth of wealth and population; and that, thus, a larger and still larger share of the product of industry tends to pass into the hands of the owners of land, not because they have done more for society, but because society has a greater need of that which they control.

184. The Primitive Tenure of the Land.—It has only been of late years that the careful and painstaking scholars of Germany, aided by two or three eminent historical students in England, have been able at last to uncover enough of the old "metes and bounds" to show how the soil was divided, and how it was cultivated, in most of the countries occupied by tribes and nations of the Aryan race. It thus appears plain that our ancestors did, to a very great extent, deal with the soil just as the advocates of land-nationalization wish us now to do. The territory of a tribe, or smaller band, was held in common; the arable land was periodically divided up among the members of the tribe, for individual cultivation; the undivided pasture and the undivided wood-land were subject to use by all the members of the tribe, either at pleasure, or according to some scale adopted by the tribe, regulating the amount of wood which any member might take out of the forest, or the number of animals which he might turn out to graze upon "the common." While this system of tribal ownership has almost universally disappeared, slight vestiges of it are still found here and there, in Europe, India and America. Many of the communes of Switzerland, for example, still hold their forests after the old fashion; while common rights of pasturage still exist in many communities of Aryan stock.

So far, therefore, as antiquity can furnish an argument, the advantage is with the advocates of land-nationalization.

185. Why was Common Ownership Abandoned?—If such was once a very common, if not the general or universal, land-policy of our ancestors, why was it abandoned? Why has it been replaced everywhere by the system of private ownership, which gives to the individual, instead of the community, the power and the right to exact economic rent?

The answer to this question is not a simple one; and here, again, the advocates of land-nationalization possess a certain advantage, from the historical point of view. It is incontestable, that the gradual passage from the condition of common ownership to that of private ownership, was promoted by chiefs and great lords, with a view to their own personal advantage; and that power joined hands with cunning to despoil the community for individual aggrandizement. Even after the chiefs and great lords had received lands, as their own, subject to public charges and to public duties, they continued at work still further to benefit themselves, until, by their power, as legislators or governors, they succeeded in ridding themselves of those public charges and public duties.

But, while the passage of the land from public to private ownership was thus, in a large degree, wrongful, I believe that candid inquiry will satisfy every historical student that what made it possible for the chiefs and great lords thus to acquire the soil, in their own names, was the fact that cultivation-in-common was exceedingly and increasingly unproductive and unprofitable. I deem it not unfair to say that this unproductiveness, this unprofitableness, of cultivation-in-common is so much in the nature of the case, is so far unavoidable, that the community fares vastly better under the private ownership of land, allowing the land-owning class to take out their rents, than it possibly could under a system of public ownership, where the whole product should go to the community.

186. The Public Advantage of Private Ownership.—The justification of the private ownership of land, if it is to be justified at all, is to be found in the public benefits it confers. Its private benefits, i.e., the interests of the landlord class, form no part of that justification. But, if it can reasonably be proved that the community is distinctly better-off by reason of private ownership, then, no matter how much individuals may selfishly profit thereby, a public benefit is shown, and the system is justified.

Now, this is exactly what the great majority of intelligent, experienced and disinterested men, in all countries, firmly believe. And, moreover, all those who hold this view also believe, without exception and without qualification, that this public benefit is not small but great; is not transient but permanent, and is, even, of increasing importance. They believe, indeed, that public benefit to be, not great merely, but enormous, inexpressible: so much so, that no calamity more dire could befall the community than a return to common ownership.

On the other hand, there is a comparatively small, though increasing, number of learned and able men, scattered through many countries, who hold that the abuses of "landlordism" outweigh its benefits. Admitting the evils which have attended common ownership, in the past, and the difficulties to which it will always necessarily be subject, they yet believe, that, as nations become more and more enlightened, and as political forms and institutions become more and more democratic, common ownership will become an altogether good thing. Especially do they urge that the acquisition, by the State, of that economic rent which now goes entire to the landlord class, will not only relieve the people from the present burden of taxation, but will afford ample means for vast public improvements, in parks and hospitals, picture-galleries and museums, libraries and schools.

The fact that those educated and experienced men who believe in the nationalization of the land are few, in comparison with those who believe that such a policy would be baleful and pernicious, by no means settles the question. Many times in human history has public opinion been on the side of public abuses and antiquated systems. Yet, notwithstanding this, the settled preponderance of intelligent opinion constitutes a powerful presumption in favor of any policy. That presumption may be overcome by argument or by experience; but until this has been done, every prudent man will hold himself strongly bound by it.

187. The Objections to the Common Ownership of Land. —Fully to discuss such a question would require more space than could be given to it in an elementary treatise like the present. The two main objections to the common, or national, ownership of land are as follows.

1st. The amount of political machinery that would be required to administer all lands, under such a system; the great number of office-holders to be appointed for the purpose; and the immense amount of corruption and favoritism which would inevitably be involved. When one considers how much evil results from the comparatively small operations of existing governments, which have to do only with a few of the concerns of the people, he cannot but be shocked and revolted at the thought of governments which should own the soil of every farm within their respective territories, which should own the road-bed of every railway and the ground upon which every man's house, shop or store was built. The periodical leasing and re-leasing of all these properties, the fixing of their respective rentals, the estimation of improvements made by outgoing tenants, would necessarily so increase the work of government, would involve such an army of officials, and would afford such enormous opportunities for corruption and favoritism, as to threaten the very existence of human society.

2d. Perhaps an even stronger objection to the common ownership of land is found in the liability to abuse of the soil, whenever it is cultivated by those who are not directly and deeply interested in preserving its fertility. It is always possible so to abuse the land, as, within a short term of years, nearly or wholly to destroy its value. Many of the once fairest tracts on earth, which formerly supported large populations in abundance, are now little better than sterile deserts, all through man's reckless, or wanton, treatment of nature.

The productiveness of the soil can only be preserved through the greatest care and pains on the part of the cultivating class. In countries, like England, where land is generally leased, owners are obliged to protect themselves against abusive or destructive cultivation, by the most stringent and minute provisions inserted in their leases; and these are not always sufficient to save the soil from injury. In countries, like France, on the other hand, where the land is cultivated mainly by those who own it, in small parcels, the soil improves from age to age on account of the deep, direct and personal interest which every cultivator feels in keeping up the value of his little estate, which was his father's before him and which shall be his children's after him.

Now, were the owner of all lands to be the State, who can believe that the government would be able to protect its landed property, spread over thousands, or hundreds of thousands, of square miles, from the most monstrous abuse: abuse which might, in no long time, permanently impair and even destroy much of that property? A single generation of abusive cultivation might cost a nation far more than the value of all the rents that would be reaped by the landlord class, under the system of private ownership, to the end of time.

It is the force of considerations like the foregoing which causes nearly all men who have wide knowledge of public affairs and who are well read in human history, to accept the system of the private ownership of land, as inexpressibly superior to collective ownership. Fully as they may recognize the injustice of the social arrangements by which economic rent goes to private individuals, and increases, not according to the exertions and sacrifices of those individuals, but according to the needs, the exertions and the sacrifices of the community, they yet see no escape from this result, except in a system which would turn government into an intolerable despotism, and would, at the same time, put in peril the permanent productiveness of the soil.*

---

* The objection to collective ownership, arising from liability to abuse of the soil, does not apply with equal force, if at all, to land upon which houses are erected and cities built. There is, here, little or no danger of permanent injury. Consequently, some economists who strenuously oppose the ownership of agricultural lands, favor the acquisition by the State of all "urban" real estate, i.e., the sites of all towns and cities. The political objection, however, remains in full force in this case, if, indeed, it is not here in greater strength than in the case of agricultural lands.

CHAPTER XX.

PROFITS.

188. The Point we have Reached.—Let us pause to note just where we are, in the theory of the distribution of wealth.

We have seen (par. 55) that four grand productive agents, viz., Land-power, Business Ability, Capital and Labor, are applied to the production of wealth, in its various forms. We have seen (par. 165) that the aggregate body of wealth, thus produced, is, in economic theory, first divided into two great shares.

Of these shares, one is equivalent to the volume of wealth *that would have been produced had all the labor and capital been employed " at the greatest disadvantage"*: that is, had all the labor and capital been applied to lands no better than the poorest actually cultivated for the supply of the market ; and been so applied by employers no more efficient than the least competent employers actually controlling any considerable part of that labor and capital. All the body of wealth thus constituted is, as we saw, to go, entire and without deduction, to capitalists and laborers, though we are not yet prepared to show how that amount is to be divided between capitalists and laborers.

The other great share of the product of industry consists of all THE EXCESS OF PRICE OVER COST. This is to go, entire and without deduction, to landlords and employers. None of it can go to either the laborer or the capitalist, as such. Of this great share of the product of industry, we have already taken into consideration one part, viz., Rent, going to the landlord, as remuneration for the use of the native powers of the soil. Normal price being fixed by the cost of production (capital and labor) upon the poorest soils actually under cultivation for the supply of the market (which lands themselves pay no rent, see par. 173), the owners of all the more productive lands realize a surplus of price over cost. We have seen, in the last chapter, that such a surplus must, in the nature of things, exist; and that it can only go to the owner of the soil, be that an individual or the State.

189. The Origin of Profits.—We now pass to consider the second of the two parts into which that great body of wealth which consists of the excess of price over cost, is divided. To this part we assign the name, Profits. It is the remuneration of Business Ability,* engaged in the production of wealth. What is the origin of profits? Why should any part of the product of industry go to the Employer? To this question every one of my readers will have an answer ready. He will say that the employer must receive some share of the product of industry, in order that he may remain an employer, at all. Whether he is to receive more, or is to receive less, he must, at the least, receive enough to keep him alive and in condition to do his work. But why should he receive any more than that? To this question, again, every one of my readers will have an answer ready. The employer must receive as much as the laborer receives. When I speak of the laborer, in this connection, I do not mean the day-laborer, or the unskilled laborer; but have reference to laborers of the higher grades, viz., superintendents, overseers, foremen, clerks, cashiers, accountants. Unless the employer is to receive, on the aver-

---

* For the definition of this industrial agent, see par. 55.

age, taking one year with another, as much, or about as much,* as laborers of this class, he will naturally prefer to become a laborer himself. In order, therefore, that there may be employers (pars. 54–55), the remuneration of this industrial agent must, at the least, be as great as the remuneration of the laborer : that is, profits must be equal to wages. Here, then, we take our start, in dealing with profits. We have, in wages, the minimum of profits. What we are to inquire about, in the present chapter, is this: how does it come about that employers, all or any of them, receive more than this minimum?

190. The No-Profits Class of Employers.—To the remuneration of the employing class, so far as it does not exceed the minimum spoken of above, we do not apply the term, profits. Profits, not in excess of wages, are not profits at all. Although received by employers, they are still nothing but wages. They are governed by the same law as wages, and should be considered as wages, and nothing else.

Now, what we have first to note is the all-important fact that there is a grade of employers who receive no profits: that is, whose remuneration does, on the whole and in the long-run, not exceed the amount which these persons could individually have expected to receive, as wages, if employed by others. In every large body of employers, there are always some no-profits employers, just as, in the lands cultivated for the supply of any considerable market, there are always some no-rent lands. This is the fact with which we start, in ascertaining the law of profits.

---

* I say, "about as much," because there is a class of men to whom the exercise of authority and the opportunity to exert marked executive ability might be, in some measure, a recompense for undertaking the duty of an employer. The number of such men undoubtedly tends to increase with the progress of civilization and the diffusion of intelligence.

If the prices of goods were so high that all employers made profits (that is, something in excess of wages), then it would inevitably happen, either that more persons would go into business and become employers, in order to secure these profits, or, else, that the existing employers would try to increase their business, so as to get more of these profits. By the operation of this simple force it comes about that competition among employers, for the profits of employment, constantly tends to bring prices down to the point where the least efficient employers make no profits.

191. The More Efficient Employers.—Starting, thus, with a class of employers whom we call the no-profits employers, we have to note the indisputable fact that above these rise, rank on rank, employers of higher and still higher degrees of efficiency in the employment of labor and the conduct of business. These are men who have, by the force of education or of experience, exceptional abilities or adaptations for commercial or industrial success. They are not always better men or better citizens than their less successful brethren; but, from whatever source they derive it, they possess peculiar power in the production of wealth. Using the same amounts of labor and of capital, they are able to produce more of wealth thereby.

I say, more of wealth: that is, a larger amount of value. This may mean more goods of the same kind; or it may mean the same amount of goods, but of a better kind. Sometimes the peculiar industrial efficiency of an employer may be exhibited in the prevention of waste in his materials, sometimes in the saving of wear-and-tear to machinery and injury to tools. Sometimes it may take the form of ability to get much more out of his body of workmen, within the usual number of hours. We have shown, in paragraph 53, that this does not necessarily mean a greater physical and nervous strain upon the laborers.

Sometimes the peculiar industrial efficiency of an employer may result in the production of a body of goods no greater, but of a finer finish, or of more durable quality, or of a more attractive shape, commanding, thus, a higher price in the market. Sometimes the advantage which one employer possesses over another, consists in a wider knowledge of men and a deeper insight into character, enabling him to avoid grave mistakes in entrusting his interests to incapable and unfaithful persons, or in selling his goods to irresponsible or dishonest parties. Sometimes the higher efficiency of employers may come from a rare commercial instinct, which enables them to tell, almost without knowing why, that prices are going to rise or to fall.

It is not necessary to extend the description of the various ways in which certain employers come to produce more of wealth than others are able to do, with the same amount of labor and capital. Those ways are not few, but many, very many. The resulting differences are not small, but great, very great.

192. The Law of Profits.—If we have correctly discerned and stated the facts of industrial society, so far as they bear on this subject, we are now in a position to lay down the law of profits.

PROFITS ARISE OUT OF THE DIFFERENCES IN PRODUCTIVE EFFICIENCY AMONG THE EMPLOYERS ACTUALLY ENGAGED IN BUSINESS, FOR THE SUPPLY OF ANY MARKET. PROFITS CONSIST OF THE ENTIRE EXCESS OF PRICE OVER COST OF PRODUCTION, AFTER RENT HAS BEEN PAID.

We shall illustrate this principle sufficiently for the present purpose, if we suppose that the required supply of goods, of a certain kind, at the existing price, would yield fifty millions of dollars; and that this aggregate has been produced, in equal amounts, by fifty employers. Now, in such a case, it is certain that some of these employers will barely be able to make themselves good for their outlay in wages, in materials, in machinery and in other ways. They will have little or nothing left to themselves, after all the care and the pains they have taken; after all the risks they have run; after all the anxieties they have endured. In the same body of employers, there will be others who have made ten thousand dollars, in producing the same amount of goods; others who have made twenty thousand dollars; others, still, who have forty, sixty, or eighty thousand dollars left in their hands, after paying all bills which are properly chargeable to that production, including deterioration of plant, wear-and-tear of machinery, interest on capital, bad debts, etc.

193. The Effects of Accident and Fraud.—It is true that, in some cases, and more or less in most cases, the force of fraud, or the effect of accidents, like fires and floods, will have had something to do with the failure of an employer to realize a larger profit, or to realize any profit at all, on his month's or his year's business. But this fact does not impair the truth or the importance of what has been stated. Were no frauds perpetrated, did no accidents take place, there would still be employers who would realize no profits out of any given amount of business; while other employers were making profits; others, large profits; others, still, monstrous profits, under the same conditions, and with the use of the same amounts of labor and capital.

Generally speaking, too, the men who make large profits, in spite of accidents and frauds, are the men who would make large profits in the absence of accidents and frauds; while the men who make small profits, or none, in the actual case, are the men who would make small profits, or none, in the hypothetical case. The ability to guard against fraud, the ability to foresee impending evil, to break its force and to repair its effects, are among the qualifications for the successful conduct of business.

194. The Analogy Between Rent and Profits.—It will be seen that there is a very close analogy between rent and profits. In dealing with rent, we begin with the no-rent lands (par. 173), and measure rent upwards from that line. In dealing with profits, we begin with the no-profits employers, and measure profits upwards from that line. In each case, we find that differences in productive efficiency (labor and capital being assumed equal) create a surplus, which consists of the excess of price over cost, price being fixed by the cost of "production at the greatest disadvantage."

That analogy we may carry on to the end. Rent, we saw, (par. 175) does not enter into the price of produce. In the same way, we see that profits do not enter into the price of produce, or of products, since the price of these is determined by the cost of their production at the hands of employers *who themselves receive no profits.* Prices must be high enough to enable this class of employers to keep up their business; otherwise, the required supply would fall short in the market. Prices being fixed so high, by this cause, those employers who are able to produce at a less cost realize a surplus. *Prices, then, are not high because profits are made; but profits are made because prices are high.*

No more is it true that profits are obtained by deduction from wages. The employers who make profits pay as high wages* as the employers who make no profits. The reason why wages are no higher than they are, is because

---

* In a certain sense, they pay somewhat higher wages, since the greater continuity of employment and certainty of payment, which belong to the laborers who work for the more successful employers, are really as good as a small addition to their wages.

the least competent employers (whose demand is essential to taking up the whole supply of labor in the market), cannot pay any higher wages and get them back in the price of their products. The existence of profits, then, constitutes no wrong to the laborer. They represent, from first to last, the creation of an additional amount of wealth, by the skill, energy and prudence of the successful employer. Wages would be no greater, were profits to be prohibited.

195. Lowering the Margin of Production.—The last point we shall note, in the analogy between rent and profits, is that, in both cases, it is for the interest of the laboring class that the "margin of production" should not be lowered. In treating of rent, we showed (par. 168) that, if cultivation be driven down to inferior soils, not only a larger actual amount, but a larger share, of the produce necessarily goes to the land-owning class, as rent. Likewise in the case of profits, it is for the interest of the laborers, as well as of the entire community, that employers of a lower grade of industrial efficiency should not be brought into the conduct of business. If the margin of production is to be lowered, in this respect, not only a larger actual amount, but a larger share, of the product will necessarily go to the employing class, as profits. Prices are determined by the productive capability of the lowest class of employers who are actually producing for the supply of the market; and all excess of those prices, over the cost of production in the hands of the more capable men of business, goes to these latter, individually, as profits.

We see, by this, how mistaken are the views and feelings commonly entertained by laborers regarding profits. Generally speaking, the laboring class have not a little jealousy and envy toward the large profits of successful employers. But, if we have correctly discerned and stated the origin of profits, the only real injury done to the laboring class is through the comparative incompetence of those employers who realize no profits from the conduct of business. When we come to speak of the effects of imperfect competition (Chap. XXIV), we shall have occasion to refer to certain causes which tend to bring incompetent men into the conduct of business, and to keep them there, at the expense of the community, in general, and of the laboring class in particular.

196. To Whom do Profits Belong?—In treating of rent, it was shown (par. 177 to 181) that, under the private ownership of land, rents must necessarily go, entire, to the owners of land, as such; and that no economic force could be invoked which would have the tendency to carry rents, or any part of them, to any other class in the community. But it was also shown that the community, the State, might, if this were thought wise, lay claim to rents, on grounds of political equity.

Could any such claim be made to profits, on behalf of the community, the State? In such a case, the community, the State, would, in effect, say to the men of superior ability: "You shall continue to carry on business, to employ labor and capital, to direct the production of wealth; but the profits you may realize belong to the State and must be paid into the public treasury. We will, perhaps, allow you some small part thereof, as an encouragement to you to do your best; but we cannot admit that you have a right to the wealth which you create by your skill, energy and prudence, over and above the wealth which other employers, of less ability, can produce with the same amount of labor and capital." We can, indeed, conceive an Asiatic government making this demand; but such a view would be so foreign and so hostile to the ideas and sentiments of our people, that it need not be discussed here.

It may, however, be said that, should any government

undertake thus to confiscate profits, it would surely find that, while it could easily prevent individuals from realizing profits, it would not bring any wealth thereby into the public treasury. The act of the man who killed the goose that laid the golden eggs, would be wisdom itself, in comparison with the folly of such a course. The fact that the employer is to realize, for his own benefit, all that is to be saved, and all that is to be gained, by his prudence, energy and skill, is of the very essence of that prudence, energy and skill. Were the reward of his exertions to be taken from him, the mainspring of those exertions would be broken.

197. The Socialist View of the Employer.—I have spoken in this chapter, and frequently throughout this book, of the part which the employer performs, in the production of wealth, as I understand it. I do not believe that I have one whit exaggerated the importance of that industrial function. Those writers, however, called Socialists, who desire to have the State do everything in the production of wealth, and who would abolish at once the private ownership of land and private enterprise in production, are naturally disposed to take a low view of the importance of the employer's work. This is, partly, because a higher view of that work would go against their own scheme; partly, because many of these writers entertain a deep prejudice and even an intense hostility towards the body of employers, whom they regard as engaged in robbing the laboring class. Few of these writers have had either the kind of education or the opportunities for observation which would qualify them to form valuable opinions on such a question.

CHAPTER XXI.

PROFITS, CONTINUED: CO-OPERATION.

198. What is Industrial Co-operation?—The contemplation of large profits realized by the employers has given rise to many movements, in this and in other countries, which have had for their object to secure to the laborers, themselves, the gains which otherwise the employer would reap. These movements may all be embraced under the general term, Co-operation. We shall devote the present chapter to considering the objects of industrial co-operation; the advantages which it would secure, if successful; the liabilities to loss and failure which co-operation encounters; the conditions under which co-operation would have the largest chances of success.

The main purpose which a body of laborers have in view in initiating co-operation is to get rid of the employer, by doing his work themselves, and thus reaping his gains. Seeing that a large amount of wealth is realized by the employing class, they, not unnaturally, say, why should we not employ ourselves? Why should we not get together freely, instead of being brought together and hired by some one else? Why should we not decide, for ourselves, in what line we shall work; buy our own materials; apply to these our own labor; sell the goods ourselves; and put into our own pockets the entire value of the product?

I have said that in co-operation the object is to get rid of the employer. Unfortunately the more usual, indeed, the general, way of putting it is that the object of co-operation is to get rid of the capitalist. This form of statement is not only erroneous; it is grossly misleading.

Co-operation is not going to get rid of the capitalist. Co-operation has no tendency to get rid of the capitalist. A body of co-operative laborers must have as much capital to use as a body of laborers working under an employer. If they have not, their failure will be assured from the start. They must have just as many and just as good tools; just as much and just as good material; just as ample and commodious rooms or buildings; just as much water-power or steam-power, for a given product. The essence of co-operation, I repeat, is that the laborers are to employ themselves. Doing, thus, the employer's work, they hope to reap his gains.

199. The Advantages Sought in Co-operation.—We have already indicated the first of the advantages sought for in co-operation, viz., to secure for the laboring class that large amount of wealth which goes annually, in profits, to employers. But there is a second advantage which the more thoughtful members of the laboring class see would result from the success of co-operation, viz., it would secure to the laborer the opportunity to produce wealth independently of the will of an employer. Under the present system, it remains with the employer to decide, not only what shall be produced, and how and when it shall be produced, and in what amounts, but, also, whether any production, at all, shall take place. The employer's motive in production is the profit he expects to realize for himself. Generally speaking, he will only produce as he sees an opportunity to make a profit.

It is true that the employer may carry on production for a while, out of sympathy for his workmen, even though the state of the market is so unfavorable that he does not anticipate making much or any profit for himself. It is true that he may even, at times, consent to carry on production at a slight loss, rather than let his customers go to others, or close his works. But these considerations cannot be relied upon to any great extent or for any long period; nor can they be relied upon at all, as against the apprehension of considerable loss. In a state of the market which causes the employer to doubt, whether, after paying out large sums for materials and labor, he will get his money back in the price of the products, the most natural course for him to adopt is to curtail production, to the extent of one-third or of one-half.

The laborers who are thus allowed to work only on two-thirds or half time, cannot rightly complain that the employer should protect his own interests. But, if they should choose, through co-operation, to take the risks and the responsibilities upon themselves, it would be in their power to keep up production continuously. No matter what the state of the market, they could remain at work, producing their goods and selling them for what they were worth, or holding them over until a better time. This might be much better for them than not working at all. On the other hand, it might be much worse for them. Whether it should be better or be worse would somewhat depend upon the nature of the business;* more, upon the judgment and good sense displayed by the co-operators. In any case, it would no longer be the interest of the one employer, but the interest of the many workmen, which should decide whether production were to proceed or not.

200. Co-operation, in the View of the General Economic Interest.—I have mentioned the two chief benefits

---

* For example, in a business where the value of the materials used was small, and the value of the product depended mainly on the amount and quality of the labor expended, such a plan would work much better than in a business where there was a large outlay.

which the laboring class look to secure for themselves by means of co-operation. In addition to these, the political economist sees in such a system three possible sources of advantage.

1st. Co-operation would, by the very terms of the case, do away with strikes. There would no longer be any one to strike against. The employer having disappeared, the workmen having become self-employed, those destructive contests, in which prejudice, passion and greed take so large a part, would disappear, as a matter of course.

2d. The workman would be incited to greater industry and to greater carefulness in dealing with materials, tools and machinery. It was stated, in paragraph 46, that whenever men take the position of hired laborers, working for wages, some part of that hopefulness and cheerfulness in labor, which are the most fruitful source of strenuous exertions, is, by the nature of the case, lost. A body of co-operative workmen, on the other hand, would have the advantage of all those inspirations and incitements which we sought to describe in paragraphs 43, 44 and 45.

3d. Frugality would be greatly encouraged. It cannot be doubted that a body of laborers, having an opportunity to invest their savings, at once and on the spot, in their own business, and, indeed, feeling strongly the need of additional capital to carry-on that business, would come under more powerful inducements to frugality than a body of wage-laborers.

201. Co-operation from a Still Higher Point of View.— In addition to the foregoing advantages which might result from co-operation, as viewed by the political economist, the moralist and the statesman can discern in this system the possibilities of still greater benefits. Co-operation, if it could be introduced and maintained, would greatly tend to educate and elevate the working classes, in all the elements of character and citizenship. It would give them a more palpable stake in the community; and thus promote peace and social order. It would train them to the discussion and decision of important questions; and thus at once increase their general intelligence and teach them moderation, prudence and respect for the opinions of others. It would strengthen the bonds of society, and would do away with many of those feelings of envy, jealousy and distrust which keep apart the members of a community.

202. The Difficulties of Co-operation.—The advantages of co-operation being so many and so great, it will naturally be asked why this scheme, proposed so long ago, sanctioned by the highest economic authority, appealing directly to the self-interest of the laboring classes, advertised extensively in discussions relating to labor and wages, has not been immediately successful, upon a large scale? How is it, that, on the contrary, of the great number of enterprises, of this character, which have been started in England, France, the United States* and other countries, only a few have achieved a decided or even a moderate success; while more have failed or been abandoned?

I answer: the difficulties of co-operation are directly as its advantages. The power wielded and profits enjoyed by employers make the working classes desire, naturally enough, to bring about a different industrial order. Yet, when a body of laborers set up for themselves, the result very soon shows that the reason why the employer wields such arbitrary power and enjoys such large revenues, is that he performs a part in modern industrial society (pars. 54 and 55) which is of supreme importance: in which any-

---

* The publications of the American Economic Association contain the most recent and reliable accounts of the many and various co-operative enterprises which have been undertaken in the United States.

thing less than the highest abilities of administration and organization involves comparative, if not absolute, failure.

203. Is Co-operation Practicable, in a Near Future?— The time may come, when a body of laborers, joined together for the purposes of co-operative production, will give as intelligent a direction, as close a supervision, as rigid a discipline, as energetic an impulse, to the work in which they are engaged, as the present successful man of business gives to the enterprises on which his fortunes and his reputation are staked. This may come about, in time; but, for one, though believing thoroughly, so far as politics are concerned, in a "government of the people, by the people, for the people,"† I see nothing which indicates that, within the near future, industry is to become less despotic than it now is. The power of the Master, " the captain of industry," has steadily grown throughout the present century, with the increasing complexity of commercial relations, with the greater concentration of capital, with continual improvements of apparatus and machinery, with the multiplication of styles and patterns, with the localization and specialization of manufactures.

No one would rejoice more heartily than the writer to see the working classes rise to the height of the occasion, and vindicate their right to rule in industry by showing their power to do it. But meanwhile it should be understood that nothing costs the working classes so much as the bad or weak or commonplace conduct of business. Industry must be energetically, economically and wisely managed, no matter who is to do it. Co-operation will only be successful as it results in the production of equally good articles, at equally low prices, with those produced in establishments controlled by individual employers.

---

† President Lincoln.

204. A Possible Field for Industrial Co-operation.—I have spoken thus strongly of the difficulties of co-operation, because I believe that only harm can come to the working classes from slurring-over those difficulties, as has, with the best intentions, been done by many writers. Not a few economists have spoken on this subject as if co-operation were the easiest thing in the world to bring about, the only difficulty being to get the working classes interested in it. It ought, on the contrary, to be clearly understood that the difficulties of the scheme are great in proportion to its advantages; that co-operation can only succeed when undertaken by intelligent and high-minded men, who will carefully study their business; who will put all envyings and jealousies and mean suspicions under their feet; who are prepared to do, to endure and to forbear much, for the good they seek; who have magnanimity enough to give a cordial support to the managers they shall choose, to trust them thoroughly, and to pay them handsomely.

In speaking thus, I have reference to industry as a whole, and especially to its larger branches, which supply general markets, and which are subject to competition at once searching and far-reaching. There are, however, portions of the field of industry where the difficulties are less formidable.

Where (1) a branch of industry is of such a nature that it can best be carried on by a small group of workmen, rather than in large establishments; where (2) the workmen so engaged are substantially on a level, as regards strength and skill; where (3) the initial expenditure for tools and the running expenditures for materials are small; and, especially, where (4) the goods are to be produced wholly or mainly for the local market, the difficulties of the co-operative system sink to a minimum, while its advantages rise to a maximum. It is, therefore, in such branches that the experiment of productive co-operation should first be tried. Success can be achieved here, if anywhere. Should success be here achieved, advantage may be taken of the experience thus accumulated and of the training thus acquired, to undertake larger and still larger enterprises.

205. Profit-sharing.—The obstacles which beset industrial co-operation are not encountered by the scheme of Profit-sharing, which has been highly recommended by many writers and which has been undertaken of late years, not, indeed, on a large scale, but in numerous instances. The advantages of this scheme, illustrated by many successful examples, have recently been stated in an excellent book by Mr. N. P. Gilman. The matter is one of economic and administrative detail, too minute to be treated fully in an elementary work of this character.

The object sought is to interest workmen in increasing production and reducing waste and breakage, by paying to them a portion of the employer's profits. It is, also, held that this system would have the effect to promote good feeling between the laborer and the employer, and to diminish the resort to strikes and labor contests.

The difficulties of profit-sharing are found (1) in the smallness of the amount which can thus be distributed among the workmen,* without unduly diminishing the employer's interest in production; (2) in the suspicions likely to arise regarding the employer's good faith, in declaring

---

* Suppose, for example, that an employer pays in wages $200,000 a year, and realizes, on his production, a profit of $15,000. Were he to distribute one-third of his profits, this would amount to but $2\frac{1}{4}$ per cent on his "pay-roll." A workman who earned $500 a year, would receive $12.50 bonus. Would he do or forbear much, for such a consideration? (See par. 209.)

the amount thus subject to distribution, unless the workmen, or a committee of them, are to be allowed such access to the books and accounts as few business men would willingly concede; (3) in the perplexing question, what should be done in the, not infrequent, cases where the employer realizes a loss.

The last of these difficulties is, perhaps, the greatest. The employer is, not unnaturally, disposed to hold that, if the workmen share his gains in good years, they should also share his losses in bad years.

206. Consumptive Co-operation.—I have, thus far, for simplicity of treatment, directed my remarks toward co-operative enterprises which undertake to produce goods for the market. To these we may, perhaps, apply the term, Productive Co-operation. There is, however, a very large department of business to which the co-operative principle can be applied with almost indefinitely less difficulty and risk. This department of business relates to supplying consumers, at retail, with the necessaries, comforts and luxuries of life. This kind of co-operation may properly be called Consumptive Co-operation.

The distinction between productive and consumptive co-operation may be expressed as follows. In productive co-operation the laborer seeks to make for himself an income. In consumptive co-operation, the laborer seeks to expend or to consume that income to the best advantage: to make each dollar of his earnings go as far as possible in providing subsistence for himself and family. The two things do not necessarily go together. A man might (1) earn his income by working for an employer, and expend that income through a co-operative society; or (2) he might earn his income in a co-operative factory, yet expend it in purchases from grocers, butchers, and shoe-dealers, here or there, according to his fancy or convenience; or (3) he might both earn his income as a member of one (productive) co-operative society and expend it as a member of another (consumptive) co-operative society.

207. The Advantages of Consumptive Co-operation.— Among the advantages of consumptive co-operation may be mentioned the following.

1st. The certainty of business. The managers know that all the members will purchase their supplies at that store or shop. It is, therefore, possible to estimate closely the amount of trade to be done, and the quantities of the several kinds of goods which will be required.

2d. The saving of advertising-expenses. It follows from the above that the managers of a co-operative store or shop are relieved from all expenditures for the purpose of attracting trade. They not only do not need to advertise in the newspapers or on the "dead walls;" they are not obliged to spend money for plate-glass windows or for rosewood counters or for electric lights. They can have their place of business on a back street, in plain quarters, at a low rent; yet their customers will come to them, all the same.

3d. Avoidance of book-keeping and losses by bad debts. In Europe, nearly all co-operative stores do business purely on the cash principle. No one is allowed to take goods out of the shop without paying for them, at the time. All the expense of recording and "posting" small purchases, and of sending-out and collecting small bills, is thus avoided. An even greater advantage is found in escaping losses by bad debts. In ordinary retail trade, under the credit system, so common in the United States, those losses are simply enormous.

208. Practical Experience with Consumptive Co-operation.—This species of co-operation has had no inconsiderable degree of success in England, in the way of shops for the sale of flour, meats, groceries, dry-goods and other articles of domestic consumption. At these shops, annual subscribers or members of the association buy goods, generally at the ruling prices of retail trade, always for cash. At the end of the year or the season, the profits, after deducting the expenses of supervision and management, are divided among the members, either equally or in proportion to their purchases. The latter is the usual rule. At the time of each purchase, a member receives a check, showing the amount paid. At the end of the year or season, he brings in his checks; and, upon the aggregate amount, he receives a dividend, corresponding to the profit upon the entire business done. In comparison with ordinary retail trading, under the credit system, a co-operator ought, with good management, to save twenty per cent of his income. Moreover, he ought, in this way, to secure a better quality of goods, as no one has any interest in cheating him.

209. American Experience.—Here, on the other hand, the scheme of consumptive co-operation has not been very widely applied; and, in most cases, has either failed or been abandoned. The causes of this small success have been the following:

1st. The indifference of our people, even of the poorest classes, towards small savings. The average American will work harder than the man of any other nation to make an income; but, in expending incomes, we are the most careless and wasteful people in the world. This is equally true whether we are buying domestic goods at the store or using them in the household.

2d. The national passion for taking credit. An American feels himself insulted if he is informed that he cannot carry goods out of a shop without paying for them. No matter how easy it would be to bring the money with him, or how thoroughly he understands the disadvantages of the credit system, he yet resents any application of the cash principle in his own case.

3d. The popular unwillingness to take pains, steadily and persistently, to secure a proper administration of trusts. The same defects of character which have allowed our municipal affairs to fall so largely into the hands of incompetent or unworthy persons, have wrecked many of the most promising co-operative enterprises undertaken in this country. Such an enterprise starts off with a great deal of zeal on the part of the members ; the best men are put in charge ; accounts are carefully supervised ; the buying and selling are well looked after. In the course of time, the interest wanes ; poorer men get in power : the administration becomes lax. The usual result is either that, after a few years or months, the store or shop is shut up ; or else, the last manager makes an offer for the goods and fixtures, and sets up business for himself. Such has been the history of thousands of "union," "granger" or "sovereigns of industry" stores, in the United States.

There is no essential difficulty regarding consumptive co-operation. Like most good things, however, it is only to be had with labor and pains. Whenever any considerable number of people care enough about the advantages of this system to give it thought, effort and a reasonable portion of time, they can, in this way, secure for themselves an important economic advantage.

CHAPTER XXII.

INTEREST.

210. The Point we have Reached.—Let us again stop to note the point we have reached, in the distribution of wealth. We have now disposed of all that body of wealth which constitutes the excess of price over the cost of production. We have seen (Chapter XVIII) that the differences in productiveness existing among the several grades of soil, actually contributing to the supply of the market, give rise to a surplus, in the case of the crops raised upon all the better grades of land, which surplus goes, under the name of rent, to the owners of the soil. Secondly, we have seen (Chapter XX) that the differences in productive power existing among the several grades of employers, actually engaged in conducting the business of the community, give rise to a surplus, in the case of all goods produced by the more efficient employers, which surplus goes, under the name of profits, to those employers. The wealth, whose distribution we are now to consider, is that which remains after the Surplus, arising from the two causes just mentioned, has been disposed of.

The body of wealth thus to be distributed is, as we have previously stated (par. 165), equivalent to that which *would have been produced*, had all the labor and capital engaged in production been applied to soils of the lowest grade actually cultivated (or to the produce of such soils); and been so applied under the direction and control of employers of the lowest grade of industrial efficiency. The body of wealth, thus made up, is to be distributed among two classes of industrial agents, viz., capitalists and laborers. To no part of this has either the landlord or the employer any economic claim. Both these parties received all they were entitled to, when they carried away the surplus which represents the excess of price over cost. All that enters into the cost of production consists of the exertions and sacrifices of capitalists and laborers; and these two classes are entitled to divide among themselves, in one proportion or another, all that part of price which represents the cost of production.

211. Capital.—In Chapter VIII, we sought to describe the origin and the industrial office of capital. It was there shown that capital arises wholly out of savings. In this fact is found an abundant justification for the claim of the individual to the full use and enjoyment of his capital. If a man's wealth is his to spend, it is equally his to save. If there be any difference between the right of a man to the wealth he is to spend and the right of another man to the wealth he is to save, that difference is in the favor of the latter, since the saving and accumulation of capital is, by general admission, greatly for the advantage of the community, affording the means for carrying-on and enlarging production.

212. Interest.—The economist applies the term, interest, to that part of the product of industry which constitutes the proper economic return to the capital employed in production. That term is equally used, whether the owner of capital himself employs it in production, or loans it to another, to be by him employed. In the latter case, there is an actual payment, by the debtor to the creditor, of a certain amount, under the name of interest, as the consideration for the loan. In the former case, the amount which the economist considers as interest is not distinctly separated and paid over under that name. But it is there, all the same; and should always be so distinguished in economic reasoning.

213. The Right to Interest.—The right to interest is found in the right to capital. We have said that if a man has a right to wealth in order to spend it, he has equally a right to wealth in order to save it. Likewise, if a man has a right to wealth which he has, by self-denial and sacrifice, saved, he has the right either to use it, himself, in further production, or to receive the proper fruits of it from another, who may wish to use it in production. Strangely enough, this right was for many centuries denied among Christian nations. The grounds for this denial will be given in the next paragraph.

214. Objections to Usury.—Until within two or three centuries, "usury," or the taking of interest upon loans, was forbidden in many countries, of which we may take England as an example. One reason for this was doubtless found in the prohibition, in the Old Testament, of the taking of usury by one Hebrew from another. But this prohibition of usury among the members of "the peculiar people" was clearly one of the means resorted to for keeping them apart from their idolatrous neighbors; and was in no sense intended as a moral precept of universal application.

Another, and perhaps more influential, reason for the prohibition of usury was found in a mistaken notion regarding the nature of the transaction involved. This mistaken notion was embodied in a dictum of Aristotle, the great Greek philosopher, that, inasmuch as *money does not produce money*, nothing ought to be exacted for the use of money.*

---

* The honor of having first exposed the fallacy lying in Aristotle's dictum is attributed to John Calvin.

The error here lies in the assumption that interest is paid for the use of money; whereas, in fact, interest is paid for the use, not of money, but of capital. Now, though money itself does not produce "after its kind," most of the things which a man can buy with money do produce after their kind. If a man borrows money and with it buys a hundred sheep, those hundred sheep may, in a few years, become five hundred. If a man borrows money and with it buys grain, that grain will, if duly sown and cultivated, bring forth "some thirty, some sixty, and some an hundred fold." If a man borrows money and with it buys merchandise, he may, by shrewd selling, make twenty or thirty per cent upon his stock. So, we see, that, if, in the case of every loan, money were actually borrowed, all the things which should be judiciously bought with that money might be made to produce "after their kind."

In the vast majority of cases, however, where interest is paid, no money, at all, is used in the original transaction. A man buys a house, and promises to pay the price, at some future time, "with interest," meanwhile. Interest upon what? Interest upon money? He has had no money. The interest promised is upon capital, invested in the house. A merchant or a manufacturer buys a stock of goods, and gives his note promising to pay the price, "with interest." Not interest upon money, for money was not used in the transaction; but interest upon capital, in the form of merchandise or materials, which have been entrusted to him and out of which he expects to make a profit, which he is to share with the owner of the capital.

In spite of all the objections of the schoolmen and the churchmen, the philosophers and the common people, the taking of interest was, about the middle of the sixteenth century, made lawful in England, although public opinion and the views of the clergy were still deeply hostile to it. But, while the law allowed interest to be paid, it undertook to fix a rate above which interest should not go; and similar enactments have been made in nearly all countries, and still remain the rule to the present time. Of the expediency of such restrictions upon the rate of interest we shall speak in a subsequent paragraph.

215. How Much Shall the Capitalist Receive?—We have seen that there is an abundant justification of interest in the fact that production is increased by the use of capital. How much of this increase shall go to the owner of the capital? Shall he receive the whole amount by which production is so increased? I answer: (1) This will not be so as a matter of course; (2) that, in fact, the amount going to the owner of capital, as interest, is only a part of that increase; (3) that, in general, the amount received as interest is but a small part of the amount by which wealth is enhanced through the use of additional capital.

What, then, determines the amount which shall be paid as interest? Properly to answer this question, we must again ask, what is interest? Interest is *the price* paid for the use of capital. What determines price, in any and in all cases? There can be but one answer to this question. Price (par. 95) is always, only and wholly controlled by demand and supply. The price paid for the use of money, interest, is, therefore, entirely a matter of the supply of, and the demand for, capital. Now, the supply of any article being determined, price must fall and continue to fall *until the demand has been found which will take up the last portion of that supply*. This is what happens in regard to the price paid for the use of capital, that is, interest.

216. The Process Illustrated.—Let us illustrate this by reference to a community which has been some time established in its present seats, and in which large amounts of capital have already been applied to production. Farms have been opened and cultivated; but there is still much good land which might be cleared of timber, and there is a large area of swamps, rich with the vegetable mould of centuries, which might, by the application of labor and capital, be drained. Mines have been opened and worked; but there are still richer mineral deposits, deeper down in the crust of the earth, or higher up among the mountains, which there has not yet been capital enough to reach. Wood and timber have been cut from the neighboring forests; but there are tracts of better timber which could only profitably be brought to market through the construction of a tramway or railway. Vegetable and animal fibres have been spun and woven for clothing; but it has been by the spinning-wheel and the hand-loom, there not having been capital enough to build dams upon the rivers, to put up mills and to fill them with machinery.

217. The Last Portion of the Supply.—Now, suppose that capital, to the value of ten millions of dollars, were to be made available for the use of the community, constituting the present supply of capital for loan. Some of this capital would be so much needed, would have the capability of so greatly increasing production, that, rather than not have it, the borrowers could afford to pay 18% per annum. If the amount which was needed in this degree was ten millions, then 18% would be the rate of interest. But if only three millions were needed in this degree, 18% would not be the rate of interest, for such a demand would not take up the whole supply. There might be other enterprises, agricultural, commercial, manufacturing, which could put additional capital to so good a use that, rather than not have it, the persons concerned would pay 12%. If, however, only two millions more were needed in this degree, neither 18% nor 12% would be the rate of interest, but something less. We might suppose that there were other enterprises which could afford to pay 10%, and others, still, which could afford to pay 8%: but neither 10% nor 8% would be the rate of interest unless the whole supply was taken up by these successive demands. That result might not be reached without applying the last million of dollars to enterprises which could only afford to pay 6%. This being so, 6% would become the rate of interest, *not for that million alone, but for the whole ten millions.* Those who could have afforded to pay 18% for the use of capital, rather than not have had it, will still get the use of it for 6%.

218. The Law of Interest.—The rate of interest is determined by the productiveness of that last (considerable) part of the supply, which is applied to industry "at the greatest disadvantage."

The productiveness of this portion determines the price to be paid for the whole. If, in the instance above given, the supply had been so great that the last portion of the demand (necessary to take up the whole supply) had to come from enterprises which could only afford to pay 4%, then 4% would have been the rate of interest on the entire body of capital.

It will be seen that the capitalist does not receive the whole amount by which production is increased through the use of capital. He receives that whole amount only in the case of those industrial enterprises from which proceed the last (considerable) portion of the demand which is necessary to take up the supply. In all other cases, the industrial enterprises concerned derive a benefit from the employment of the additional capital, for which they pay only in part.

219. The Inexpediency of Usury Laws.—We have, I think, gone far enough in our subject to be in a position to see the inexpediency of laws, such as exist in most countries and in most states of the American union, prescribing a rate of interest which it shall not be lawful to exceed. The reason for these laws is found in the feeling that it is very hard that persons who wish to use capital productively should be obliged to pay a high price for its use. And so it is. But what is *the real cause* of this hardship? It is that capital is scarce in that community. The rate of interest will only be high when capital is scarce, in comparison with the demand for its productive use.

But, if the scarcity of capital is the trouble, is this to be cured, or is it to be made worse, by laws which prevent the owners of capital from getting the full price for it? Clearly, the latter. If the scarcity of capital creates a high price for its use, the true way to cure the evil is to let that price be freely paid and received. Then, every one who is in a position to accumulate capital will set himself to do so with double eagerness, in order to get the benefit of that high price. Moreover, men in other communities, where capital is more plentiful, will send their capital thither, to get the higher rate. In this way, the painful need of capital, which is indicated by excessive interest, will be supplied as rapidly as, in the nature of the case, is possible. A high rate of interest, freely allowed, is the best and speediest cure for the evil of a scarcity of capital.

220. Evasions of Usury Laws.—I have spoken, above, of the importance of allowing interest to be freely and openly paid, whatever the rate which existing economic conditions may determine. As a matter of fact, usury laws can always be evaded, in any one of many ways. This may be done by a *bonus*, or premium, upon the loan; by a commission to an agent, who turns over the greater part of it to the lender, as extra interest: by selling goods at a fictitious price, the excess over the real price being in the nature of extra interest; by "dry exchange," as when a note is made payable in another city, and "exchange" (pars. 124–126) is charged for bringing the money home, although in fact the note has not left the city where the loan was made.

The effect of these and many other modes of evading usury laws is simply to make it harder for the man who already finds it hard enough to borrow. They really enhance the price to be paid for the use of the capital which belongs within the community; and they serve as a great obstacle to bringing in capital from communities on the outside. In a high degree, therefore, usury laws defeat their own object.

221. False Interest: Insurance of the Principal.—We have thus far spoken as if, in the same market, there could be but one rate of interest at a given time. Yet we know that, in any market, notes are discounted every day, at varying rates of interest. How is this? I answer, a great deal which goes under the name of interest is not true interest, but is in the nature of Insurance upon the capital, or principal sum lent.

For example, a capitalist has thirty thousand dollars which he intends to loan. Ten thousand of this he "places" upon a "bottom mortgage," at 5%. Here he has for his security improved real-estate, which is worth at least twice as much as the sum lent. This 5%, then, is the true rate of interest, at that time and place. With another ten thousand dollars, the capitalist buys first-class business-paper, bearing 6% interest. The security here is good; yet all merchants are liable to fail, through the bankruptcy of others, through embezzlement by their clerks or cashiers, or through some tremendous fall of prices. Consequently, an insurance of one per-cent is here demanded, over and above the true rate of interest. On the same day, the capitalist buys ten thousand dollars in the bonds of a new railroad company, which promise 7% interest. Here the investor takes the risk that the railroad may not prove a success, either through being badly located or being badly managed; and for this risk he demands an insurance of two per-cent, per annum, upon the principal.

The total amount of this false interest or real insurance, in case of loans, is very great. On the very day when British "three per-cents" are selling at par, Russian "five per-cents" and Turkish "ten per-cents" may be at a discount. The man who lends to the British government runs no risk worth thinking of. The man who lends to the Russian government runs a considerable risk. The man who lends to the Turkish government runs a frightful risk. On the very day when first-class business-paper is discounted at 5%, the notes of doubtful firms are being "shaved" at all the way from ten to twenty-five per-cent.

222. Extra-hazardous Loans.—Speaking generally, the amount promised as extra interest on very hazardous loans and investments, is less than the proper premium of insurance for the risk taken. The losses through such loans and investments, in any considerable term of years, are enormous, far exceeding the value of the extra interest received. The people who make such loans and investments are gambling; and, like most gamblers, they lose.

Persons who, in a community where the proper rate of interest is 5%, buy bonds which promise to pay ten or fifteen, do not commonly act upon anything like a real judgment as to the probabilities that the bonds will be paid when due. They are simply tempted beyond what they are able to bear. The offer of an extravagant rate of interest overcomes their prudence. They buy a very poor thing because they can buy it at a very low price; and almost invariably find they have been cheated, at that. They receive one or two payments of interest, which the managers make in order to hook the last gudgeon in the pool; and, after that, their bonds are mere waste-paper. No prudent person will ever invest any money which he cannot easily afford to lose, in any enterprise which promises a rate of interest greatly above that which is paid by well-established business houses.

223. Differing Rates of Interest in Different Markets.— We have said that, in the same market, at the same time, there is but one rate of true interest, the apparent differences being due, either to payments in the nature of insurance upon the principal, or else to the effects of ignorance, misrepresentation, etc. Broadly speaking, this is true. In different markets, however, at the same time there may be widely differing rates of interest. Thus, twenty years ago, the loan of capital could be obtained, upon what was locally regarded as good security, for 4% in London, as freely as for 6% in New York; or 8% in Chicago; or 12% in Iowa or Kansas.

Whence these differences? In some degree, doubtless, these successive additions of interest, as capital passed westward, were in the nature of insurance. In each case, the security might be as good as could ordinarily be obtained in that community. Security, however, is a relative term: what would be deemed ample security in one place might not pass the scrutiny of lenders, without question, in another. Generally speaking, the older a country is, the greater the permanence of economic relations; the more does industry settle down within traditional limits; the higher is the value assigned to commercial reputation; the more carefully are the men selected who are to control the agencies of production and trade; the fewer are the chances of revolutionary changes in business.

224. Disinclination of Capital to Emigrate.—But not all, or even the greater part, of the differences which have been noted, are due to this cause. It is the disinclination of capital to emigrate, which allows such wide differences in local rates of interest. In part, this disinclination is due to a suspicion that strangers may not be fairly dealt with by courts and by officers of the law, in case of seizures or foreclosures. In part, it is due to a fear of war, which would necessarily cause a suspension of interest-payments, if not forfeiture of the principal. In part, it is due to the fact that investments made at a distance must generally be made through an agent, whose bad faith or weak judgment may cause the loss of the whole sum invested.

The main cause, however, of the disinclination of capital to emigrate is found in (1) the *inertia* of capitalists, making them ready to accept lower rates upon the spot than could be obtained through effort and inquiry at a distance; and in (2) the *ignorance* of capitalists, from the necessary lack of information as to the rates of interest prevailing elsewhere.

The disinclination of capital to emigrate is something which changes greatly, with changing moods of the public mind. At times, the owners of capital are buoyant and confident, and feel little hesitation in investing their capital at a distance. At times, the owners of capital are even credulous; and are readily "taken in" by plausible promises and prospectuses from abroad.

The disinclination of capital to emigrate, moreover, tends to diminish from age to age, as the communication of news, by post and telegraph, becomes easier; as the peoples of different cities and different countries know more about each other ; and as nations learn to treat foreigners with greater fairness. Consequently, there is a constant tendency to reduce local differences in the rates of interest.

225. Contrasts between Rent and Interest.—We are now in a position to contrast rent and interest with each other, in certain important respects.

First, we have seen (par. 173) that the whole theory of rent rests on the assumption that there is a body of no-rent lands. These serve as The Base, from which to measure upwards the successive degrees of productiveness of lands which bear a rent.

In the theory of capital, there is nothing corresponding to this. The economist does not find any no-interest capital. In theory, all capital bears an interest; and all portions of capital bear an equal interest. If one portion, in fact, brings its owner no interest, or brings an interest below that obtained by other portions, this is because of ignorance or accident or fraud or mistaken calculations. It is not due to the nature of the capital itself.

226. The Rate of Interest Tends to a Decline.—The second marked difference between interest and rent may be expressed as follows: Rent tends to increase with the increase of population and with the progress of wealth. On the contrary, interest tends to decline. This is because the amount of capital which can be created, in any country, is not, like the amount of land, a fixed quantity. There is no natural limit to the wealth which can be saved and accumulated, within any district, by the industry and frugality of an intelligent, skilful and enterprising people. Even within a single generation, we have seen the rate of interest decline in New England from six per-cent to four and a half, and even four; while, in many parts of the West, the decline, during the same period, has been greater. In England, interest upon the best security does not now exceed three per-cent; while additional capital applied to the land hardly returns as much as two per-cent.

227. A Popular Fallacy.—We close this chapter with a reference to an erroneous notion which is always likely to be widely spread in certain stages of industrial society. This is the notion that the rate of interest can be artificially lowered by the manufacture of large amounts of paper-money. What we have seen regarding the nature of interest ought to show the fallacy of this opinion.

A scarcity of capital means a deficient supply of tools, implements and machines; of live-stock; of materials for manufacture; of food and clothing, to support men while laboring on public works, or otherwise engaged in productive industry. It means that much-needed roads and bridges, wharves and warehouses, dwellings and barns, mills and factories have yet to be constructed, with scanty means for doing it. A more bountiful supply of paper-money is not going to bring these things into existence; and, consequently, can do nothing to meet the real wants of the community. On the contrary, by unduly exciting speculation and causing great and rapid fluctuations in prices (par. 144) an excess of paper-money is certain to disturb and impair production, and to divert consumption from more to less useful objects.

CHAPTER XXIII.

WAGES.

228. The Residual Share of the Product of Industry.— We have now reached that share of the product of industry to which I venture to apply the term Residual. I call wages the residual share, not because it is the last in order of treatment, but because, in my view, wages comprise the residue (or all which is left) of the product of industry after the three other shares have been taken out, the amount of those three shares being determined by economic laws which I have sought to state.

We have seen (par. 165) that the landlord and the employer divide between them all that part of the product of industry which we call the Surplus. That is, rent and profits together take all of price which is in excess of the cost of production. This leaves the capitalist and the laborer to divide between themselves all of price which represents cost of production.

Starting from this point in the last chapter, we inquired what part of this total amount the capitalist should receive. We found that the sum which should go to capital, as interest, is determined by the productiveness of the last (considerable) portion of the supply of capital which finds a borrower. The rate of interest, thus determined, is paid upon all the capital in the market, and no more, except so far as risks to the principal sum lent require additional payments, in the nature of Insurance. Interest having been thus taken out of the product of industry, all that remains belongs to the laboring class, as wages.

229. A Position of Vantage.—If the laborer's position, in the distribution of wealth, is really that of the residual claimant, that position is clearly one of vantage. If I, with three others, own the whole of a thing, and if the shares of my fellows are fixed, by agreement or by law, anything which makes that thing more valuable, as a whole, inures entirely to my benefit. Now, we shall see in what follows (taken in connection with what was said in Chapters VI and VII, regarding the efficiency of labor), that it is always within the power of the laboring class, by greater energy, carefulness and skill, to increase the product of industry. It is, therefore, always in their power to improve their own condition; and, if they duly look after their own interests in distribution, they will reap the entire fruit of whatever additional exertions and sacrifices they may make in production. This certainly is the most hopeful view that can possibly be taken of the economic position of the laborer.

230. The Productiveness of Labor is the Source of Wages.—When an employer hires labor, it is wholly with a view to the product of that labor. He hopes that the product will be large enough to leave a profit to himself. We have seen (par. 190) that there are always some employers who are destined to be disappointed in this expectation: employers, who, after all their care, pains and anxiety, will realize no profits, properly so called. Competition will surely bring this about. It will inevitably bring prices down to the point where the least efficient employers supplying the market can only get back what they have expended, with a bare living for themselves: a living no better than that obtained by the more fortunate members of the laboring class.

But whether any individual employer does or does not

realize a profit, it is only in this expectation that he employs labor at all; and it is only out of the product of labor that he can hope to realize a profit. All employers in the market, then, competing among themselves for the profits of employment, the price of labor, i.e. wages, will, if the laborers properly look after their own interests, rise to the point which is determined by the productiveness of labor at the hands of the least competent employers. All which these employers can produce by means of labor, they will be obliged to pay over in wages, subject only to the deduction of rent and interest. If, then, the productiveness of that labor be, by any cause, increased, the employers can afford to pay correspondingly higher wages; and this they will be compelled to do, if, as we said, the laborers properly assert their own interests.

The rate of wages, determined by the productiveness of labor at the hands of the least competent employers, will become the rate of wages for all labor. The more efficient employers will pay the same wages for labor; and will make a profit corresponding to the productiveness of labor under their superior management. This, then, is the law of wages.

231. How the Productiveness of Labor may be Increased. —It is not necessary to repeat here what has been said at so much length in Chapters VI and VII. We have there enumerated the principal elements which make up the efficiency of labor. Most of those elements, it is clear, are largely within the control of the laborers themselves. If they will put more zeal into their work; if they will be more careful of materials and machinery; if they will study their trades and make themselves thorough masters of their business, they can greatly increase their productive power.

Doubtless the chief reason why the laboring classes, as a whole, have not been more anxious and earnest to increase their industrial efficiency, is because they have failed fully to appreciate, in many cases have failed at all to apprehend, the true relation between the productiveness of labor and the rate of wages. For this failure there are two causes.

First. They have been taught, and they have generally believed, that their wages came out of a fund * which the employing class held for their benefit, instead of their wages being their own creation.

Secondly. Because they worked for wages stipulated in advance they have thought that all they had to do was to earn their wages for that piece of work.

But why were the stipulated wages no higher? Because the productiveness of their labor, as understood by their employers, was no greater. An increase of their productiveness would, of course, not give them higher wages under their present contract; but it would constitute a sufficient economic reason for higher wages under their next contract, and under all succeeding contracts. Employers, I repeat, will always be obliged to pay wages corresponding to the (known or anticipated) productiveness of labor at the hands of the least competent employers; and laborers have only to cause it to be known, or reasonably anticipated, that their labor will be more productive, in order to secure higher wages.

All the foregoing reasoning assumes, as we gave notice in par. 162, that perfect competition exists throughout industrial society. We shall see, in the next chapter, what is required for perfect competition; and what are the consequences of a failure to meet those requirements.

232. Particular Wages.—What we have thus far said, concerning wages, has all borne upon the question, what part of the total product of industry shall go to the laboring class as a whole. To this subject we might apply the

---

* Called by most English and American economists The Wages Fund.

term, General Wages. There remains to be briefly considered the subject which we may call Particular Wages, under which we discuss the question why wages in one employment are higher or lower than in other employments; and attempt to account for such differences.

The range of wages, between highest and lowest, in any community, even among able-bodied men, is very great. The theoretical minimum of wages is, of course, the amount necessary to keep the laborer alive and in strength to work, and also to rear children to take his own place in the industrial order. At least as much as this the employing class must pay for any kind of labor, because, otherwise, they could not long have labor at all.

This minimum of wages, viz., necessary subsistence, is hardly known at all in this country. There are few American families, which have not lost the "bread-winner," but could actually support life upon from one-half to one-third of the amount which they have to spend. Of this any one can readily satisfy himself by observing how the Italians and people from other foreign countries, where a low standard of living prevails, eat, dress and house themselves, when they first come among us. It is not, then, necessary that the actual minimum of wages shall be equal only to the cost of bare subsistence. Whether it shall be so, or not, depends upon causes which are mainly within the control of the working classes themselves.

In the distribution, among the several classes of laborers, of that total amount of wealth which the whole body of laborers are to receive, demand and supply are the all-effective agents. Generally speaking, the lowest wages, as among able-bodied men, are received by those who have nothing but muscular strength to offer; who are able to lift and carry heavy loads, to strike powerful blows or to wield the shovel for hours without tiring; but who have little general intelligence and no technical skill. Such persons, who are commonly spoken of as day-laborers (whether actually employed by the day or not), generally receive the lowest wages paid. This is simply because the supply of such labor is very abundant. The great majority of all who grow to manhood can do this sort of work. It is only as a man is able to do some kind of work which the great majority of laborers cannot do, that he lifts himself out of this class, and his wages rise above those of a common laborer.

How high they shall rise, will depend (1) upon the demand for the special service which he is qualified to render, and (2) upon the number of persons who compete with him for the privilege of rendering that service. A distinguished economist once told me that he had seen, in the books of a brass-manufacturing concern of this country, entries which established the fact that a certain brass-moulder had for a long time received wages averaging eighteen dollars a day. All around this man, were other moulders, men of great skill, who were glad to earn four or five dollars a day. This man was able to do something which they, with all their trying, could not effect. Everything which he touched took on a grace, which was worth money in the market. The ordinary brass-moulders, again, were receiving wages two or three times as large as those received by the day laborers and heavy porters of the same factories. This was because, and only because, with a given demand for such work, the supply, i.e. the number, of persons capable of doing it, was closely limited. That work requires great nicety of touch, accuracy of perception, sound judgment and executive force. The man who is to do it well, must not only have a good hand and a good eye; but he must also have a good head. A stupid, unobservant person, is not fit to undertake it; and no employer could afford to allow such a person to do the work, were he willing to do it for nothing.

Had we such a system of public education as we ought to have, by which all the powers and faculties of the child were called into exercise and taught to work together harmoniously and enthusiastically, much of the difference that now exists among the wages of the laboring class would disappear; the number of those who were capable of performing the higher parts in production would be vastly increased.

We must put altogether aside the notion that labor is compensated according to some scale of dignity or moral worth. Some kinds of work, which peculiarly require the use of the noblest of the human faculties, such as taste and imagination, or which bring into special exercise the greatest of the human virtues, such as patience, fidelity and the spirit of self-sacrifice, are more meanly compensated than others which make no such requirement. It is all a question of demand and supply. Some occupations which are peculiarly loathsome and revolting in their character bring very high wages, because the nature of the work to be done diminishes the number of those who will offer themselves for the service.

Dangerous employments sometimes yield very high wages. This should always be so; but the multitude of "broken men" in every community, that is, men who have been made desperate or reckless by misfortunes or by bad habits, constitute a reservoir from which, at any time, may be drawn those who will render the most dangerous services at wages which afford no adequate compensation for the risk to life and limb.* Just so far as the moral and intel-

---

* The reader may be interested to glance over the figures which show the comparative hardships and exposure to accidents and disease in different kinds of labor and professional service. Doctor Neison, an

lectual condition of the laboring class is improved, and, especially, as the vice of drunkenness is banished, will those laborers who are required, for the benefit of society, to perform work which is dangerous, painful, or exceptionally disagreeable, receive additional compensation therefor.

233. The Wages of Women.—A great deal of attention has been directed, in these late days, to the wages received by women who are obliged to leave their homes and go into "the market for labor," to earn their bread; and a great deal of very bad reasoning has been indulged in upon this subject. On the one side, philanthropists and sentimentalists have talked of what working women *ought* to receive, as if the question of wages were an ethical instead of an economic one; and have railed at employers because they paid women at the rates current in the market, as if it were the business of employers to do anything else. On the other hand, economists have been too apt to sneer at efforts to advance the condition of working women; and have talked of "demand and supply," as settling the whole question of women's wages, without recognizing the fact that *there are moral and intellectual elements in supply and in demand,* which are subject to man's volition and conscious activity.

---

eminent actuary, states that the mean annual mortality in England, between twenty-five and sixty-five years, is, in the clerical profession, 1.12 per cent; in the legal, 1.57; in the medical, 1.81. In domestic service, the mortality among gardeners is only .93 per cent; among grooms, 1.26; among coachmen, 1.84. Of the several branches of manufacture, paper shows a mean mortality of 1.45; tin, 1.61; iron, 1.75; glass, 1.83; lead, 2.24; earthen-ware, 2.57. Among the different kinds of mining, iron shows a mean mortality of 1.80; tin, 1.99; lead, 2.50; copper, 3.17.

In some of these cases, the extraordinarily high mortality is due to the poisonous fumes which are given out; in others, to the fact that the air is filled with fine particles, which penetrate the bronchial tubes and lungs, causing early death; in others, to the intense heat in which the work has to be done.

The supply of women's labor is, unfortunately, not greatly within control. That depends chiefly upon the needs of women. Generally speaking, women will, if they are free to choose, prefer to remain within the household, devoting themselves to making the home comfortable and beautiful, rearing and training the young, and enjoying social pleasures. If women are driven out into the market for labor, it will generally be because of misfortunes, the sickness or death of "the bread-winner," or the scantiness of the wages which the father or brother is able to earn.

But while the supply of women's labor is, thus, not greatly subject to control, the demand for that labor can be very much influenced by human choices. We have, in our day, seen an enormous extension of the field open to women, which has been due to a better understanding of the subject; to the improved education of women themselves; and to a more generous consideration of the wants of those, of this sex, who are obliged to earn their own bread. This good work can go on almost indefinitely. Many an employer could, if he saw a little more clearly on the subject, and felt a little more deeply concerning it, readily find a place for women in his works; and every such instance would make it more easy for women to find room in other establishments.

Nor is it alone the employers of labor who can contribute to this result. The greater the respect and sympathy for working women, on the part of the general community, the easier will it be for the young and unprotected to find employment and maintain themselves in it. It is hard enough, at the best, for a woman to go about and solicit work, perhaps in strange places, certainly from strangers; and to go and come, at early and at late hours, through quarters not free from disorderly elements. The more public interest is aroused in working women, the more man's instinctive chivalry is appealed to on their behalf, the larger will be the opportunities of work open to them, the better their chances of obtaining the employment they need. This is what I mean by "the moral and intellectual elements of demand and supply."

CHAPTER XXIV.

THE ECONOMIC EFFECTS OF IMPERFECT COMPETITION.

234. The Assumption of Perfect Competition.—In paragraph 162 it was said that, in the chapters immediately following, a state of perfect competition would be assumed. We should, thus, seek to show what would be the distribution of wealth, did each man, in his place in the industrial order, high or low, fully understand his economic interests, and unfalteringly pursue those interests, as thus discerned. We have now seen what I believe to be a complete and consistent theory of distribution, constructed upon this basis.

The assumption that competition is always and everywhere perfect, implies a great deal. How much it implies, let us, for a moment, stop to see. It implies, not only that a man has the general intelligence and the special information to enable him to know, at any time, just what would be for his own true, permanent, economic advantage; but, also, that he will not be hindered by law or force or custom or public opinion, or by his own ignorance, indolence, fear or poverty, from seeking that object, steadily and firmly, until he reaches it. Should his interest require him to leave home, country and friends, he will not hesitate to do so. Should better opportunities offer themselves in other avocations, he will change his work, not less than his place, in order to secure those advantages.

235. The United States as an Example.—It will be seen that perfect competition requires a great deal: more, indeed, than was ever found among any people. But, while nothing less than this will answer all the requirements of competition, something much less than this will yet answer those requirements so far as to secure a reasonably harmonious and beneficent distribution of wealth.

Let us take the Free States of the American Union before the War of Secession, as an illustration. Here a system of public education had bred a population in which the elements of knowledge were every man's possession. Not only was the ability to read, write and cipher universal; but the genius of the people was singularly alert, active and inquisitive. What the American of those days did not know about his own business, he was sure to know about that of his neighbor. Political suffrage being universal, the whole population had become accustomed to public discussion; and all had learned freely to communicate their own views, quickly to gather the opinions of others, and to take part, with confidence, in the decision of important questions.

This people, moreover, had an instinctive aptitude for tools and a remarkable readiness for turning themselves to any work which offered. The American farmer was a good all-round mechanic; while the professional mechanics could, if necessary, change their trade, almost over-night. The habits of the population favored the freest movement. From the first settlement of the country, men had made less of going from the seaboard to the frontier than the men of some countries make of going from one village to the next. At the time of which we are speaking, not less than one-fourth of the population were living in States other than those in which they were born; another fourth, probably, in Counties other than those in which they were born.

We have only to add that, in a new country, as yet only

half settled, the "margin of living" had been so large as to admit of almost universal saving: no man was too poor to migrate, if he learned of superior advantages elsewhere, and of these he was almost certain to learn, through newspapers that went into nearly every house and cabin.

Under conditions such as the foregoing, every economic advantage was quickly discerned and keenly pursued, and, so, the actual distribution of wealth came very near to the theoretical distribution which has been outlined in the preceding chapters.

236. An Illustration of Defective Competition.—In contrast with the Americans of that period, let us take, as an illustration of how far competition might fail, among a people of the same race, the England of 1824. Here no system of public education had made the elements of knowledge free to all. The heavily taxed newspapers were for "gentlemen's reading," alone. The great body of the working classes were excluded from the suffrage; and had never been invited to the deliberations and decisions of public policy. Twenty years of war, combined with heavy duties laid on foreign breadstuffs, had forced cultivation, within the island, down to almost the poorest soils, and had, thus (par. 168), largely increased the share of the produce going to the landlord class; while enormous taxes, due to war and to war-debts, raised the price of the necessaries of life to an intolerable pitch. The "margin of living" had long been so small that savings were few; and the great majority of working men were too poor to migrate, even within the kingdom, had they been disposed.

In fact, however, their ignorance was so great that good opportunities, existing elsewhere, were most unlikely to come to their notice. It only needs to be added that, for hundreds of years, it had, by law, been a crime in England for laborers to combine together to raise the rate of wages, or to shorten the day of labor, while masters had been, all th· time, free to combine to lower the rate of wages and to lengthen the day of labor. The laborers, thus, unaccustomed to act in concert, were without mutual intelligence and without mutual support, if not jealous and suspicious of each other, as rivals for employment. The masters, strong in their position, their wealth and their knowledge, formed a resolute and compact force, whether for defence or for offence.

237. The Consequences of Defective Competition.—Such was industrial England, in 1824. The lamentable defects of so extensive a failure of competition could only be adequately depicted in a volume. Wages had gone down and down, and with them had gone, to an inconceivable depth, the moral character and even the physical vigor of the population. The laborers in the fields obtained a meaner and scantier subsistence than the paupers in the almshouses.* Pauperism was, indeed, the best refuge for the able-bodied. Even when opportunities for employment existed in more favored localities, the peasants were too ignorant to learn of it, and too poor to migrate, had the intelligence been brought to them.† Within the districts where labor was in excess, wages were whatever the masters chose to offer. The power to resist had utterly departed from the laborer. With every successive reduction of wages, physical vigor declined; self-respect and social ambition received heavier and still heavier blows; disease came in with

---

* The Poor Law Commissioners of 1833 reported that, while able-bodied paupers received 151 oz. of food per week, the agricultural laborer consumed but 122 oz.

† Even at a later period, a well-known statistician says: "A laborer's wages in Dorset or Devon are barely half the sum given for similar services in the North of England." And this state of things continued for a generation, without a movement of labor sufficient to correct the inequality.

deadlier power; intemperance grew with misery; shameful vice * became ever more obtrusive.

It is no hostile picture which I have drawn. More grievous statements could be borne out by hundreds of volumes written by Englishmen: many of them, official "blue books." What has been described is simply the natural effects of one-sided competition. On their part, the masters, actuated by no ill-feeling toward their laborers, but earnestly seeking their own interests, and often sorely crowded by each other, kept pushing, pushing, pushing against their laborers, who, on their part, were utterly unable to resist the fatal pressure. Had the men been alert, active, aggressive, with equal rights of combination, thoroughly "posted" as to the conditions of industry, confident in themselves and trusting each other, the harder the masters pressed against them, the better for all. What was wanted was, not that the masters should be mild and yielding, but that the workmen, too, should be resolute and firm.

238. A Loss which No Man Gains.—It is not, even, for the interest of the employing class that their workmen should easily give way, under pressure from them. If the employers, themselves under a painful strain from competition (and it is always to be borne in mind that many employers can, at the best, only hope to make both ends meet), crowd hard upon their laborers, in the matter of work and wages, and the latter give way, immediate relief is, indeed, afforded, but that relief is only temporary, while, in the end, the effects are destructive.

Wages having, under pressure, fallen, prices follow them down to the point where the least competent employers can, again, only just get back their outlay in the sale of their

---

* "In many districts," says Miss Martineau, in her History of the Peace, "it was scarcely possible to meet a young woman who was respectable."

goods. This having been brought about, these employers are no better off than before. But how is it with the laborers concerned? Upon them the loss of wages, which means scantier subsistence and meaner conditions, operates to reduce at once their physical strength and their social and industrial ambition (pars. 37-41 and 43-45); and they are soon worth their lower wages no more than they were formerly worth their higher wages. Here, then, is a loss which no man gains. The employer is no better-off because the laborer has been driven to lower wages and meaner conditions, and deprived of much of his physical vigor and self-respect. The laborer is infinitely worse-off. The State, too, has sustained a painful and irreparable loss, in the character of its citizenship.

239. Self-Assertion on the Part of the Laboring Class is Essential to General Well-Being.—Nothing, economically speaking, can save industrial society from progressive degradation, except the spirit and the power in the working classes to resist being crowded-down. The crowding must take place. It is in the nature of trade and production. If the workmen are active, alert, aggressive: strong in their self-respect and confident of their cause, that pressure will do them no permanent harm.

Suppose you strike with a hammer into a bin of barley. You bury the hammer up to your wrist in the barley; yet you do not crush a single grain. Why not? Because the whole mass was free to move; and no single grain had to receive any considerable part of the blow. Lay one of those grains upon a plank, and strike a blow a tenth part as hard: you will smash it into a paste. Why? Because the grain was not free to move; and consequently had to suffer the blow without escape. Let the stoutest ship which ever rode-out a hundred gales, be lodged in the sands, or caught between rocks; and the waves which smite her. as she is held fast in position. will, in a few days or hours, break her up. and scatter mast and plank, crew and cargo. in wreck along the shore.

A laboring population which is alive to its own interests and prompt and strong in maintaining them. cannot be crushed by any sudden calamity, or even by unremitting pressure from the master class. If employment fails at one point, hundreds or thousands will go to the places where business is flourishing. If industry is prostrate all over the land, such a population will be found to have reserves, in savings banks or in real estate, which will carry them through to better times. If the conditions of industry grow harder and harder, from year to year, such a population will withhold their increase, and thus gradually reduce the supply of labor.

But a population such as we have described, in the England of 1824, only breed the faster, the more miserable they become; only cling the closer to their place, the harder their lot. Upon such a population industrial blows are sure to fall, thick and fast; and each blow does a damage never to be repaired. There is almost no limit to the industrial and social degradation which may come in this way.

240. Lowering the Industrial Character of the Employing Class.—I have said that it was of no permanent advantage to the employer to reduce wages by economic pressure; while it was of great and lasting injury to the laboring class. There is another effect of imperfect competition, as between laborer and employer, which deserves to be noted. The inevitable result is to bring into business a poorer class of employers; and thus to reduce the margin of production, in this respect; and thus (par. 195) to still further injure the laboring class and the whole community.

If the laboring class are active, alert and aggressive in the pursuit of their interests, the employing class will be continually sifted; its weakest members will be thrown-out; and the whole class will undergo an unceasing education, in all that relates to their business. If, on the other hand, the laborers are ignorant, stupid, inert, great numbers of incompetent men will get into the control of industry, and sustain themselves there, at the expense of the community, and of the laboring class in particular. The poorer the man, the poorer the master. The unprofitableness of slave labor was not due more to the inefficiency of the slave than to the shiftlessness of the management. Men will become the employers of poor labor who would never become the employers of good labor, and who ought not to be the employers of any kind of labor.

241. The Repeal of the Corn Laws.—An excellent illustration of the effects of increased competition, in improving the character of the employing class, is to be found in the history of English agriculture, before and after the repeal of the Corn Laws, in 1846. While Parliament was discussing that measure, there were numberless farmers who could appear before committees, or write letters to the newspapers, showing that they were only just able to make both ends meet, at existing prices for produce. If, then, prices were to be lowered, by allowing foreign breadstuffs to come in free, it was as clear as the nose on your face that English agriculture would be ruined.

As to the facts, there could be no question. These farmers were perfectly honest in their statements. Nevertheless, Parliament repealed the Corn Laws. Was English agriculture ruined? Far from it. Many of the old ignorant, hard-drinking, horse-racing, fox-hunting farmers were, indeed, driven out; but their places were more than taken by a new race, who studied their business, worked hard, bought superior machinery; introduced improved breeds of cattle; frequented the agricultural fairs, not for a "good time," but to get hints for the management of their farms. As a result, English agriculture gained more during the twenty-five years which followed 1850, than during the seventy-five years which preceded it.

242. Other Causes which Help to Swell the Proportion of Incompetent Employers.—There are many other causes which help swell the proportion of incompetent employers. Shilly-shally laws relating to insolvency do this; bad money does this, in a high degree; truck (that is the payment of workmen in goods, at the employer's store, instead of in money) does this; protection, also, in my opinion, does this. Each of these causes enables employers to escape the consequences of incompetency, and to hang miserably on to business, where they are an obstruction and a nuisance.

243. The Influence of Defective Competition upon Rents. —We have seen that the normal rent of any piece of land is determined by the excess of its productiveness over that of the least fertile lands contributing to the supply of the same market, at the same time. In theory, rents cannot exceed the amounts thus determined. Should the landlord attempt to exact a higher rate, tenants will move to the no-rent land (whether found at home or in some distant country); and thus protect themselves against such exactions. Under perfect competition, rent can only carry away the proper Surplus, as we have defined it. But how if competition be imperfect?

244. Rents in Ireland.—We have illustrated the effects of imperfect competition upon wages, by a reference to the condition of the working classes in England, prior to 1825. Let us illustrate the effects of imperfect competition upon rents by a brief reference to the condition of the tenant class in Ireland, prior to 1850. Unfortunate as were the relations between laborer and employer in England, at the time spoken of, the relations between landlord and tenant in Ireland were even worse.

In the first place, the Irish peasant was peculiarly ill fitted for a close competition with his landlord. He was, by nature, sanguine, impulsive, careless in expenditure, perhaps it is not too much to say, improvident. He was not much given to looking far ahead; while, in the present, he was sociable and generous to a fault. Had, however, the landlord class been of his own race and bound to him by common sympathies, the peculiarities of the Irish temperament might not have resulted in serious harm. Most unfortunately, the landlords of Ireland, at this time, were largely of a different race and a different religion. The two classes were not only, thus, alien to each other; they had been made hostile by mutual injuries.

Even this was not the worst of the case. A large part of the Irish landowners were "absentees," expending in foreign lands the rents which were wrung from the peasantry by middle-men, or agents resident on the soil. Generally speaking, these middle-men and agents were a peculiarly hard sort of men. They had been selected for their skill in searching-out every possible means of exaction, and for their unflinching resolution in exacting the last penny, even by "distraint" or eviction. The hatred with which they were regarded by the peasantry only made them the harder. The dangers to which they were exposed, in their cruel work, destroyed every feeling of compassion in their hearts.

245. Over-Population.—We have said that the Irish peasantry were peculiarly ill qualified for such a competition by their national characteristics. But that which put them at the greatest disadvantage was the recklessness with which they increased their numbers. The more miserable they were, the earlier they married, the more freely they brought forth children. By this it came about that population soon came to be greatly in excess; and the wretched peasantry were driven to compete with each other, with ever increasing eagerness, for the poor privilege of cultivating each small parcel of ground.

It was through such a state of unequal competition, that the Irish peasantry were reduced to that condition of universal and hopeless poverty which the great famine of 1846-7 brought so vividly to public attention, filling the world with horror. Rents had been increased, step by step, until, in a large proportion of instances, the sums which the peasants had promised to pay were, incredible as it may seem, actually in excess of the whole produce of the soil! Of course, such rents could not be paid. The peasant had to live; and consequently the landlord had to allow him something on which to live. But his food was of the most scanty and miserable character; rags were his clothing; his bed, a heap of straw; his hovel, a pen only fit for swine. Even so, the peasant was always in arrears to his landlord, which fact gave the agent still greater power over him, and made it still harder for him to improve his lot.

CHAPTER XXV.

WHAT MAY BE DONE TO HELP THE WORKING CLASSES.

246. What was Done in England.—If such are the evil consequences of an economic pressure to which the laboring classes are unable adequately to respond, the question arises, what, if anything, can be done, in such a state, to help them ? We shall, perhaps, best answer this question by telling, very briefly, what actually was done in England.

247. Trade-Unions.—In 1824–5, Parliament, under the enlightened leadership of William Huskisson, repealed the laws which had forbidden workmen to combine to raise wages or shorten the day of labor, or alter the terms or conditions of employment. Of this the working classes at once took advantage, to form Trade-Unions, in which men of the same trade joined together to promote their common interest. These Unions collected money from their members, through weekly or monthly fees ; kept up correspondence with other unions, in other places ; assisted the sick and disabled of their own number ; and, when they deemed the occasion propitious, made demands upon the employing class, which demands they stood ready to enforce, if necessary, by Strikes, that is, by concerted refusal to work at the old terms.

In the miserable condition to which they had been reduced by the causes indicated in paragraph 236, ignorant, poor, unfamiliar with affairs, the laborers, in their new efforts, for awhile made many and great mistakes. Noisy and turbulent, or sly and plausible, men got the leadership, as is always the case at first. These misled the well-meaning and excited the bad. Demands were made upon employers which could not properly be granted; and those demands it was sometimes sought to enforce, not only by strikes, which were lawful and right, but also by violence, which was unlawful and wrong. In many of the contests which ensued, the laborers were beaten; and, after suffering untold losses, were obliged to go back to work, at the old wages and for the old hours. Still they persisted, with wonderful courage and admirable fidelity to each other. Beaten again and again, they again and again returned to the attack. Even when they were beaten outright and completely, the masters were yet learning to fear and to respect them, as they had never done in the times when it was the theory, alike of the law, and of the master, and of the economist, that laborers had nothing whatever to do with fixing their own wages, but should take whatever was offered them, in silence and thankfulness.

248. Education of the Working Classes.—Meanwhile, the working classes were learning both their own power and the limitations of that power; were coming to have confidence in themselves and in each other; were beginning to see the difference between noisy demagogues and true leaders. Better men were coming to the front among them. The times taken for making demands were more wisely chosen. The demands themselves were more reasonable. The tone and manner in which these demands were made were more conciliatory and respectful. More and more, demands thus made were conceded without a contest, or won after a hard fight. But, whether the working men won or lost the particular thing they were struggling for, they were, all the while, gaining knowledge of themselves and commanding the respect of the employing class

249. Factory-Acts Passed.—While this series of industrial insurrections was going on, Parliament, moved by many enlightened and philanthropic men, was doing what it could to raise the condition of the people. Factory-Acts, so-called, were passed, which limited the hours of labor to what was consistent with health and strength; which restricted the employment of young children; which forbade women to work underground in mines, or in other avocations unsuited to their sex; which required dangerous machinery to be fenced or guarded, so as to protect life and limb; which provided for the sanitary regulation and inspection of factory buildings.

250. Other Remedial Legislation.—Acts were also passed which established banks to protect the first small savings of the very poor; the suffrage was extended; taxes which pressed with peculiar hardship on the masses were repealed; the stamp duties were removed from the newspapers. Measure after measure, conceived in the true spirit of statesmanship, TO HELP THE PEOPLE TO HELP THEMSELVES, became laws, in quick succession. Aided, thus, by judicious legislation, but striving ever more and more to aid themselves, the British laboring class climbed upward, out of "the horrible pit and miry clay" in which they had been left by the abuse and neglect of centuries; and began to take their true place in society.

There was still a great deal of drunkenness, riot and coarse vice, a great deal of wastefulness and foolish expenditure of means hardly earned. But, in spite of all, the long history of mankind has no other chapter which is so full of promise, as that which tells of the rise of the working classes of England from 1825 to the present time. The British laborer of to-day differs as widely from the British laborer of the early time, as if he were, in the phrase of Edmund Burke, "a different species of animal."

251. Factory-Acts Considered.—The present Duke of Argyle, in his Reign of Law, declares that the necessity and economic benefit of factory legislation, like that of England to which we have referred, constitutes one of the greatest discoveries of the nineteenth century, in the science of government. Certainly, although these acts were at first opposed by many statesmen and by most economists, they have been, in the result, approved by experience, and have been copied, with more or less of change, by nearly all civilized governments. It has now passed beyond question, that it is desirable that mill-owners and large employers of labor, should be, by law, restrained from doing (whether under the impulse of avarice, or under painful pressure from competition) certain things which are clearly prejudicial to their operatives, and which can, in the long run, do no good to themselves. Such acts, if wisely conceived and sensibly administered, are a protection not less to the employer than to the laborer. They do no harm to any, but only good to all. The master class themselves ought to be glad that it is forever put out of their power to do the things* which are prohibited by these measures. Within the limits where the law still leaves them free to act, the ablest of employers will find abundant scope for the exercise of all his energy, enterprise and skill.

To the laboring class, on the other hand, seeking their

---

* The beginning of the present century found children of five, and even of three, years of age, in England, working in factories and brickyards; found women working underground in mines, harnessed with mules to carts, drawing heavy loads; found the hours of labor whatever the avarice of individual mill-owners might exact, were it thirteen, or fourteen or fifteen ; found no guards about machinery, to protect life and limb; found the air of the factories fouler than language could describe, even could human ears endure to hear the story.

own interests through much perplexity and against many obstacles, factory legislation gives a certain definite, solid, unshakable ground, on which they can securely build, in their further efforts. Below this, the force of competition, the effects of shocks and catastrophes cannot come. This much, at least, is secure.

252. How about Freedom of Contract?—The objection made to factory legislation has been that it interferes with the freedom of contract. But what is freedom,* so far as practical men are concerned with it? Is it an empty right to do something which you cannot possibly do? or is it a real power to do that one, out of many things, which you shall choose? If one course gives a man a legal right to do anything, but results in his being so helpless, and brings him into such miserable straits, that he can, in fact, do but one thing, and that, a thing which is most distressing; while another course, though it keeps a man from going hither and thither, actually conducts him to a position where he has a real choice, among many and good things—which course affords the larger liberty?

In the case of a poor and ignorant population, the absence of factory-acts, while it nominally leaves the operative free to go anywhere and do whatever he likes, really results in his staying where he is, and doing what he particularly dislikes. He becomes the slave of the mill, bound fast to the great wheel which turns and turns below. Theoretically, he will not work in any factory in which the sanitary arrangements do not suit the most fastidious tastes; in which machinery is not fenced, to prevent murder and

---

* "The modern English citizen, who lives under the burden of the revised edition of the Statutes, not to speak of innumerable municipal, railroad, sanitary and other by-laws, is, after all, an infinitely FREER, as well as nobler, creature than the savage who is always under the despotism of physical want."—PROF. JEVONS.

mutilation; and in which the hours are not agreeably short. Theoretically, too, he will place himself with reference to the comfort of his family, and to the education of his children for a career better than his own.

Practically, he will have no choice but to work as long as the great wheel turns, be that twelve hours or fourteen, or else go out to starve; he will every week see some of his companions bruised and mangled by unguarded machinery; he will breathe air which is deeply laden with poisonous particles or gases. Practically, too, he will, under the pressure of dire necessity, put his children into the mill just as soon as he can get them there; and in the mill they will stay until they die. This is what will come to most laboring populations, without factory-acts. Are such populations really freer than populations which are protected by laws like those which we have described?

A crutch acts only by *restraint*; and, to a perfectly sound man, would be only a hindrance and a nuisance. But is a cripple without a crutch a freer man than a cripple with a crutch? In his case, does not the crutch correspond to an existing infirmity, in such a way that he has a much greater liberty and power of action and of movement, through its help: that is, through the restraint it exercises?

253. Trade-Unions Considered.—In the elevation of a laboring population, long abused and deeply abased, trade-unions may perform a part of much importance, although always at the risk of doing harm rather than good. That risk, however, men have frequently to take in the pursuit of a desirable social object: and the history of industry shows that, on the whole, the good has predominated over the evil, in the work of trade-unions.

Trade-unions, as means for advancing the condition of the working classes, are subject to drawbacks which do not attend factory-acts. There is no reason why the effects of the latter should not be altogether for good. The things which are to be prohibited are things which, in any broad view, are seen to be injurious to all. The things which are required are things which really benefit both parties to the contract for labor. Within the lines drawn by factory legislation, the laborer and the employer are left free to seek their several interests, and to exercise each his own powers in his own way. But in the case of trade-unions, there is a real and a great danger that mischief will be done. There is a strong and a constant liability to begin courses which can only result in injury to the general community, and to both parties to the contract for labor: most of all, to the laborer himself. The trade-union is not only an edged but a two-edged tool, which is highly dangerous to those who wield it carelessly or wantonly.

254. Abuse of Trade-Unions.—Trade-unions, viewed merely as Friendly Societies, insuring their members against the effects of sickness or accident, promoting good fellowship and exerting a certain social influence throughout the craft, are, of course, beyond objection. But trade-unions, as bodies seeking to legislate concerning the ways in which industry shall be carried on, and to enforce that legislation by industrial war, are subject to many evil liabilities.

It would greatly surprise one who had not studied the subject to read the foolish and mischievous rules which many trade-unions have established for the government of their own members, and have attempted to enforce upon employers. It would be difficult to say, in regard to some of these codes, whether gross ignorance as to the primary conditions of production, or a spirit which delighted in humiliating and harassing employers, had played the greater part. In not a few instances such regulations have led to bitter contests, in which the interests of both parties have been sacrificed.

I prefer to say the worst that is to be said regarding trade-unions, at the beginning, rather than at the end. In addition to extreme instances of folly or mischief-making, there is a great deal in the regulations which trade-unions, in America, in England and elsewhere, have undertaken to enforce, which has borne with unnecessary severity upon the employing class; has been unfair to the outside mass of labor, waiting to be employed, and has been, perhaps in no sudden and violent way, prejudicial to industry and to the well-being of the community.

255. Education through Experience.—Whenever a body of men have suddenly come into the possession of power, they are apt to deem that power irresistible, and to presume greatly upon it. They are likely to fall under the influence of the less moderate and fair-minded of their own number. Only experience in affairs, with both good and evil fortune, can teach men to use power without abusing it. That experience is expensive; but it is the price of industrial, as of political, freedom.

In England, where trade-unions, in their modern form, first arose, there has been a steady progress towards moderation, sound judgment and fairness, in dealing with questions arising between laborer and employer. The character of the men chosen as leaders has continually improved; their constituencies have grown in knowledge, in prudence and in the respect paid to good advice. Strikes have diminished from decade to decade; the proportion of disputes adjusted by arbitration has increased.

Whether there is, or has ever been, any real industrial occasion for trade-unions in the United States, is fairly a matter of question. There certainly was none before the War of Secession. If such an occasion has since arisen;

if the welfare of the laboring classes now requires the existence of such associations, this is wholly on account of the vast numbers of persons, not born upon our soil, not bred under our laws, not educated in our schools, whom the great prosperity of the country and the force of our tariff-laws have drawn across the ocean, to make their home here.

256. Strikes Considered.—The possible utility of strikes has long been the subject of dispute. There was a time when most educated men held that strikes were only and always of evil. A somewhat different view has recently come to prevail.

Strikes are the insurrections of labor. Like insurrections in the political body, they are justifiable on the part of men whose rights or whose interests are threatened with the gravest injury. In such a case, no one should, merely for the sake of peace, wish to have any body of men too weak or too cowardly to resist. For myself, I believe that the fierce series of industrial revolts which, in England, followed the repeal of the Combinations Acts were absolutely necessary in order to break up the power of fear, of tradition and of poverty, by which the minds of the working classes of the kingdom had been so long held in bondage; absolutely necessary, in order to create among the laborers the self-confidence, the social ambition and the sense of mutual interest, which were needed for their development into industrial and political manhood; absolutely necessary, in order to teach the master class to respect their workmen; absolutely necessary, in order to secure a fair competition, equal on the two sides.

But, while strikes are, thus, under certain circumstances, useful, it is only in the earlier stages of industrial progress. Strikes have no positive virtue. They do not create wealth, but only destroy it or impede its production. As soon as a body of workmen have fairly "pulled themselves together;" have taken the first steps in their own advancement; have got a little ahead in the world, they ought to find better means than strikes, for securing their further progress. They can generally, by active, energetic competition, take a shorter and a surer way to economic prosperity, than through industrial warfare.

257. Strikes, the Last Resort.—Yet, behind all friendly negotiations, all arbitrations and compromises, the strike will always remain as the last resort, to give seriousness and earnestness to the efforts of both parties to reach satisfactory results, by mutual agreement. Perhaps the state of things which at the present time exists in England represents, as fairly as could be expected, the true use of this agency. Strikes now seldom take place in that country. Both parties have reason to dread them and to shrink from them. Long and bitter experience has made each party painfully anxious to avoid that resort. In consequence, the claims of laborers for advance of wages in good times, the propositions of masters for reductions of wages made necessary by bad times, are considered with an earnest desire to find a solution satisfactory to both parties.

In such a state of the public mind, lightness, arrogance and wantonness, disappear from the debate. The working men are careful not to put forward demands which they cannot make good, for that would injure their cause. Masters are anxious to concede whatever can be fairly shown, to impartial judges, to be reasonable and right.

Such has been the improvement of the laborer's condition, through the causes already recited, that the two parties are now not unevenly matched, in point of power. Either party is strong enough to win the fight, if its cause commands the sympathy, the respect, and, if needed, the

pecuniary support of the outside community.* On the
other hand, neither party can expect to win if it is manifestly
seeking to crowd the other "into a corner," or carries
on the conflict by unfair means. This is what should
be. Such an equilibrium between the two parties in interest,
with the general sense of all disinterested people and
all lovers of fair-play coming-in to turn the scale, is, perhaps,
the best result we can hope to attain, while the organization
of industry remains substantially as at present.

---

* The effect of this has been shown, to a most remarkable degree,
in the great London strike of the present year—1889—when nearly
all the men of high position, in society, in business, and in the
church, gave open approval and support to the laborers, as against
the dock-companies; and when large contributions of money flowed
in from all parts of the kingdom, and even from foreign countries.

CHAPTER XXVI.

THE "PAUPER-LABOR" ARGUMENT FOR "PROTECTION."

258. Are Low Wages Infectious?—It was said, in paragraph 156, that, not until we had passed through the whole theory of the distribution of wealth, should we be in a position to take up, to advantage, the argument for Protection which is known as the Pauper-Labor argument. We may now briefly consider this subject.

The plea made, from this point of view, in favor of the policy of protection, is that populations among which wages are high and a respectable standard of living is maintained, cannot freely import the products of countries where wages are low and the laboring classes are deeply degraded, without, in time, losing their own economic position of vantage, and becoming reduced to the same low level as the least fortunate peoples with whom they trade.

259. Not between Non-Competing Countries.—It is, in the first place, to be noted that any such lamentable result need only be apprehended in case the more fortunate and the less fortunate peoples are engaged in producing the same kind of goods, or, else, goods which can largely be substituted for each other in use.

For example, the United States produce no tea. It cannot, therefore, matter to us, except on grounds of humanity, how miserably the peoples of the tea-producing countries live. If wages in those countries are low, *in proportion to the work done,* the people of the United

States only get their tea the cheaper thereby. In the same way, the tropical fruits which come hither will only cost us less, the more miserably those who, in distant lands, produce them, are compensated for their labor.

The evil effects which are anticipated can only occur when the two peoples concerned are competing with each other in selling the same kind of goods, or goods so nearly alike in their uses that one kind can be substituted for another. Manifestly this is so; and it is to this state of things, only, that the Pauper-Labor argument applies.

260. How about Competing Countries?—But, if two peoples are thus competing, is there danger that the low wages and the miserable standard of living in one will tend, through the course of trade, to infect the other? On this point two things are to be said.

First, we must recur to the principle which governs Normal Price. In Chapter X, we saw that the normal price of any kind of goods is fixed, not by the cost of producing this or that portion of the supply, but solely by the cost of producing the last (considerable) portion of the supply which is produced "at the greatest disadvantage."

If, then, a foreign nation produces a portion of the supply at greater advantage (let us, for argument's sake, say, through employers being able to hire labor at lower wages), this will not necessarily affect the price of those goods. So long as the full supply of that kind of goods requires that any considerable portion should be produced at a comparative disadvantage (due, let us say, to the payment of higher wages) in other countries, the price will be determined by the cost of production in these countries, and not in the former country.* It would not, then, be until the

---

* Here we have a sufficient reply to the objection which is made to allowing "convict labor," in prisons and reformatories, to be employed in making goods for the market. It is said that, as this labor

former country could so increase its production as to bring forward the whole supply required, that prices would fall to a point corresponding to the low wages there paid.

Secondly. But do low wages necessarily, or generally, constitute an advantage in production, which would allow the countries where such wages prevail to undersell those in which high wages prevail? On this point we refer to considerations pointed out in Chapter VI.

261. High Wages: Low Cost of Production.—There is apt to be a great deal of confusion in the public mind regarding the difference between high or low *wages*, and a high or low *cost of production*. The cost of production may be low when wages are high, because the laborers may be so energetic and efficient, so skilful and so careful, that the employer may get back even those high wages in the price of his product.

The cost of production may be high when wages are low, because the labor purchased thereby may be so unintelligent, shiftless and wasteful, so lacking in energy and inspiration, that the employer may find it difficult, perhaps impossible, to get back those wages, mean as they are, in the price of the product. Not only may this be so; but it often, and, indeed, generally, is so. High wages are commonly, habitually, found associated with a low cost of production. Low wages are, quite as generally, found associated with a high cost of production.

262. Practical Illustrations.—The English cotton-spinner receives as many shillings, a week, as the East India cotton-

---

costs little (the State being obliged, for the public safety, to subsist the convicts, whether employed or not), the wages of honest, free labor will be reduced by such competition. But the goods produced by convict labor, in general, constitute a small, often an inconsiderably small, part of the supply. Their cost of production, at a relative advantage (through a low cost for labor), does not, therefore, fix the price.

spinner receives pence; yet English cottons undersell Indian cottons in Indian markets. The German iron-maker receives two or three times as much wages as the Russian; yet German iron has to be kept out of Russia by heavy duties. On the other hand, the English iron-maker receives two or three times the wages of the German; yet Germany feels under a terrible necessity to keep out the iron of England.

Illustrations might be multiplied; but one more will suffice. In a report made by Mr. Blaine, as Secretary of State, June 25, 1881, occurs the following statement regarding the cotton manufacture of England and the United States:

"It thus appears that each American operative works-up as much raw material as two British operatives; turns out nearly $1.50 worth of manufactures to the British operative's $1 worth; and, even in piece-goods, where the superior quality and weight of the American goods are so marked, the American operative turns out 2.75 yards, to 2.50 yards by the British operative."

263. The Reason for the Rule.—The reason for this association of high wages with low cost of production is perfectly plain. As shown in Chapter VI, the laborer's efficiency is, in great part, the immediate product of his wages. So far as the laborer's efficiency is the immediate product of his wages, that efficiency should increase at least proportionally with his wages. In fact, it will, within wide limits, increase more than proportionally, very much more. An underfed and ill-clothed laborer (and most of the laborers of the world are underfed and ill-clothed) does not develop labor-power in proportion to the meagre subsistence allowed him. A laborer receiving 150 ounces of solid food a week, can perform not merely one-half more of effective work than a laborer receiving 100 ounces: he can probably do twice as much. So far as food, alone, is concerned, it is unquestionably true that, until the economic maximum has been reached (and that maximum is very unlikely to be reached), productive power is developed at a continually increasing ratio. So far, therefore, as wages go to food, there is the best possible reason why high wages should be associated with a low cost of production.

How is it with the other elements of personal consumption, to which wages are applied? That the same principle operates in respect to that portion of wages which is applied to clothing and to securing comfortable and wholesome lodging is, I believe, abundantly established. But how about those parts of wages which go to what we may call the decencies and luxuries of life? Do these constitute a force, of which efficiency in labor is the direct and necessary product?

Generally speaking, it has been shown, on the widest scale, that the self-respect, the domestic and social ambition, the hopefulness and cheerfulness, which arise out of such enjoyments and the further prospect of such enjoyments, on the part of the laboring classes, generate an industrial force (pars. 43–5) which as fully repays its cost (that is, the price of such enjoyments) as does any equal expenditure upon the necessaries of life. I should regard any person as very unfortunate in his opportunities for the observation of human life, or still more unfortunate in the spirit he brought to that observation, who should deny that the foregoing statements are largely, and even generally, true.

264. Does this Rule hold Universally?—But is this principle, that industrial efficiency (within reasonable limits, of course) increases at least proportionally, and tends to increase more than proportionally, to increase of wages, temperately and virtuously applied, a principle of universal applicability? Is it equally true, when the increase is large and sudden, coming to men who have previously lived in squalor and who have comparatively little susceptibility to moral and intellectual motives, as when the increase of wages is moderate and gradual, coming to men who have heretofore been accustomed to decent and comfortable habits of living?

Is it equally true, when the increase of wages occurs within a branch of industry where the work is such as gives little opportunity for the exercise of intelligence, of care in the use of tools and machines, of ingenuity and prudence in the prevention of waste, and where the rate of the laborer's motions is practically determined by the movements of machinery, as it would be, were the increase of wages to occur within a branch of industry offering large possibilities to the physical, moral and intellectual activity of the laborer?

265. To Come Down to Particular Cases.—Is it equally true that an increase of wages would produce a corresponding increase of working power, in the case of Hungarians, or of Poles, or of South Italians, as in the case of native Americans or of Scotchmen or of Saxons? Is it equally true in case of men employed in a cotton mill, as in the case of men working in a shoe shop, or a watch factory, or a machine shop? If this be not so, I am not sure that the answer which the free trader has habitually made to the protectionist, at this point, is quite as conclusive as people of my own general way of thinking have been accustomed to regard it.

As to the universality of the principle, that high wages mean a low cost of production, I confess I am not confident. That among a generous and well-bred people, socially ambitious, self-respectful and intelligent, successive advances of wages, by moderate degrees, would, up to a certain, high, point, generate increments of productive force proportional, or even more than proportional, I entertain no doubt whatsoever.

266. Conclusion.—If the proposition of the free trader, that industrial efficiency increases correspondingly to increase of wages, is universally true, then the protectionist has no ground to stand upon. No case exists such as he assumes. If American wages, for example, are exceptionally high, then it must be true that the foreign manufacturer pays as much, and probably more, FOR THE SAME AMOUNT OF WORK, OF THE SAME KIND AND QUALITY.

If, on the other hand, the principle laid down be not universally true, then the case which the protectionist has in mind may arise, viz., where the American manufacturer, in branches of industry peculiarly unresponsive to the physical, intellectual and moral invigoration of their operatives, does, in fact, pay higher wages, for a given amount and kind of work, than is paid abroad. In this case, there would be a real, no longer a merely nominal, disadvantage in the cost of production, on the part of American manufacturers. That disadvantage the protectionist would seek to counterbalance, by weighting down the corresponding foreign products by means of customs-duties.

But, in such a case, the question would arise as to the wisdom of the legislation which brought such industries into being, in a country whose people were fitted for higher work, and which invited, and, in a sense, compelled, to come to our shores such large numbers of persons whose descent, education and early experiences only fit them to take part in industries which are, as we said, "peculiarly unresponsive to the physical, intellectual and moral invigoration of their operatives." If government lets industry alone, in a country having an intelligent, spirited and frugal population, only those branches of manufacture will arise which are of a nature to allow relatively high wages to be paid without increasing the actual cost of production.

It will be seen that, in the view taken above, protection is, at the best, only a means of defending the working classes against the effects of a competition to which they are unequal, by reason of their ignorance, or indolence, or lack of self-respect and social ambition, or by reason of abuses and wrongs to which they have been subjected in the past. This chapter, then, is really a part of Chapter XXV. Among a generous, self-respectful, well-bred and well-educated people, applying themselves to the higher departments of industry, no such artificial protection, or support, will be required.

CHAPTER XXVII.

THE CONSUMPTION OF WEALTH

267. The Meaning of the Term.—By the term, Consumption, in political economy, we signify the use made of wealth. We have seen how wealth is produced and exchanged. We have inquired respecting the forces which distribute the product of industry. We are now to ask, what men shall do with the shares they receive in that distribution.

The consumption of wealth is not identical with its destruction. To be sure, most forms of wealth that are put to use do, sooner or later, disappear ; but to most of them this would happen, in time, whether they were used or not. We do not wait until an item of wealth has been destroyed by use, before we speak of it as consumed. It is, in the economic sense, consumed when it is *put to its destined use*, although the material of it may last for a long time thereafter. Cloth is consumed, as cloth, when it is made into garments. The garments are consumed, in the economic sense, when they pass to their destined wearer, although they may still be good for years. Iron beams and bars and rods are, in the economic sense, consumed when they are built into the frame of a bridge. The bridge, however, remains to carry passengers and freight for generations.

268. The Importance of Consumption.—Many, indeed most, economists have left consumption altogether out of their treatises, holding that it was not their business to go into that subject. But, surely, if we are studying political economy because of the importance of wealth to human welfare, or to the strength and stability of the State, we cannot afford to pass-by the questions of consumption. In the case of any people, the ways in which they are consuming their wealth—that is, the uses to which they are putting it—are of far more consequence than the present amount of that wealth. In the case of a nation, as of an individual, very large accumulations, with foolish or vicious modes of expenditure, may intimate a less prosperous future than a moderate stock, which is being used temperately and wisely.

Existing wealth may be applied to ends which inspire social ambition, which restrict population within limits consistent with the general welfare, which increase the efficiency of the laborer and supply instruments for making his labor still more productive; or it may be used in ways which encourage the undue increase of population, bringing-in poverty, squalor and disease; in ways which debauch the laborer, morally and physically, striking at both his power and his disposition to work hard and continuously. The completeness with which the French people, through their temperance, frugality and industry, made up in a few years the terrific fines and losses of the German war (1870–1), affords a very striking illustration of the virtue there is in the labor-power of a country rapidly to replace its capital, provided only a right consumption of wealth be assured.

The secret of a nation's rise or decline in prosperity is not to be found chiefly in its situation and natural advantages for commerce; not in its soil and climate; not in its good or evil fortune; not in the malice of its enemies or in the help of its allies. That secret lies in the use which the nation makes of the wealth, be that ample or scanty, which its powers and resources enable it to produce.

"What will he do with it?" is the question which is asked (not spoken) of every man, at every turn of life: what will he do with the new opportunity: how will he meet the new danger: to what use will he put the treasure that has fallen at his feet? Eminently, in regard to the wealth of nations, "What will they do with it?" is the question of questions.

269. Population.—The use which, in a primitive community, is most likely to be made of existing wealth is to support an increasing population. Let us take the case of a tribe, occupying a district of moderate extent, cultivating the soil of the fertile valley of their native stream, pasturing their cattle and sheep on the mountain sides, and practising certain rude mechanic arts. Now, in such a state, *the instincts and appetites which lead to the multiplication of numbers* will be those which are earliest and most strongly felt, after the appetites which crave food and warmth. The food may be coarse, all of one kind, prepared without skill, eaten on the ground. The desired warmth may be obtained in close hovels, or possibly in caves, amid the foulest of air and the grossest of filth. These things matter not. As soon as food and warmth have been obtained, even in such a miserable way, the appetites which lead men to marry and to breed after their kind will make themselves felt; and will thereafter practically take possession of all the remaining wealth of the community, to use it for their own purposes.

Now, the capabilities of human increase are vastly in excess of the capability of supporting life, within any defined field. Mankind have, over and over again, shown that, under favorable conditions, population can be doubled in twenty-five, in twenty-two, and, perhaps, even in twenty years, in spite of sickness, accidents and premature deaths. If, then, the tribe we are speaking of numbers one thousand, it may, at the end of one century (assuming that population doubles itself in twenty-five years) contain sixteen thousand souls. Had the valley and the mountain sides been but sparsely settled at the beginning of the century, the sixteen thousand, who would occupy these seats at the end of the century, might be no more than a comfortable population. Indeed, the sixteen thousand might, owing to the advantages of the division of labor, live better than the one thousand did.

But, even if so, the quarter of a million of persons (256,000), who, at the end of another century, would take their place, should increase go on in a geometrical ratio, would probably be reduced to the last stages of human misery, through the operation of the principle of Diminishing Returns in agriculture (Chap. V). Did famine, fever or internecine war not come in to check the growth of population, the quarter of a million would, at the end of still another century, have grown to (4,096,000) more than four millions! That population would, of course, be impossible. To prevent such a result, famine and the fevers which feed on the half-famished, would, every year or every few years, sweep through the valley, cutting-off thousands at a time; or, else, the unhappy inhabitants, driven to despair through lack of food, would prey upon each other, or, under some bold leader, would pour out of their valley, a great devastating horde, to fight with neighboring tribes for the possession of their land.

Such are the capabilities of human increase.* If, then,

---

* The law of population, thus briefly set forth, bears the name of Mr. Malthus, an English clergyman. The doctrine is called Malthusianism. Mr. Malthus was, at the time, roundly abused for his

the instincts and appetites which lead to the multiplication of numbers are to remain (as they always are at the beginning) the appetites which come next, in order and in strength, after the desire for food and warmth, the history of every tribe of men will be what we have described, and no other. All the wealth which is left-over, after feeding, clothing and housing, in the meanest manner, the existing population, will be continually used-up in the attempt to support an increasing population. There is, speaking broadly, no other consumption of wealth known to the savage or the barbarous man. Even so, as we saw, all the wealth available will not suffice to carry-on the natural process for more than a century or two, without giving rise to the most hideous physical evils.

270. Higher Economic Desires.— The question, then, whether there is to be any other consumption of wealth— whether, in fact, the beginnings of civilization are to become possible— is the question, whether other economic desires shall come to force themselves in front of the appetites which lead to the multiplication of numbers. If this is not to take place, no economic improvement will be possible; and all religious and social influences for the better, which may be exerted from the outside upon any such tribe, will be feeble and transient, like marks made upon the sands which have been uncovered by the tide.

Observe: there are two reasons why it is to be desired that other economic desires should come in, and, in some degree, crowd-out the appetites which lead to the multiplication of numbers.

---

plain speaking. But people have now learned that the whole truth should be spoken on this subject. If men will breed like vermin, they must die like vermin. If men will be "lords of the universe," they first must be lords of themselves. If they would be masters of their conditions, they must be masters of their appetites.

First, simply because only in this way is the frightful round of over-population, famine, disease and internecine war, with all its chaos of horrors, to be prevented. From this point of view, it does not matter whether the new economic desires are higher in their moral and social character, or not. Almost anything is better than that the increase of population should not be, by some cause, restrained. Secondly, because such other economic desires are likely to be, or in time to become, higher and more beneficent than those which they replace.

And, yet, those new desires are not likely to be, at first, much higher. Mankind do not make progress by leaps, but, at the best, by slow and painful steps, which often slip, and often lead to falls. No great advancement is to be expected, in the beginning, from people in the stage of life which we have been considering.

The early economic desires of different communities vary greatly. In one, the first want felt, after the absolute necessaries of life are obtained, is of ornament and decoration. Even when men are hardly covered from the cold and scantily nourished, the passion for display makes its appearance. In another community, the first want felt, after the claims of bare subsistence are met, is of a store for the future, as a provision against the caprices of the seasons and the casualties of life. The first want emerging in the life of another community may be of wealth to be expended in worship and in honor of the national or local deity. Millions of men may consent to live squalidly, in order that a few temples may shine like the sun, their altars smoke with unending sacrifices, their priests walk resplendent with embroidered and jewelled vestments. In still other communities, the new want may take the form of a desire for a diversified diet, or for leisure, or for some costly drug or drink, like the opium of the East Indian or the Chinaman, or the "fire-water" of the North American Indian.

271. A Diversified Diet.—Doubtless, the want which has been efficient on the largest scale, at once in promoting labor and in restraining population, is the craving for a diversified diet. Once let the sole diet of the barbarian, be it fish, or flesh, or grain, be crossed by other species of food, exciting the pleasure which resides in variety; and an economic force has been introduced into the life of the community which is capable of producing mighty results. Probably this has been the lever by which more tribes and races of men have been raised and kept, one degree at least, above the condition of a population pressing all the time upon the limits of subsistence, than by any other.

Although a diversified diet doubtless contributes, in some degree, to health and vigor, it is yet a pure luxury, in the sense that it is not sought upon that account, but wholly for the gratification of appetite. It will seem strange to the reader that a desire for objects of luxury should be spoken of as having greater power to promote effort and to check population than the fear of privation and actual misery. Yet so it is; and, as we go up the scale of human wants and desires, we shall find that, in general, the higher the want or desire, morally considered, the stronger it proves to be. In an advanced civilization, mere sentiments and tastes, which involve the gratification of no physical sense, impel men to the most painful and protracted exertions, and hold in check the strongest passions of the lower nature.

272. A Rising Scale of Expenditure.—Contemplating a community which has grown above the low desires which control and completely master the barbarian; and which has, by the force of higher personal wants, attained the power of checking population, otherwise than through disease and famine, we say that the entire future of such a community depends upon the further growth of economic wants among its members. If they are to remain content with a low scale of personal expenditure, they will waste in idleness or sport all the time which is gained for them by improvements in the arts and by the discovery of new resources in nature.

There have, indeed, been tribes of men who could remain on such a low scale of living, and yet cultivate arts, letters and philosophy, and apply their leisure to social and intellectual improvement. Even so, however, such a civilization is highly transient; liable to be swept away by every wave of foreign force, or broken-up by a single outburst of domestic sedition. Generally speaking, it is only the nations that are eager to improve their material condition which cultivate the arts and increase in knowledge and in refinement. It is such nations, alone, that can found a permanent civilization. The reason for this is threefold.

First, the physical and mental activity to which men are incited by the desire for greater wealth, with which to purchase more of the comforts, decencies and luxuries of life, constitutes, itself, the greatest of all means of intellectual and moral education. By it, the faculties of the barbarian are awakened from a torpor which is akin to death; are stimulated to the highest pitch; are trained by appropriate exercises. through which they continually gain in strength, in suppleness, in persistency. By it, the low desires, the brutal cravings, the gross vices of the barbarian are repressed; while nobler motives and higher tastes come into consciousness and become, increasingly, the law of life. It is in this way that the small-brained have grown into the large-brained races. It is in this way that timid and indolent peoples have developed into peoples that delight in encountering danger, in overcoming difficulties, in enduring hardships; and whose spirit mounts with opposition.

273. Civilization.—Secondly, wealth, in its various forms, furnishes the tools and the materials for the finer arts and the higher studies; furnishes, also, the means by which the results of those arts and studies are extended and brought to the knowledge and enjoyment of all.

Thirdly, every civilization which is not embodied in institutions, in permanent structures, in accumulated resources, is always liable to fall rapidly away, under the influence of physical disaster, or foreign hostility, or through the mere force of weariness and disgust. It is institutions, permanent structures, accumulated resources, which enable each successive generation to hold firmly on to the past, to go strongly through its own difficulties and dangers, and to transmit the arts, tastes and powers which it has inherited, unimpaired to its natural successors.

Man is distinguished from the other orders of animals by his susceptibility to new desires. Those desires may, by appropriate influences and by the course of experience, be made to increase almost indefinitely, both in number and in variety; and it is generally true that the latest desire becomes the most urgent and persistent of the series. The man of the modern state toils, night and day, to procure for his children articles which do not minister to any bodily sense, but are required by the existing standard of social decency. The man of the primitive state will run the risk of suffering and famine, to him and his, rather than make the most moderate exertions and sacrifices to provide a store for the future.

In this matter, as in everything else, "it is the first step which costs." The greatest difficulty is in introducing into the life of a people any tastes or desires, whatever, beyond those fundamental wants of which we have spoken.

Once let a community be lifted out of the mire of existence, by this lever, and new wants will come, thick and fast, upon them. As soon as any new want is felt, their condition will seem to them intolerable, unless that want can be supplied ; and, so, the elevating and ennobling process will go on, without a stop, unless some great catastrophe, or some great debasing cause, shall enter to throw them back into hopeless misery and social degradation.

CHAPTER XXVIII.

SOME MISTAKEN NOTIONS ABOUT CONSUMPTION.

274. Prevalence of False Notions.—There is probably no subject in political economy which is so much beset with false notions as is the consumption of wealth. Persons who have never thought much about the production, the exchange or the distribution of wealth, are almost certain to have their own ideas about its consumption; and these ideas are very apt to be erroneous. There would seem to be something in the nature of the subject which makes it difficult for men to see more than one side of any question which concerns consumption.

275. The Destruction of Wealth.—We have seen that most forms of wealth are necessarily destroyed, sooner or later, by being used. Such a destruction of wealth is, of course, neither to be rejoiced over nor to be regretted, since these forms of wealth are produced with this very result in view. But there is, among very large numbers of persons in every community, a disposition to look at the premature destruction of wealth by any cause, as something either good in itself or, at any rate, having advantages to counterbalance the loss sustained. In the common phrase, it is supposed to "create a demand for labor;" to "encourage industry," etc.

The notion mentioned above is seldom found among agriculturists. Men who have taken part in raising crops are not much disposed to look at the destruction of those crops, or of the barns which shelter them, or of farming implements or machines, as bringing good to any one. Among commercial and manufacturing populations, however, this belief is very prevalent. Working men are apt to hold it; domestic servants are perfectly sure that their breakage "makes trade good;" even many highly educated people cannot free themselves from the instinctive feeling that the abrupt removal of existing wealth quickens industry and promotes the general welfare.

276. Destruction Sometimes Means the Removal of Obstruction.—There are, of course, situations, where the destruction of wealth may have the effect to secure a larger production, in the future. Thus, a man may occupy a "water privilege" with an old-fashioned badly-built mill, which he cannot find it in his heart to tear down. He may know that it would be better to do so; but he puts it off from year to year, doing what he can with the old mill and its old machinery. Every year he gets further and further behind, as new and better mills are built all around him. One night a fire breaks out; and a year later, a fine, large, new mill occupies the site, in which a great deal more and a great deal better work can be done. It is not unlikely that, in five or ten years, the manufacturer, himself, will be richer than he ever could have been with the old mill; while a larger number of operatives are engaged, at higher wages, producing goods which are required for the clothing of the community.

Again, two towns, on opposite sides of a river, may long have put-up with a mean, narrow, unsafe and inconvenient bridge, which has always been an obstruction to traffic. A flood comes and carries the bridge down the river: whereupon the towns unite in building one fully suited to their needs, broad and firm, with ample approaches from both sides. This may give such an expansion to the industrial activity of both towns as, in a short time, to more than repay the cost of the new bridge.

Still again, it is an undoubted fact that the destruction, by fire, of the old and crooked parts of certain cities, filled with "rookeries" and tumble-down houses, repulsive in aspect and almost impassable to traffic, has led to a large increase of wealth. It had long been known that that "quarter" was a nuisance and an obstruction to the growth of the city and to the development of its trade. But each property-holder felt that it was of no use for him to pull-down his own miserable houses and to build better, so long as his neighbors were not ready to do the same. Thus, one man waited for another; while all were disposed to put-off the day of making improvements at so great an expense. A conflagration comes; burns down the rickety houses, foul with the accumulated filth of generations; and in a few years that wretched quarter has been replaced by broad streets and convenient and wholesome houses. The city is wealthier and healthier for the change; and even the individual property-holders may be richer than before.

277. What We See and What We Don't See.—But the disposition to rejoice in the destruction of wealth is not confined to instances like the foregoing, where nuisances and obstructions are removed. It extends to cases where the existing forms of wealth were well answering the purposes for which they were created. That disposition is due to the fact that those who rejoice see only one side of the effect. They see that, where wealth is destroyed, other wealth generally flows-in, to take its place; and labor and capital are soon actively, perhaps hurriedly, employed in repairing the waste. What they do not see is that this labor and capital are drawn from other avocations and from other places, where, but for the fire or the flood, they would be engaged, though without making so much stir, in producing new forms of wealth, wholly in addition to those which have been destroyed, thus increasing the total sum of wealth to be enjoyed by the community.

278. Luxurious Consumption.—Regarding the consumption of wealth in what we may call, without attempting closely to define it, Luxury, two popular notions are prevalent. These two notions are largely opposed to each other; yet they may both be equally erroneous. Both are often held by the same persons, at different times, according to the mood in which their minds are, at the moment.

One false notion concerning the consumption of wealth is that which regards all personal expenditure which is very greatly above what the mass of people can indulge in, as an injury to the community and as a wrong to the laboring classes in particular. Now, in order to get a plain view of this matter, let us take the case of a manufacturer who produces goods to the value of five hundred thousand dollars annually, out of which he realizes a profit of twenty-five thousand dollars. Let it be conceded that five thousand dollars would furnish decent and comfortable subsistence for the manufacturer's family, including proper education for his children. But he is not satisfied with so moderate a scale of personal expenditure. He spends another five thousand dollars upon things which, while they are not essential to comfort and decency, are yet not so far out of the common as to attract public attention and to make him and his family conspicuous. In addition to all the foregoing, he expends ten thousand dollars in display and self-glorification, in luxuries of the most extravagant cost, upon pleasures of the most ephemeral nature. This leaves him but five thousand dollars to put into his business, or to lay up in bank.

Now, it does not need to be said that it would be better were the manufacturer in question wise enough to save a larger portion of his profits, either as a means of increasing his business, or as a reserve against the future. Again, it does not need to be said that it would be better, in case he is to expend twenty thousand dollars of his income, were he wise and generous enough to spend that sum in ways which would bring more good to his fellow men, do more credit to himself, and afford a better training for his children. But the question is not, whether something much better might not have been done with this amount of wealth, but whether such a use of it constitutes a positive injury to the community, or is, in any sense whatsoever, a wrong to the laboring classes.

The point which is overlooked in the popular view of this question, is that, this manufacturer's tastes, habits, ideals, ambitions being (by force of nature and of education) what they are, the power of indulging in such expenditures is a great part of the motive which leads him to carry on business and to apply perhaps great abilities, with untiring energy and unflinching courage, to the production of wealth. It is, of course, a pity that the man has not simpler tastes and higher ambitions; but we have to take the man as we find him. Deny him the opportunity to indulge his own impulses in the expenditure of his wealth, and you destroy or largely impair the energy which he would otherwise bring to the conduct of business. As it is, he pays out several hundred thousand dollars a year for labor and for materials which are mainly the product of labor. The fact that he has realized twenty-five thousand dollars in profits is proof that he has conducted his business with great energy, skill and prudence. Other men have had control of equal amounts of labor and of capital, and have realized no profits.

We conclude, then, that luxurious expenditure, even though its objects are not altogether well and wisely chosen, may be far from injuring the community or wronging the laboring class, since it may furnish the motive required for securing the most intense and unremitting application of Business Ability to the work of production.

On the other hand, there is a disposition very frequently manifested, to applaud luxurious expenditure, even in its most extravagant forms, as a good thing in itself, because it "makes trade good," "puts money in circulation," "gives employment to labor," etc. Whenever any great exhibition of extravagance is given, there are always found those who approve it for such reasons.

Again we say, those who take this view of the expenditure of wealth, see only one side of the case. While most forms of extreme luxury do, at the time, give employment to labor and give "a fillip" to trade, there is almost always some use to which that wealth might have been applied which would have proved, in the long run, much more beneficial to the community at large and to the laboring class in particular.

Let us suppose that a well-to-do manufacturer, who might have provided a decent, comfortable and even handsome home for his family, at a cost of twenty-five thousand dollars, is moved by vanity and love of display to put one-hundred thousand dollars into his dwelling, with greenhouses and stables. It is true that the additional seventy-five thousand dollars is expended for labor, or for materials which are mainly the product of labor. It is true, also, that, so long as the estate is properly kept-up, a few additional servants, gardeners and grooms will be employed. But, had the seventy-five thousand dollars been applied to the building of a new factory or to the improvement of a large tract of agricultural land, an equal amount of employment would have been given to labor, in the first instance; while, through all succeeding time, employment would be afforded to a number of laborers ten, twenty or perhaps thirty times as many as those who would be employed in keeping-up the fine house and grounds.

279. Government Expenditures.—Another subject, in regard to which public opinion is very apt to go wrong, is the expenditure of wealth by government. In approaching this subject, it needs to be said, in the first place, that there are many and large occasions, in every highly civilized community, for government to consume wealth for the general welfare. Not only must the State preserve the public peace and protect person and property, at a great cost for judges and jails, for policemen and soldiers, but there are many things which nearly all citizens are now agreed should be done by the State, which are not so much of a protective, as of a productive, character.

The streets of cities and the highways which cross the country should, for the best effect, be laid out by the government. The bridges, by which the public roads are to cross streams and rivers, should be built by the State; and it is by some made a question whether the docks and wharves, at which vessels are to load and to unload, should not be provided in the same way. Whether this would be wise or not, it is certain that the improvement of rivers and harbors, at enormous cost, the maintenance of a lighthouse system and the construction of breakwaters, are the proper work of government. The water supply of cities is largely provided by public authority, out of public revenues, and in some cases, also, the gas supply. In nearly all countries, the telegraphs and in many countries the railroads, also, are owned and operated by the government. In addition to these and similar works which government undertakes, the State has vast expenditures to make for elementary schools and, perhaps, also, higher institutions of learning; for museums and libraries; for parks and pleasure grounds.

The popular error regarding governmental expenditures is not in approving the consumption of wealth which is actually required for carrying on useful works; but in looking at government expenditures as good in themselves, as "putting money into circulation," and as having a kind of virtue to "promote trade and industry." There are found, in every community, many persons, otherwise intelligent, who are ready to applaud "liberal" expenditures on the part of the government, not as the necessary price of things which actually require to be done, but as being beneficial in themselves.

The trouble with these people, also, is that they see only one side of the matter. They see that, at whatever point government disburses its revenues, there is a distinct increase of activity in production and in trade. They fail to note the less intense but much wider effects which are produced upon production and trade, all over the land, by the taxes through which the government collects those revenues. Every dollar which the government expends with one hand, it must take away from somebody with the other hand. Indeed, that the Treasury may have one dollar to spend, it has to take from the people a dollar and ten cents, or a dollar and twenty cents, because of the expenses of assessment, collection, disbursement and public accounting. In order, therefore, to encourage one person or set of persons by its expenditures, to the extent of one dollar, government has to discourage another person or set of persons, by its taxes, to the extent of a dollar and ten, or twenty, cents. This constitutes no sufficient reason why government should not collect money for great public works which individuals could not construct at all, or could not maintain to advantage; but it does constitute a very strong reason why government expenditures should not be made any larger than is necessary, from any vague notion of encouraging trade and industry thereby.

280. Over-Production.—All the erroneous notions regarding the consumption of wealth, which we have pointed out in this chapter, spring largely out of one fundamental error, which is very widely spread in the public mind, and which finds its expression in the familiar phrase, Over-Production. There is a very common tendency to think of wealth, after it has once been produced, as somehow getting in the way, so that other wealth cannot be produced until this has been consumed. The fact is, physically speaking, men might go on producing wealth to the end of time, and not consume any of it, without encumbering the earth thereby, or blocking the way to further production. Of course, morally speaking, men will produce wealth only as they expect it to be consumed, or used. It is our business, then, to inquire whether there is any natural limit to the amount of wealth that can be consumed. If there is not, then such a thing as true over-production cannot take place.

Let us look around. We see, in the community in which we live, men who earn three hundred dollars a year, on which to support their families; others, four hundred; others, five or six hundred; others, still, one thousand, two thousand, or three thousand; still others, perhaps, five thousand, ten thousand, or twenty thousand. Is there any family, now expending three hundred, or four hundred, or five hundred dollars, which could not, and would not gladly, expend twice or three times as much, if they had it? Do not the members of those families know the very things they would like to purchase, with added means: things, probably, which would be not only harmless, but actually, and perhaps highly, beneficial? Is there any man, now expending one thousand or three thousand or five thousand or ten thousand dollars, who could not, and would not gladly, expend twice or three times as much, if he had it for the purpose? Let the reader try to put himself in the place of persons of these different classes, in succession; and he will soon be satisfied that it is idle to suppose that more wealth is likely to be produced than men would be ready and glad to consume. Yet just this is what is meant by over-production.

But, while universal over-production is thus seen to be practically impossible, it not infrequently happens that over-production takes place *in certain lines*. This we should call Partial Over-Production. For example, we might suppose the production of woollen goods to be enormously increased. Let us say that it is doubled within a year. Even so, it is not probable that there would be more woollen goods in existence than people would like to use, for no community was ever so well clothed but that a great many more garments would be welcome. But, when a poor family have bought a certain quantity of woollen goods, they do not want to buy any more of these until they have a certain amount of cotton goods and of linen goods. In the case supposed, therefore, there would be a relative over-production of woollen goods: an over-production, that is, in comparison with the amount of cotton and linen goods produced. Hence, there might be no "market" for a portion of the stock of woollen goods; and, consequently, some of the woollen mills might have to remain idle for months.

We might suppose, again, that the increase of production had taken place through all the branches of the textile manufacture, in silk, linen, and cotton, as well as in woollen goods. There would, perhaps, be no more textile fabrics in existence than people would be glad to use; but, after people have bought a certain amount of textile goods, they do not want to buy any more until they have a certain amount of glass ware, of china, of wooden ware, of iron ware, of carriages, of pictures, etc. There might, then, in the case supposed, be an over-production of textile fabrics, in general: an over-production, that is, in comparison with other kinds of manufactured goods.

Over-production might even be extended to all kinds of what we call manufactured goods. Not that there would probably be more of manufactured goods than people would be glad to consume, if they had them; but that there would be more of manufactured goods than people would be willing to purchase until they had bought more of agricultural produce, or until they had built themselves better houses, or until they had been able to construct more roads and bridges.

It will thus appear that partial over-production may be carried a great way. The history of industry also shows that over-production is *very likely to take place,* in one line, or in several lines, sometimes in many lines together. If the price of a certain article, or of several articles, has for some time been high, owing either to a falling-off from the usual supply or to a sudden and large increase of demand, employers of labor and owners of capital are very likely to rush-in, almost tumultuously, and build many more mills or works, in order to take advantage of the high price. Soon it is found that the "plant" is much greater than is needed; yet each mill-owner for a while tries to keep his machinery and his hands employed. The result is over-production, followed by a long period of stagnation, perhaps by many failures in business.

The reader will be prepared for the remark that, the further the division of labor is carried, the more widely trade is extended, the greater the localization and diversification of industry, the more numerous become the

opportunities for this MISUNDERSTANDING BETWEEN PRO-
DUCERS AND CONSUMERS. That misunderstanding is the
price which the world has to pay for the great advantages
of industrial civilization. That price is, indeed, very high.
It implies, at times, a frightful waste of capital and great
suffering to the laboring class, from the failure of employment in those lines where production has been over-done.
Whether, in the further progress of industrial society,
means will be found for preserving all the advantages resulting from the widest division of labor and the largest
use of the machinery of production, and at the same time
reducing the great loss which men now have to suffer
through partial over-production, is a question which no
one is wise enough to answer.

THE END.

INDEX.

☞ The references are to numbered sections, not to pages.

Absentee landlords of Ireland, 244.
Abstinence, the creator of value, 60; interest, the reward of abstinence, 213-6.
Accident and fraud: influence upon profits, 193.
Accumulation, how influenced by the rate of interest, 219-20.
Adams, Henry C., Prof.: Outlines of Lectures upon Political Economy, preface, page vi.
Adaptations, Industrial, of different peoples, 42, 149.
Advertising expenses, saved in Co-operation, 207.
Agriculture, subject to the law of Diminishing Returns, Chap. V; chiefly controlled by soil and climate, 148. (See Land and, also, Rent.)
Agriculturists not prone to regard the destruction of wealth as a good, 275.
American economists, erroneous views regarding the relation of capital to wages, 231.
Americans, their industrial aptitudes, 42, 209, 235, 262.
Amsterdam, bank of, 110.
Andrews, E. B., his Institutes of Economics: preface, page vi.
Apprenticeship, time saved by division of labor, 48.
Argyle, Duke of: restrictions on the contract for labor, 251.

Aristotle on usury, 214.
Art: political economy as an art (a branch of statesmanship) distinguished from political economy as a science: preface, page v.
Assertion by the laboring classes of their own interests, essential to general well-being, 239, 247, 255, 257.
Australia, gold discoveries, 109.
Authority, legal, excluded from our definition of value, 3, 4.
Automatic regulation of metallic money, 140; political money not so regulated, 142.

Balance of trade, 124-7.
Banks, Chap. XIV.
Banking functions, the, 116-24; the banking agencies, 128.
Bank-money, 113-5, 129-141; its volume, how regulated, 141.
Bankruptcy laws: in early times, very severe, 101-2; if ill-considered, may increase the proportion of incompetent employers, 242.
Barter, the primitive form of exchange, 86-93, 133.
Belgium, underfed laborers, 40.
Bill brokers, 128.
Bi-Metallism, 107-9.
Birth-rate, its possibilities, 269; diminished by increase of economic desires, 270-2.

Blaine, Secretary: report on the cotton manufactures of the United States, 262.
Brabazon, Lord: inadequate food of French factory-hands, 40.
Burke, Edmund, quoted, 250.
Business Ability, one of the four agents of production, 22, 55, 80, 188, 278; its remuneration (profits), 163, 189, Chap. XX.
Business-paper (see Commercial paper).

Caird, Sir James: houses in Scotland, 41.
California, gold discoveries, 109.
Calvin, John, on Usury, 214.
Cancellation of indebtedness by banks and clearing houses, 120.
Capital, one of the four agents in production, Chap. VIII, pars. 22, 78, 163, 188; Capital invested in land, 171–2; circulating *versus* fixed capital, 63–4; remuneration for the use of capital (interest), Chap. XXII; relation of capital to the scheme of co-operation, 198; relation of capital to wages, 231; the use of capital enters into the cost of production, 77, 79; how capital comes into a bank, 117; accumulation of capital as influencing the distribution of industries, 148, 150.
Capitalist, the (see Capital), a claimant in the distribution of the product of industry, 163; has no right to any part of Rent, 180; his share of the product, Chap. XXII; not to be gotten rid of by co-operation, 198.
Cash Principle, in retail trade, 207.
Cattle, as money, 96.
Cereals, as money, 96, 104.
Chadwick, Edwin: the cellar populations of English cities, 41.

Cheap money—is inconvertible paper money cheap? 131–46, cheap money does not make a low rate of interest, 227.
Cheerfulness, as contributing to labor power, 43, 263–5.
China, underfed laborers, 40.
Circulating *versus* fixed capital 63–4.
City Real Estate, differs in an important particular from agricultural land, 187.
Civilization tends to diminish the sum of values, 60; how civilization is made permanent, 272.
Clearing house, the banker's bank, 121.
Climate: influence on the distribution of industries, 148.
Clothing, its relation to subsistence, 62, 263.
Coin basis of bank money (see Reserve).
Coincidence, double, of wants and of possessions, 87, 133.
Comfort, ideas of, developed in the progress of society, 9, 59, 270–2.
Commerce: old-time theory that it could be beneficial to but one party, 11.
Commercial paper, its discount, 221.
Common Ownership of Land (see Nationalization, etc.).
Competing countries: influence upon each other in the matter of wages, and of the standard of living, Chap. XXVI.
Competition, 49; what is involved in perfect competition, 162, 234–5; effects of imperfect competition, Chap. XXIV; what can be done to remedy the effects of imperfect competition, Chaps. XXV and XXVI.
Concentration of manufacturing industries, tendency to, 150–1.

INDEX. 315

Congress of the United States, its unfitness for tariff legislation, 155.
Consumers of agricultural produce have no right to any part of Rent, 178.
Consumers and producers, possible misunderstandings between, 280.
Consumption of wealth, 59, Chap. XXVII; consumption, how influenced by bad money, 146; mistaken notions regarding consumption, Chap. XXVIII.
Consumptive *versus* productive co-operation, 206; advantages of, 207; practical experience, 208-9.
Contract for labor: interference by law with, 75, 249, 251-2.
Contract for labor: what determines the price at which this is made, i.e., wages? 231.
Convertibility of paper money (see Redeemability).
Convict labor, 260.
Co-operation, Chap. XXI; an effort to get rid of the employer, 198; erroneous conceptions of many economists, 198; anticipated benefits, 199-201; practical difficulties, 202-4; consumptive *versus* productive co-operation, 206; special advantages of consumptive co-operation, 207; practical experience, 208-9.
Corn-rents, 104.
Corn-laws (English), 241.
Cost of production, its relation to normal value, Chap. IX; rent does not enter into the cost of production, 164, 175; profits do not enter into the cost of production, 194; wages and interest alone constitute the cost of production, 165; relation of cost of production to the distribution of wealth, 165, 188, 210, 215-7; low cost of produc-

Cost of production—*continued*.
tion compatible with high wages, 261-5.
Credit, commercial, largely managed by banks, 116.
Credit sales, their great importance in modern industry, 100-2; make necessary a standard for Deferred Payments, 103; the Multiple or Tabular Standard, 106.
Creditor class, 100-2.
Custom, effect on price, 75.

Dangerous employments, how compensated, 232.
Debtors, laws regarding, 100-2.
Debtor class, their demand for paper-money issues, 138.
Debts, Bad, loss by, 207.
Debts, scaling down, 138.
Decency, Ideas of, developed in the progress of society, 9, 59, 270-2; power to check population, 270-2; desire for decencies promote efficiency in labor, 263-5.
Deferred Payments, Standard for, 103-5; political money as the standard, 134-42 (see Tabular Standard).
Degradation of the laboring class, through unequal competition, 236-8, 263.
Demand and supply, 15, 215, 232; intellectual and moral elements of, 233.
Demand, Causes which affect, 69.
Denominator of Values, 89.
Deposit and discount, the great banking function, 116-7.
Depreciation, not a necessary result of the inconvertibility of paper money, 133, 143.
Desires, economic: their development in the progress of mankind, 9, 59; their influence in retarding the growth of population, 270-2.

Destruction of wealth: popular notion that it stimulates production, 275-7.
Deterioration, liability to, as affecting price, 74.
Diet, diversified, taste for, as antagonizing the procreative force, 271.
Diminishing Returns in Agriculture, Chap. V.
Disadvantage, production at: preface, page v, Chapter X, pars. 160, 188, 215-18; influence on the distribution of wealth, 165, 188, 194, 210, 215-18, 230.
Discount and deposit, the great banking function, 116-7.
Distribution, the Problem of, Chap. XVII; the several shares in distribution, Chaps. XVII and XVIII.
Distribution, geographical, of money, how effected, 140.
Division of Labor (see, also, Territorial Division of Labor): how it arises, 47; how it becomes a source of productive power, 48-54; evil possibilities attendant upon, 280.

East India, inefficiency of its laboring population, 35, 262.
Economic Association, American: preface, page vi, also par. 202.
Economics (see Political Economy).
Economics, Quarterly Journal of: preface, page vi.
Education of the working classes, through their own efforts to improve their condition, 201, 248.
Education, popular, effects upon industrial aptitudes, 42, 232, 235.
Efficiency of the individual laborer, dependent upon several causes, 36-46, 263; relation to wages, 230-1, 263-5; efficiency of bodies of labor, promoted by the organization of industry, 47-54.

Emigration of capital, 224; of labor, 235-7, 239.
Employer, the: his industrial function, 55, 197, 203; his remuneration, 163,189 (see Chaps. XX and XXI.
Employer, the least competent: the productiveness of labor, at his hands, determines wages, 85, 190, 192.
Employers, incompetent, how their control of business affects the distribution of wealth, 195; causes which tend to increase the proportion of such employers, 241-2.
Employed Laborer (see Laborer).
Encouragement of Manufactures, the, 153.
England: insufficient food and shelter of agricultural laborers, 39-40; contrasted with India and Russia as to the efficiency of its laboring population, 35, 262-5; banking agencies, 111; aristocratic holding of the soil, 187; co-operative enterprises, 202, 208; usury laws, 214; government securities, 222; mortality in certain avocations, 232; defective competition, 236, 237; corn-laws, 241; remedial labor legislation,246-50; strikes, 257.
English economists: their erroneous views regarding the relation of wages to the product of industry, 231; they oppose Factory Acts, 251.
Environment, Industrial, influence of, 52.
Esprit de Corps in industry, 51.
Exchangeability, the test of value, 3-8.
Exchange, the old-time theory that it could be beneficial but to one party, 11.
Exchange, as a department of political economy, Part I.
Exchanges, foreign, 124-7.

Factory laws, 249, 251-2.
Fashion, Changes of, as affecting demand, 69.
Fawcett, H.: insufficient food of West of England laborers, 40.
Fiat money (see Inconvertible Paper Money).
Financiering, as a banking function, 110.
Fiscal motives to excessive issues of paper money, 136.
Fixed vs. Circulating Capital, 63-4.
Food (see, also, Subsistence): its relation to labor-power 37-40, 237-8, 263; the primary form of capital, 62; its relation to population, 269.
Force, Productive, cannot be lost out of nature, but may be lost out of man's reach, 25.
Forced circulation, generally a characteristic of government paper money, 133.
Form value, 20.
France: underfed factory hands, 40; bimetallic system, 108-9; rapid recovery from effects of German war, 268; popular tenure of the land, 187; co-operative enterprises, 202.
Fraud and accident: influence on Profits, 193.
Free Trade vs. Protection, Chap. XVI; the Pauper Labor argument against free trade, Chap. XXVI.
Freedom, real vs. nominal, 252.
Frugality, awakened by ownership of land, 45; the creator of capital, 60; encouraged by Co-operation, 200.

Gains which no man loses, 238, 263.
Gains, Unearned, do little good to any, 104, 144-6.
Geometrical progression in population, 269.
George, Henry, his "Progress and Poverty," 182.

Germany: has to protect itself against England, while Russia protects itself against Germany, 262.
Gilman, N. P., Profit Sharing, 205.
Girdlestone, Canon: diet of the laborers of Devonshire, 40.
Glut (see Over-production).
Gold (see Precious Metals. See, also, for its relations to silver, Bi-Metallism).
Government, as producer and consumer, 279; restraining greed and imposing conditions upon industry, 251-2 (see The State).
Government expenditure, how far to be encouraged, 279.
Grain, as money, 96.
Gratuity, its relation to value, 60.
Greed, often antagonistic to the enlightened pursuit of wealth, 11, 251-2.
Greenbacks, so called, of the United States, 137, 143.
Ground-rents, 159, 163, 187.

Habit, influence on price, 76.
Hazardous risks of capital, how compensated, 221-3.
Health is not wealth, 6-8; effect upon health of certain avocations, 232.
Hebrews, ancient, usury forbidden, 214.
Hireling, the, lack of interest in production and in care of wealth, 46 (see Co-operation).
Holland, underfed laborers, 40.
Honesty: its relation to punctuality, 123.
Hopefulness in labor, as an element of productive power, 43, 263-5.
Huskisson, William: repeal of the English laws against Combinations, 247
Immobility of Capital and Labor (see Emigration, etc.).

Improvements made upon the Land; the returns to them should be distinguished from Rent, 171-2.
Inconvertible paper money, Chap. XV; its multiplication does not reduce the rate of interest, 227; increases the proportion of incompetent employers, 242.
Increment, the Unearned, of land (see Rent).
Indebtedness, Cancellation of, 120.
India: the efficiency of its laboring population contrasted with that of England, 35; underfed laborers, 40.
Inertia, Mental, influence on price, 76; on rate of interest, 224.
Inflation (money), Chap. XV; effects of Inflation, 142-6.
Inglis, H.: the city houses of Ireland, 41; industry of peasant proprietors, 45.
Institutions, essential to civilization, 272.
Insurance of the principal, an important element of interest, 221-3, 228.
Intellectual elements of supply and demand, 233.
Intelligence is not wealth, 6-8; a source of productive power, 42.
Interest, as a share of the product of industry, 163, Chap. XXII; what determines the rate of interest, 215-6; justification of interest, 213-4; interest is not paid, generally speaking, for the use of money, but of capital, 214, 227.
Interest contrasted with Rent, 225; rate of interest tends to decline, 226.
International Distribution of Money, 140.
International Division of Labor (see Territorial, etc.).

Invention facilitated by the division of labor, 48.
Investment of Capital, 63-4; as affecting the supply of commodities, 73.
Ireland, peasants' houses, 41; rents in, 244-5.
Irish, their industrial aptitudes, 45, 244-5.

Jevons, W. S., Prof, quoted, 252.
Joint stock banks, 128.

Knies, Prof.: his classification of values, 17.

Labor: how related to value, 14; employed in agriculture subject to the condition of Diminishing Returns, 26-31; not so when employed in mechanical industries, 32-3; one of the four agents of production, 22, 188; varying efficiency of labor, 35-46; division of, 47-54; relation of labor to value, 67; to cost of production, 77-8, 165.
Laborer, the, as laying claim to a share of the product of industry, 163; the residual claimant upon the product of industry, Chap. XXIV.
Laborers, their mistaken notions regarding Profits, 195; their efforts to improve their own condition, Chap. XXV.
Laborers, agricultural, have no right to any part of Rent, 179.
Land, one of the four agents of production, 22, 79, 188, Chap. IV; land a fixed quantity, 24; liable to grave abuse, 187; its capability of increased production, Chap. V; remuneration for the use of land (see Rent); the Tenure of Land, Chap. XIX (see, also, Nationalization of the Land).

Landlord, the, as laying claim to a share of the product of industry, 163; Chaps. XVIII and XIX.
Latin union, so called, its monetary league, 109.
Laws, regulating the contract for labor, 75, 249, 251-2.
Legal Tender, 133.
Lincoln, President, quoted, 203.
Loans (see Interest and Usury Laws), Interest, in the economic sense, is received by capital, whether actually loaned or not, 212; interest on extra-hazardous loans, 222.
Loss, which no man gains, 238, 263.
Losses, undeserved, work great injury to industry, 104, 144.
Locock, Mr., quoted, 40.
"Log-rolling" in legislation, 155.
Lombard Street Banks, 111.
London Banks, 111; London the centre of exchange-operations for the world, 127.
Luxurious consumption: its economic character, 278.
Luxury, ideas of: their influence in retarding the increase of population, 270-2.

Machinery: great differences among different peoples in the capacity for using it, 42, 149; its introduction renders necessary the employer, 54; tends to set producers and consumers apart, 280.
Mahon, Lord, quoted, 35.
Maine, Sir H. S.: use of "living money," 96.
Malthus, T. R.: the law of population, 269.
Manufactures: not subject to the condition of diminishing returns, 32-3; how far affected by soil, climate, etc., 148-50.
Margin of Production: as to land, 168; as to Business Ability, 195.

Market value, its relations to normal value, 68.
Marriage: discouraged by economic desires, 270-2.
Marshall, Alfred, and Mary Paley, the "Economics of Industry," preface, page vi.
Martineau, Harriet: Female chastity in England, how affected by the degradation of labor, 237.
Massachusetts, its colonial paper money, 138.
Mastership in production, 54 (see chap. on Profits; also, chap. on Co-operation).
Materials, the third form of capital, 61; waste of, an important element in production, 42, 191, 200, 231; materials vs. products, in tariff legislation, 155; value of, as affecting the success of co-operative enterprises, 199, 204.
Measure of Value, so called (see Denominator of Values).
Mechanical industry, not subject to the condition of diminishing returns, 32-3.
Medium of exchange, money serves as the, Chapter XI; how about paper money? 133.
Metals, as money, 98.
Metals, the Precious, as money, 99; the irregularity of their production, 105, 107 (see, also, Bi-Metallism and Tabular Standard).
Middlemen in Ireland, 244.
Mill, John Stuart, his Political Economy, Preface, page vi; distinction between fixed and circulating capital, 63.
Mining industry, nature fixes the limits within which they may be pursued, 148.
Mobility of capital and labor (see Emigration, etc.).
Money, defined, 92; discussed, in its various forms, Chapters XI-

Money—*Continued.*
  XV; banking economizes the use of money, 118; interest paid, in general, not for the use of money, but of other forms of capital, 214; to increase the amount of money is not to lower the rate of interest, 227 (see, also, Bank Money, Inconvertible Paper Money, Political Money, Bi-Metallism).
Monometallism (see Bi-Metallism).
Monopoly: land a monopoly, 24; not so, capital, 225-6.
Moral elements of supply and demand, 233.
Mosaical code prohibits usury, 214.
Multiple standard for Deferred Payments (see Tabular Standard).

National Banks of the United States, 128.
Nationalization of the land, 182-7.
Neighborhood Industries, 151.
Neison, Doctor, varying mortality of the several trades and professions, 232.
New countries, 40, 235; their characteristic industries, 150.
New England, its paper money, 138.
No-Profits Employers, 190, 230.
No-Rent Lands, 167, 173, 175.
Nominal *versus* real cost of labor, 261-5.
Normal value: its relation to market value, 68, 260; determined by cost of production at the greatest disadvantage, 81, 160.

Occupation, change of, as a means of relieving the labor market, 235-6.
Occupations of the people, how affected by soil, climate, etc., 148-50; wages in different occupations, 232.

Opinion, public: influence on wages, 233.
Organization of industry, Chap. VII; affecting price, 72.
Over-Production: how far it is possible, 280.
Over-population: industrial and social effects of, 239, 245, 269.

Pakenham, Mr., quoted, 40.
Paper money (see Bank money and Inconvertible paper money).
Par of exchange, 125.
Particular Wages, 232.
Pauperism, 237.
Pauper Labor argument for Protection, 156, Chap. XXVI.
Place value, 19.
Plant, so called, its existence as affecting price, 73.
Political economy, the Science of Wealth, 1.
Political money, Chap. XV (see Inconvertible Paper Money).
Politics and economics, 235-6.
Population: effect of the increase of population in driving cultivation down to inferior soils, 169 (see Subsistence); effects of over-population, 269.
Possessions, double coincidence of wants and, 87.
Precious Metals (see Metals, Precious).
Premium on Gold, its cause and effects, 142-4.
Price, its relation to value, 95; price, the agent in the international distribution of money, 140; price, as affecting distribution, 160; relation of rent to the price of agricultural produce, 175; relation of profits to the price of manufactured goods, 194; the price to be paid for the use of capital, 215, 218, 221.
Price current, need of, 89, 91.
Procreative Force, the: capabilities of, 269; antagonized by economic desires, 270-2.

Produce, its price not affected by Rent or Profits, 175, 194.
Product of Industry, divided into shares, 163, 165, 188-92, 228.
Production of wealth, defined, 16; modes of production, 17-20; agents of production, 22; relation of cost of production to value, Chap. IX; production at the greatest disadvantage, Chap. X, 161, 188, 215-8.
Producers and consumers, misunderstandings between them, 280.
Productive co-operation (see Co-operation).
Production, cost of, of what made up, 165, 188.
Productiveness, of Labor, the Source of Wages, 230; how that productiveness may be increased, 231 (see also Chapters VI and VII).
Profit-Sharing, 205.
Profits, the employer's share of the product of industry, Chap. XX; how profits are gained, 189-191; the Law of, 192; profits and rent are species of the same genus, 194-5; profits do not form a part of the price of manufactured products, 194; are not obtained from deduction from wages, 194; economic justification, 196; in Co-operation, laborers aim to secure the employer's profits, 198.
Protection *versus* free trade, Chap. XVI; protection tends to increase the proportion of incompetent employers, 242; the "pauper-labor" argument for protection, Chap. XXVI.
"Protest" of commercial paper, 122.
Punctuality in payments, promoted by banking, 122.

Real *versus* nominal cost of labor, 261-3.

Redeemability of paper money, what it implies, 114-5, 118, 129, 141.
Reflux, the (Bank Money), 129, 141.
Rent, a share in the distribution of the product of industry, 163; the law of rent, its source and its measure, 166-70, 174; to be distinguished from the return to capital invested in improvements of land, 171-2; No-Rent lands, 173; rent does not form a part of the price of agricultural produce, 175; is not obtained by deduction from wages, 176; does rent belong in equity to the community? 177-83 (see, also, Nationalization of the Land); analogy between Rent and Profits, 194; contrasts between Rent and Interest, 225-6; rents, how affected by imperfect competition, 243-5.
Reproduction, of wealth, cost of, 67.
Reserve, specie, of bank money, 114-5, 141.
Residual Share of the Product of Industry = Wages, 228.
Retail trade, the friction of, 75-6.
Revolutionary paper money, U. S. and France, 137.
Russia, the efficiency of its laboring population contrasted with that of England, 262; its Government Securities, 221.

Safe deposit, as a banking function, 111.
Sanitary conditions, as affecting the efficiency of labor, 41.
Saving (see Abstinence).
Savings Banks, 250.
Science, distinction between political economy as a science and as an art, preface, page v.
Scotch, once an idle people, 45.
Scotland, inadequate shelter of the laboring population, 41

Sentiments, personal, excluded from definition of value, 3–4; sentiment as modifying the influence of competition, 233, 244.
Services of the possessors of health, skill and intelligence may be the subjects of exchange, though those qualities cannot be, 6, 7.
Shelter, its relation to subsistence, 41, 62, 269.
Sheep as Money, 96.
Silver (see Precious Metals; see, also, for its relation to gold, Bi-Metallism).
Skill is not wealth, though it may become the means of acquiring wealth, 6–8.
Slave labor, the cause of its inefficiency, 44.
Smith, Adam: his Wealth of Nations, effect upon the relations of States, 11; unprofitableness of slave labor, 43; division of labor, 48.
Socialist writers, their disparaging view of the employer's function, 197.
Soil, the, a fund for the endowment of the human race, 24–5; influence upon the distribution of industries, 148; subject to abuse, 25, 187.
Soldiers, their services economic in England, non-economic in Germany, 4.
Speculation, aggravated by bad money, 144–6.
Specie Reserve of Banks, 114–5.
Standard of Deferred Payments, usually called standard of value, 103–5; how about paper money? 134–42; how about bimetallic money? 107–9 (see, also, Tabular Standard).
State, the, its obligation to control the issue of bank money, 115; its right to Rent, 181; its intervention in the contract for labor, 76, 249, 251–2.

Stock, influence of a stock of a commodity upon its price, 70.
Storage, necessity of, as affecting price, 74.
Strength is not wealth, 6–8.
Strikes, 247; justification of, 256–7; co-operation would abolish strikes, 200.
Subsistence, one form of capital, 61; its relation to wages, 232, 238; its relation to population, 269.
Substitution of one commodity for another in use, as affecting price, 71.
Suffrage, political, its influence upon the distribution of wealth, 235–6, 250.
Sumner, W. G., Prof., his Problems of political economy; preface, page vi.
Supply and demand, 15, 215, 232; intellectual and moral elements of, 233.
Supply, causes which affect, 69–76; supply of money, 129, 134–42.
Surplus, the, above cost of production, of what made up, and how distributed, Chap. X, pars. 164–5, 188–192, 194, 228.
Sympathy with labor (see Opinion, Public).

Tabular Standard for Deferred Payments, 106.
Tariff, Protective (see Protection).
Taxation (see Government Expenditure).
Tenure of the Soil, Chap. XIX.
Tender, Legal (see Legal Tender).
Territorial division of labor, 147–51.
Three Cornered Exchange, 127.
Time value, 18.
Tobacco, as money, 93.
Tools, the second form of capital, 61.

INDEX. 323

Trades unions, their formation in England, 247; their economic influence, 253–4.
Transferability, essential to value 6.
Transportation, its relation to value, 19; to prices, 140; to rent, 170; as affecting the distribution of industries, 151.
Truck, 242.
Turkey, its government securities, 221.

Unearned increment of land (see Increment, etc.).
United States: the laboring population well fed, 37, 40; capable of using delicate and intricate machinery, 42, 149; Banks and Bank money, 112–6, 128–9; its government paper money, 137, 143 (see, also, Greenbacks); agriculture, 148, 171–2; co-operative enterprises, 202, 209; competition in the U. S. before the War of Secession, 235; trades unions, 255.
Usury and usury laws, 213–4, 219–20.
Utility, how related to value; useful, in economics, does not mean beneficial, 12.

Value: related to wealth as attribute to substance, 2, 21; defined, 3; relation to utility, 12–13; to labor, 14; is governed by the relation of demand and supply, 15; how cost of production stands related to value; Chap. IX; value of money, Chap. XV.

Virginia, the Colony of, tobacco as money, 93.

Wage fund theory, 231.
Wages: a share in the product of industry, 163; are not diminished by the sums received by the landlord class as rent, 176; or by the sums received by the employing class as profits, 194; wages constitute the residual share of the product, Chap. XXIII; effect upon wages of Imperfect Competition, 236–242; what may be done to remedy the evil, Chaps. XXV–XXVI.
Wants and Possessions, double coincidence required in Barter, 87.
War, paper money in, 137.
Waste of materials (avoidable), an important element in production, 42, 191, 200, 231.
Waste of soil, 25, 187.
Water privileges, rent of, 159, 163.
Water powers, effect upon the growth of manufactures, 148.
Wealth: the subject-matter of political economy, 1; relation to value, 2, 21 (see, also, throughout, Capital)
Webster, Daniel, quoted, 19, 146.
"Wildcat" Banking, 115.
Women: the causes which determine their wages, 233.

Young, Arthur: ownership awakens industry, 45.

American Science Series

1. **Astronomy.** By SIMON NEWCOMB, Professor in the Johns Hopkins University, and EDWARD S. HOLDEN, Director of the Lick Observatory, California. *Advanced Course.* 512 pp. 8vo. $2.00 *net.*
   The same. *Briefer Course.* 352 pp. 12mo. $1.12 *net.*
2. **Zoology.** By A. S. PACKARD, JR., Professor in Brown University. *Advanced Course.* 722 pp. 8vo. $2.40 *net.*
   The same. *Briefer Course.* 338 pp. 12mo. $1.12 *net.*
   The same. *Elementary Course.* 290 pp. 12mo. 80 cents *net.*
3. **Botany.** By C. E. BESSEY, Professor in the University of Nebraska. *Advanced Course.* 611 pp. 8vo. $2.20 *net.*
   The same. *Briefer Course.* (*Entirely new edition*, 1896.) 356 pp. 12mo. $1.12 *net.*
4. **The Human Body.** By H. NEWELL MARTIN, sometime Professor in the Johns Hopkins University. *Advanced Course.* (*Entirely new edition*, 1896.) 685 pp. 8vo. $2.50 *net.* Copies without chapter on Reproduction sent when specially ordered.
   The same. *Briefer Course.* 377 pp. 12mo. $1.20 *net.*
   The same. *Elementary Course.* 261 pp. 12mo. 75 cents *net.*
   The Human Body and the Effect of Narcotics. 261 pp. 12mo. $1.20 *net.*
5. **Chemistry.** By IRA REMSEN, Professor in Johns Hopkins University. *Advanced Course* (*Inorganic*). 850 pp. 8vo. $2.80 *net.*
   The same. *Briefer Course.* (*Entirely new edition*, 1893.) 435 pp. $1.12 *net.*
   The same. *Elementary Course.* 272 pp. 12mo. 80 cents *net.*
   Laboratory Manual (*to Elementary Course*). 196 pp. 12mo. 40 cents *net.*
   Chemical Experiments. By Prof. REMSEN and Dr. W. W. RANDALL. (*To Briefer Course.*) *No* blank pages for notes. 158 pp. 12mo. 50 cents *net.*
6. **Political Economy.** By FRANCIS A. WALKER, late President Massachusetts Institute of Technology. *Advanced Course.* 537 pp. 8vo. $2.00 *net.*
   The same. *Briefer Course.* 415 pp. 12mo. $1.20 *net.*
   The same. *Elementary Course.* 423 pp. 12mo. $1.00 *net.*
7. **General Biology.** By Prof. W. T. SEDGWICK of Massachusetts Institute of Technology, and Prof. E. B. WILSON of Columbia College. (*Revised and enlarged*, 1896.) 231 pp. 8vo. $1.75 *net.*
8. **Psychology.** By WILLIAM JAMES, Professor in Harvard College. 2 vols. *Advanced Course.* 689 + 704 pp. 8vo. $4.80 *net.*
   The same. *Briefer Course.* 478 pp. 12mo. $1.60 *net.*
9. **Physics.** By GEORGE F. BARKER, Professor in the University of Pennsylvania. *Advanced Course.* 902 pp. 8vo. $3.50 *net.*
10. **Geology.** By THOMAS C. CHAMBERLIN and ROLLIN D. SALISBURY, Professors in the University of Chicago. (*In Preparation.*)

Postage on NET books 8 per cent. additional. Descriptive Catalogue of Educational Books, or of Works in History, Political Economy, and Philosophy, or of Works in General Literature (Ill'd), or Contents *Educational Review* (Vols. I.–XII.), free.

HENRY HOLT & CO., 29 W. 23d Street, NEW YORK.

www.ingramcontent.com/pod-product-compliance
Lightning Source LLC
Chambersburg PA
CBHW021155230426
43667CB00006B/408